RETHINKING DEPRESSION

NOT A SICKNESS
NOT A SIN

DANIEL R. BERGER II

ALETHIA
INTERNATIONAL
MINISTRIES.

Rethinking Depression: Not a Sickness Not a Sin

Library of Congress Control Number: 2019900853
Trade Paperback ISBN: 978-0-9976077-6-5
Cover Artwork by: Elieser Loewenthal
Edited by: Laurie Buck

Unless otherwise noted, all Scripture references in this book are taken from the English Standard Version, copyright © 2001 by Crossway, Inc. Used by permission. All rights reserved.

Published by *Alethia International Publications* - Taylors, SC

www.drdanielberger.com

Printed in the United States of America.

A mis queridos suegros,

Urbano e Hilda:

Gracias por encomendarme a su hija

y por todo su apoyo, pero sobretodo,

gracias por amarnos pese

a todos nuestros defectos.

ENDORSEMENTS

"Daniel Berger's book provides a thorough apologetic for the sufficiency of Scripture in dealing with the spiritual issues described by the psychiatric label 'depression.' He delivers an enlightening discussion of the pervasive influence of the secular psychiatric world in 'medicalizing' the experiences of depression and bipolar, including the difficult subject of mania. Citing both secular and biblical sources, this scholarly book provides an important perspective for anyone who desires to more fully understand this common human suffering. The book will promote confidence for those utilizing biblical truth to counsel those afflicted with despair. We highly recommend this resource for every Christian's library!" - **Pamela Gannon**, RN, MABC and **Dr. Daniel Gannon**, MD; *Dan is a retired orthopedic surgeon, living in Montana with his wife, Pam, who worked as an RN clinical specialist in surgical critical care and studied medicine for two years at Michigan State University. She has served as a biblical counselor at Grace Bible Church in Bozeman since 2000. She is co-author of the book,* **In the Aftermath: Past the Pain of Childhood Sexual Abuse.** *She and her husband are frequent speakers on medical issues for ACBC conferences, are both ACBC certified and serve as adjunct professors at Montana Bible College.*

"Dr. Berger unveils the various masks of the cultural depression narrative. The current construct of depression is challenged not merely with questions but answers to bring clarity, amid the ambiguity, that has been so prevalent in our current Christian thinking. Utilizing respected secular authors, he makes a clear case that competing philosophies have been held in high esteem for far too long and that we should recover a biblical view of the very real human experiences of sadness, sorrow, and deep despair. The fruit of Berger's labor has the potential to shift paradigms held tightly in our Christian circles for nearly eighty years. We know that ideas always have consequences and Berger's work kindly cautions us to connect the dots between our theology, philosophies, and counseling practices." – **Dr. T. Dale Johnson**, *Executive Director, ACBC and Associate Professor of Biblical Counseling, Midwestern Baptist Theological Seminary.*

"Dr. Berger brings bold courage and biblical compassion to the conversation surrounding depression. He approaches everyman's struggle, not with a shaking finger of denial or a list of seven laws, but with light and love. Sorrow is welcomed and soothed, despair is bathed in hope, and guilt meets healing. Berger clarifies misconceptions so popularly embraced and marches them right to the cross where enemy tactics surrender to absolute truth, if we but bend the knee." - **Ruth Froese,** *MABC, Director of Women's Biblical Counseling at Faith Fellowship Biblical Counseling Center, and author of **Reseda** and **The Darkest Valley: Biblically Understanding and Responding to Suicide.***

"When it comes to understanding depression and caring for the depressed, we have used the shovels of human wisdom and shallow religion to dig a deep, dark hole for ourselves. Though books abound and expound upon the subject, we are as confused as we have ever been. Sadly, depression-as-disease and depression-as-sin seem to dominate the conversation in the church. *Rethinking Depression* surveys the research to chronicle how we got here, then offers a few critical steps for choosing a better direction. I appreciate how Berger brings the experience of sorrow, hopelessness and guilt back onto the landscape of normal human life, and even better, onto the landscape of gospel-centered ministry." – **Dr. John Henderson**, *pastor, author, and counselor*

"This is a biblically-based book and is a most relevant topic for both the church bringing Christ's healing to believers, and as a public testimony that the Bible is fully sufficient for matters of faith and the soul. I would place this book on the same shelf as Puritan soul doctors, such as a Sibbes and Baxter; but in particular, I would place it right next to Dr. David Martyn Lloyd-Jones's *Spiritual Depression*, a godly spiritual classic." – **David Conroy**, *Manager of Sola Scriptura Counseling Group*

"In *Rethinking Depression*, Dr. Berger has accomplished a goal many have tried, but is often failed; he successfully lives up to the title of his book and its stated goal — doing so with biblical integrity, culturally relevant and reliable research, and excellent scholarship. To say that it is a must-read for the exclusively biblical counselor, the Christian-integrated counselor, and the secular clinician would not be an overstatement.

Dr. Berger clearly articulates the fullness of modern thought on the subject of depression, and systematically unpacks it in such a way that the reader approaches the actual rethinking of depression from a thorough standpoint of understanding. In doing this, he gives an extensive treatment to the etymology of thought behind the current medical model of treating depression, its subtle influence on Christianity, and how it is that the Christian and counselor alike must objectively rethink this issue from a biblically correct worldview.

The book is thoughtful in detail, yet not overwhelming. It is grounded in biblical truth, and rooted by agreeing research from both secular and biblical thought. It is an essential addition to any counselor's library, and creates a new gold standard within the counseling movement for competent counsel on depression."
- **Stephen Ganschow**, *PhD candidate, Pastor of Counseling Ministries, Bethel Church Crown Point, Indiana.*

"In *Rethinking Depression*, Dr. Berger makes a compelling argument for understanding deep sorrow, hopelessness, and guilt that are involved in depression to be normal human experiences in this fallen world. He goes on to show how true hope, purpose in suffering, and freedom from guilt are found in a meaningful relationship with Jesus Christ." - **Dr. Anne Dryburgh**, *author of **Debilitated and Diminished: Help for Christian Women in Emotionally Abusive Marriages**, is an IABC* *and ACBC certified biblical counselor, a council member of the Biblical Counseling Coalition and has been a mission worker in Flemish-speaking Belgium since the early 1990s. She is also a guest lecturer at Tilsley College in Scotland, an external reader for doctoral candidates at the Masters International University of Divinity, a frequent contributor to the blog Biblical Counseling for Women, and coordinates the European hub of the Biblical Counseling Coalition.*

"In the counseling world many voices have spoken and continue to speak on depression, bipolar, and standards of normalcy. In this gracious, well-documented, thought-provoking book, Dr. Daniel Berger II enters the discussion, giving voice to a much over-looked philosophy of counseling. All counselors would do well to read Dr. Berger's book and give pause to ponder this well-reasoned, hope-filled approach to handling a common-to-man struggle. I was greatly blessed by the content of this book."
-Pastor Blake Shaw *Pastor of Counseling Ministry, Grace Bible Church, Bozeman, Montana; instructor of biblical counseling at Montana Bible College, Bozeman, Montana; ACBC certified biblical counselor*

"A wise counselor will listen more than he talks at the beginning of a counseling relationship. He does this because he wants to genuinely hear what the other person is saying so he understands fully and can bring competent biblical care to the individual. Dr. Daniel Berger listens well to how the world describes depression and their solutions. He then brings biblical insight, clarity, and hope to this universal problem.

There are two vital decisions that you will have to make upon reading this book. The first is your presupposition and the second is your process. Two competing presuppositional worldviews are vying for authority on the issue of depression in your life. One is human-centered, and the other is God-centered. How you choose will determine your point-of-departure in understanding, explaining, and engaging depression.

Your second decision is whether or not you will implement Dr. Berger's conclusions into your life or if you're going to go against objective evidence and continue practices that do not bring hope or transformative help. If you do not have a bibliocentric worldview on how to think about depression, this book will help you get there. But more than that; it will help you bring measurable positive change to those you serve." - **Rick Thomas,** *President, the Counseling Solutions Group, Inc. and author* ***of Change Me: The Ultimate Life Change Handbook*** *and* ***Suffering Well: How to Steward God's Most Feared Blessing***.

CONTENT

ACKNOWLEDGMENTS

This book was made possible by many friends, family, and professionals who sacrificed time and gave effort to read early drafts and offer me valuable feedback. Specifically, I would like to thank my wife, Oriana, and my parents, Dan and Gail Berger, who are always supportive and helpful along the way. I wish to also thank a group of professionals, counselors, and pastors for their time and insight: Dr. Jay Adams, Mr. Donn Arms, Mr. David Conroy, Dr. Anne Dryburgh, Mrs. Ruth Froese, Dr. Dan Gannon, Mrs. Pam Gannon, Dr. John Henderson, Dr. Dale Johnson, Mr. Elieser Loewenthal, Mr. Blake Shaw, and Mr. Rick Thomas. As always, I am grateful for my editor, Laurie Buck, who deserves much credit in helping the book to arrive at its final product. Finally, I want to thank all those who, over the past many years, have allowed me to be a part of their lives in offering them scriptural wisdom that enables them to have life more abundantly, to progress in allowing God to restore their minds, to possess genuine lasting hope, and to endure through the many sorrows of this life.

DISCLAIMER

The material contained in this book is the result of years of experience, research, and professional interviews, but it is not intended in any way to be taken as medical advice. Rather, the views and material expressed in this book are written in order to provide truth and hope to those who want proven help for their hopelessness, sorrow, and guilt.

ABBREVIATIONS

APA   American Psychiatric Association

CCNT   *Christian Counselor's New Testament*

DSM-IV   *Diagnostic & Statistical Manual of Mental Disorders IV*

DSM-5   *Diagnostic & Statistical Manual of Mental Disorders 5*

ESV   *English Standard Version of the Bible*

ICD-10   *International Classification of Diseases 10*

KJV   *King James Version of the Bible*

NASB   *New American Standard Bible*

NEJM   *New England Journal of Medicine*

NIH   National Institutes of Health

NIMH   National Institute of Mental Health

SSRIs   Selective Serotonin Reuptake Inhibitors

WHO   World Health Organization

OTHER BOOKS BY AUTHOR

CHAPTER 1

INTRODUCTION

"My soul melts away for sorrow;
strengthen me according to your word!"
Psalm 119:28[1]

The Purpose

This book emerged from my heartbreak as I see hurting people
in need of genuine help in dealing with mental issues and from
my great joy in seeing individuals recover from their hopeless
condition through an unconventional and seemingly new
perspective. The excitement to share a consistently reliable
approach to the human conditions most often referred to today
as depression and bipolar disorder has fueled me in this
endeavor.

Embracing a new approach will, of course, necessitate
abandoning ineffective, though popular, ways of dealing with
these problems. Both scientific research and Scripture will be
examined and mined to this end. These sources are not in
conflict as holders of the current secular paradigm assert that
they are. In fact, God's Word provides the only infallible and

---

[1] The *ESV* is used throughout this book unless otherwise noted.

reliable lens by which to interpret, study, and understand the natural world and all of human nature.

In truth, this new approach is not my theory or that of another; it is the approach that God establishes in His word in accordance with how He created us. In this way, this so-called new paradigm is actually an old approach that has never been disproven or failed when genuinely applied. Still, it has been set aside and hidden from the view of many, as well as denied by evolutionists who wish to establish the biological paradigm or medical model in its place.

While it is important to reconsider the construct of depression, Christians desperately need to consider and discern whether much of our understanding of the psyche/soul is sourced from evolutionary thinking and theory cloaked in scientism or if it is from the creation account recorded in Genesis 1-3. Like a bottle that has been buried in mud for centuries, our understanding of the true nature of the human condition has become muddled, and the necessary remedy ignored or disregarded. I am hopeful that as you read this book, the only reliable and efficient answers to the human struggle known today as depression will become vividly clear. In this regard, divine illumination, rather than human enlightenment, is vital to our discovery and acceptance of the only truly effective remedy to depression.

As I have counseled and met with many people from around the world, I am finding that the current most popular approaches to depression are clearly causing worse distress and pain. Though these approaches are not healthy, I wish to make it clear that I am not accusing secular clinicians and many well-meaning Christians of not caring or genuinely wanting to help. But truth and love must not be separated in providing genuine hope to a hurting soul.

From the outset, then, I also wish to make it clear that this book is not a condemnation of those who struggle with or who are being crushed under the weight of sorrow and hopelessness. You will not find the common but false judgmental narrative that being depressed is a sin. Instead, my desire in writing this book is to provide a gracious invitation to those who are crushed and weighted down to discover genuine hope and truth and to be freed from false theories and ways of thinking. At the same time, I wish this book to provide a resource for those who labor in helping others who are sorrowful and hopeless.

What should result from a biblical and scientifically objective discussion (these sources of revelation are never in conflict) is a clear understanding of our common human struggle. More importantly, when we better understand our suffering and human condition, we can then also discover essential hope and the application of truth that alone can remedy our souls.

Furthermore, I want to be transparent with you, as this book is a personal testimony of how the truth of the gospel has given me strength to endure the trials and heartaches of my life. I have lost loved ones, had my dreams crushed, grieved the death of my unborn twin children, struggled with a chronic painful illness and numerous surgeries. I have been deeply hurt by injustice and false accusations, withstood traumatic events, and experienced painful rejection throughout my life. This book represents God's leading by His grace in providing me with clear truth that alone can sustain me. This same comfort that has given me joy despite great sorrow and pain is the gospel which I wish to share with you. If you receive nothing else from reading this book on depression, I hope that you will come to realize that the gospel is not the believer's condemnation; it is our essential deliverance.

Finally, I wish to offer you genuine hope. Hope is the essential remedy that transcends all perspectives on depression and one which we can agree upon from the start. But we will need to examine carefully what saving hope truly is. Secular clinicians, therapists, authors, politicians, false religions, and even TV ads offer hope, but these are hopes that cannot genuinely deliver a person from deep impairing sorrow and hopelessness. Instead of temporal or failing hopes, what I wish to communicate in this book is the comforting reality that gospel hope is not a fleeting or false hope, and it is not merely a pleasant philosophical theory without practical applications. This book does not endorse the notion that all you need to do is trust God and pray more and your sadness will vanish away. Instead, my prayer is that you walk away from this book understanding that the gospel is comforting, empowering, transformational, practical, and that Christ is precisely the reliable deliverance we need from what is framed within psychiatry as depression.

I do not wish only to claim that Christ is sufficient to meet your needs. Instead, I also want to share with you practical truths that show just how sufficient Christ is to restore your soul and to provide you with truth to live by, joy despite sorrow, and hope despite your circumstances. As with any hope for deliverance that you will choose, however, gospel hope requires your faith. It also demands the rejection of what is false. Nonetheless, each of us must establish a hope in our lives to deliver us from our fallen human condition and the vexations of our lives, framed in today's terminology as depression.

The Need

The number of people who admit to struggling with and who seek treatment for depression is increasing exponentially.[2]

[2] One example can be observed in the "record numbers of college students [who] are seeking treatment for depression and anxiety." Katie Reilly, "Mental Health: A New Understanding," *Time Magazine* Special Edition (November 2018), 28.

Leading secular psychiatrists now insist that "depression is the world's largest health problem, accounting for more disability than any other disease worldwide."[3] The World Health Organization (WHO) found in 2017 that the number of people reporting depression yearly has increased 18% over the last decade.[4]

To make matters worse and a discussion about depression more urgent is the fact that the suicide rate continues to rise at an astonishing pace. It is not just that suicides are being reported in the news anymore; we are now faced with trying to understand our neighbors', family members', and friends' suicidal ideations and completions. The preferred theories and practices, which are widely claimed to help people, continue to fail. Psychiatrist Allan Tasman explains,

> In spite of improved understanding of risk factors and increased vigilance for suicide risk among mental health and other medical practitioners and families of those at risk, the suicide rate in the US continues to go up. . . . Between 2006 and 2016 the overall US suicide rate went up from 10.97 to 13.26 per 100,000 people. Those numbers may seem small, but they reflect an increase of just over 20% in these 10 years. And, the trend lines don't look much different going back to 2000.[5]

[3] James Murrough, "Addressing Depression: The World's Largest Health Problem," *Psychiatric Times Online* vol. 35, no. 7 (July 31, 2018): http://www.psychiatrictimes.com/depression/ addressing-depression-worlds-largest-health-problem.

[4] World Health Organization, "Depression Tops List of Causes of Ill Health," *WHO Online*, April 7, 2017, http://www.who.int/campaigns/world -health-day/2017/en/.

[5] Allan Tasman, "The Wrong Way on a Long and Winding Road: Suicide in the US," *Psychiatric Times Online*, February 20, 2018, http://www.psychiatric times.com/couch-crisis/wrong-way-long-and-winding-road-suicide-us.

Psychiatrist William Basco, Jr. also notes how suicidal ideation, suicide attempts, and suicide completions continue their trend upward in adolescence despite alleged scientific advances and increased knowledge about depression:

> Suicide is the third leading cause of death among adolescents in the United States; sadly, these rates of completed suicide are increasing. Both suicide ideation and suicide attempts are markers of increased risk for later completed suicide.[6]

Without some meaningful change, both depression and suicide rates will continue to rise.

What these statistics reveal in part is that what is being taught and accepted in both secular society and within the church surrounding the idea of depression is not genuinely helping to remedy the very real struggles undergirding the syndrome. Materialistic theories are widely accepted and defended, but since these theories of depression were first implemented several decades ago, the number of people seriously struggling in our culture has only intensified.

Many psychiatric researchers, though,[7] have begun to admit that the current approach to people as biological machines — a "mechanistic approach" or the medical model — lacks understanding and is not as effective in treating depression as advertised.[8] Yet, society in general has come to believe that

---

[6] William T. Basco Jr., "Suicide Ideation and Attempts in Children and Teens," *Medscape Psychiatry*, November 13, 2018, https://www.medscape.com/viewarticle/903921?nlid=126207_424&src=WNL_mdplsfeat_181120_mscpedit_psyc&uac=264124BV&spon=12&impID=1806863&faf=1.

[7] James Murrough, Associate Professor of Psychiatry and Neuroscience and Director of the Mood and Anxiety Disorders Program at the Icahn School of Medicine at Mount Sinai in New York City, provides one example.

[8] Murrough, "Addressing Depression."

depression is a mechanistic problem – a biological disease.[9] Despite popular beliefs and psychiatric claims to dogmatically know causes and reliable remedies, the statistics reveal that depression is a growing problem both individually and corporately rather than a disease that is being remedied or even properly managed. Other highly respected psychiatrists, such as Harvard-trained former professor and former full-time consultant for the National Institutes of Mental Health (NIMH) Peter Breggin, have also arrived at the conclusion that it is wrong and counterintuitive to view and approach depression from the currently popularized medical perspective:

> Unfortunately, the medical approach to depression has influenced many people to completely ignore the real bases for feeling depressed. . . . Although depression is experienced as emotional or psychological suffering, medically oriented scientists and practitioners have tried to redefine these feelings into something that looks more like a biological disorder.[10]

Still others point out that scientific research has undermined the popular but wrong biomedical narrative that is widely accepted to explain depression. For example, in accordance with the 2017 World Health Day campaign (which focused on the construct of depression and which was sponsored by the World Health Organization [WHO]), Dainius Pūras – representative for the Office of the United Nations High Commissioner for Human Rights (OHCHR) – asserted his own conclusions about the "biomedical" approach:

---

[9] The mechanistic approach is also called the medical model, biomedical approach, reductive neurobiological paradigm, and biological psychiatric theory. It is a presuppositional faith based upon the philosophy of *materialism*, which teaches that human mindsets, emotions, and behaviors must be theorized and framed to be the products of purely physical and deterministic realities.

[10] Peter Breggin, *The Anti-Depressant Fact Book* (Cambridge, MA: Perseus Books Group, 2001), 16; 19.

Evidence and the experience of rights-holders now tells us that the dominant *biomedical narrative of depression* as a "burden" on individuals and societies is shortsighted and insufficient for developing appropriate responses in policy and in practice. . . . The longstanding *biomedical tradition* of medicalizing various forms of psychosocial distress and human suffering has cast a long shadow over the importance of addressing the social and underlying determinants of health. This not only undermines the right to health, it also ignores a rapidly growing evidence base [emphasis added].[11]

In his statement, Pūras recognizes the need to reevaluate the construct of depression, but he also acknowledges that maintaining the current theory or "dominant biomedical narrative"/"biomedical tradition"/"reductive neurobiological paradigm" — which frames depression as a biological disease — is actually keeping people from the help that they need rather than leading them to it. He goes as far as to say in the official OHCHR statement that a person must deny compelling scientific evidence in favor of "misinformation" in order to maintain the false belief that depression is an illness:

Regrettably, recent decades have been marked with *excessive medicalization of mental health* and the overuse of biomedical interventions, including in the treatment of depression and suicide prevention. The biased and selective use of research outcomes has negatively influenced mental health policies and services. *Important stakeholders, including the general public, rights holders using mental health services, policymakers, medical students, and medical doctors have been misinformed.* The use of psychotropic medications as the first line treatment for depression and other conditions is, quite simply, unsupported by the evidence. The excessive use of medications and other biomedical interventions, based on *a reductive neurobiological paradigm causes more harm than good, undermines the right to health, and must be abandoned* [emphasis added].[12]

[11] Dainius Pūras, "Depression: Let's Talk about How We Address Mental Health," United Nations Human Rights Office of the High Commissioner, April 7, 2017, https://www.ohchr.org/EN/NewsEvents/Pages/Display News.aspx?NewsID=21480&LangID=E.

[12] Ibid.

In other words, asserting depression to be a medical condition and approaching human struggles with drugs is more of a belief in scientism and a means of maintaining the medical model than it is a scientifically sound theory. Sadly, the empirical evidence available, as Pūras acknowledges and as we will discover in this book, exposes that the medical model is an unsubstantiated approach to human nature that "causes more harm than good."

Pūras also rightly notes, which cannot be overlooked, that all of the theories and practices which frame and attempt to treat depression as a disease or biological disorder are "based on a reductive neurobiological paradigm." Secularists must attempt to reduce all human nature to biological causes and explanations according to their evolutionary worldview when they insist upon the medical model (e.g., "mental illness"). This philosophical approach — reductionism — is a key aspect of the broader philosophy of *materialism*, which views all of human nature and existence as confined to the physical rather than considering mankind to be both spiritual and physical — *dualism*. The philosophy of materialism undergirds the widespread belief that depression is a sickness — a point that we must reconsider.

Whether or not you agree with the aforementioned assertions at this point, the need is clearly urgent to discuss and seriously reconsider what has become common belief about the psychiatric construct known as depression. There is substantial empirical evidence to conclude that the current paradigm, sourced in evolutionary beliefs, has overwhelmingly failed. Psychiatrist at the prestigious University College London Joanna Moncrieff, psychologist and researcher Mark Rapley, and professor of psychology Jacqui Dillon share their own perspectives after years of believing in the current paradigm,

> We are compelled to conclude that the effort to codify various forms of misery and disturbing conduct as if they were physical diseases, far from being another triumph of modern science — carving nature at its joints a la Linnaeus or the periodic table (Mendeleev, 1901) — is,

rather, best regarded as fiction or, more kindly, in Barthes' sense, as mythology.[13]

The medical model of depression has not just failed; it is a fictional and damaging belief that must be discarded at its philosophical and practical levels.

As we reconsider our human condition, it is not simply enough to look for new causes and treatments. Rather, we must as a society discuss an alternative paradigm or presuppositional belief from which to foundationally understand, approach, and remedy the recognized features of what is known today as depression.

While the most common secular theories on depression are doing far more harm than they are providing help to people in need, Christians, too, have not been free from accumulating and forming their own false paradigms and accepting the scientism of evolutionary thinking. There exist many false and harmful beliefs in the church which are assumed to be both biblical and scientific. Some of these approaches attempt to wed perceived biblical truths with the current psychiatric paradigm, while others rest on legalistic concepts which appear biblical but are not.

What is also troubling is that many people view these harmful approaches as altruistic, effective, and necessary avenues for healing. In fact, many believe that questioning popular thinking and exposing the biomedical model — despite the accepted theory's clear failures — is uncharitable, unethical, and unscientific. On the contrary, clinging to a clearly ineffective strategy for dealing with serious and life-threatening problems

[13] Mark Rapley, Joanna Moncrieff, and Jacqui Dillon, *De-Medicalizing Misery: Psychiatry, Psychology and the Human Condition* (Hampshire, England: Palgrave Macmillan, 2011), 2.

which often have eternal consequences undervalues the widespread suffering of those dealing with what is commonly referred to as depressive disorders and indicates a lack of true compassion and understanding. We must choose to either genuinely help people or choose to uphold a theory that is hurting them.

A large part of the current failed paradigm about depression is the belief that it is an abnormality and not an integral part of normal human nature. But as we will discover in the chapters to come, struggling with deep sorrow and a sense of hopelessness is far more prevalent than most people realize. In fact, the National Institute of Mental Health (NIMH) estimates that 16 million American adults and far more adolescents are struggling with impairing depression each year.[14] While these numbers are staggering and rising, many studies — such as the one conducted at Columbia University in 2018 — have found that "up to two thirds of all depression cases are undiagnosed."[15] These statistics are estimates and not necessarily representative of the same people each year. Yet, these numbers — taken from secular research — reveal that what is framed as depression is far more common than typically acknowledged or perceived.[16]

Despite the commonality of people struggling with depression, many assume that normal people are generally happy and full of hope. When normal people do struggle with sorrow and hopelessness, they are thought to be able to find deliverance.

[14] National Institute of Mental Health, "Mental Health: A New Understanding," *Time Magazine* Special Edition (November 2018), 74.

[15] Markham Heid, "Mental Health: A New Understanding," *Time Magazine* Special Edition, November, 2018, 78.

[16] "Depression is a common mental disorder," (World Health Organization, "Depression Tops List of Causes of Ill Health," *WHO Online*, April 7, 2017, http://www. who.int/campaigns/world-health-day/2017/en/).

Americans, as one illustration, regularly struggle with deep impairing sorrow and identify themselves as unhappy. Steven Pinker professor of psychology at Harvard University discusses his research in one of the chapters of his book, *Enlightenment Now: The Case for Reason, Science, Humanism, and Progress*,[17] which he claims exposes just how unhappy Americans are despite their alleged unmatched wealth, privilege, and scientific advancement. His findings indicate that the increase of knowledge and temporal possessions often comes with more sorrow. Americans are more enlightened and technologically advanced than many other countries, and yet many of us identify as being unhappy. Such perspectives further reveal that our failure to understand and treat depression is in large part due to a wrong philosophical starting point of missing or denying both the fundamental nature of humanity and the construct of depression.

The need to reconsider the foundational philosophies, current popular theories, and mainstream practices is urgent. I invite you to join me in rethinking the construct of depression.

---

[17] Steven Pinker, *Enlightenment Now: The Case for Reason, Science, Humanism, and Progress* (New York: Penguin Random House, 2018).

CHAPTER 2

UNDERSTANDING DEPRESSION

"Our current concept of depression is left over from times when we didn't really understand it very much."[18] – Bruce Cuthbert, director of research and treatment development at the NIMH

Before we can discuss the causes and remedy for depression, we must first understand what the current psychiatric constructs of depression describe or attempt to explain. The various labels created by the American Psychiatric Association (APA) and listed in their catalog of constructs called the *Diagnostic and Statistical Manual of Mental Disorders, 5th edition* (hereafter referred to as the *DSM-5*)[19] provide little value in this discussion

---

[18] Bruce Cuthbert quoted by Jenny Chen, "Why Depression Needs a New Definition," *Atlantic Online*, August 4, 2015, https://www.theatlantic.com /health/archive/2015/08/why-depression-needs-a-new-definition/399902/.

[19] American Psychiatric Association, *Diagnostic and Statistical Manual of Mental Disorders*, 5th ed. (Washington, DC: American Psychiatric Publishing, 2013), 20. The World Health Organization and the World Psychiatric Association both use the *DSM-5* and the *International Classification of Diseases*, 10th edition (*ICD-10*) to classify and label alleged mental disorders. These books are both based upon Emil Kraepelin's original classification system, which he published in the late 1800s. The *ICD-10* will not be addressed separately, since it is so similar to the *DSM-5*.

since they merely identify, describe, and categorize common human struggles. The criteria the labels seek to represent are the genuine substance of distress and pain that we must carefully study and seek to remedy.

The psychiatric labels are descriptive monikers that have changed over the last two centuries. For example, what is now thought of as depressive disorders by secularists were in the early 1600s called *melancholia* (from the Greek meaning "black bile") because of the false belief that the kidney or spleen caused people to be sad, hopeless, and even manic.[20] Other terms such as *neurasthenia* and *moppishness* have also been utilized by secularists to describe the same human struggles.[21] *Affective psychosis* (meaning "the emotional condition of the soul"; including unipolar and bipolar depression) was a term created by the German psychiatrist Emil Kraepelin in the late 1800s and was commonly used until the APA began to describe these struggles as "depressive reaction" and "manic-depressive reaction" in the *DSM-I* (1952).[22] This history leads us to today's current primary labels of *depression* and *bipolar*: [23]

> "Depression" was first used in physical medicine to describe a reduction in cardiovascular function and was afterwards adopted by early psychiatrists to indicate emotional states that were considered to be the opposite of excitation. During the early years of the twentieth century the term intruded into the language of ordinary

[20] The APA still utilizes the term *melancholia* in the *DSM-5* to describe an alleged sub-set of depression.

[21] Richard Bentall, *Madness Explained: Psychosis and Human Nature* (New York: Penguin, 2003), 214.

[22] Ibid., 58.

[23] For more on the history of the term *depression*, see G. E. Berrios and Roy Porter, eds. *Mood Disorders: A History of Clinical Psychiatry* (London: Athlone Press, 1995).

people, so that we now think of "depression" as a natural label for how we feel during times of loss.[24]

The diagnoses of *unipolar* and *bipolar* depressions are simply labels or constructs that identify common mindsets and behaviors which are framed as disorders and categorized in the *DSM-5*. Setting aside the psychiatric theory the labels represent and discussing the genuine problems is the necessary starting point if we are to have a worthwhile discussion and consider other perspectives. For some, this first step of accepting the diagnostic labels as unimportant may be difficult. But finding a remedy will only occur if the current failed theory is side-lined.

In accordance with this realization, the National Institute of Mental Health (NIMH) has introduced what they call *Research Domain Criteria* (RDoC) in order to consider criteria apart from psychiatric labels. Many psychiatrists and clinicians are now realizing that the labels limit and hinder necessary discussions and consideration of construct features (criteria) on their own:

> Measurement of symptoms domains and their response to treatment in relative isolation from diagnosed mental disorders has gained new urgency, as reflected by the National Institute of Mental Health's introduction of the Research Domain Criteria (RDoC).[25]

Not only do psychiatric labels, which seek to summarize common human conditions that are impairing or distressful obscure important considerations and remedies, but they also further enable faith in the medical model and sustain the speculative biological theory. Taking all of this into consideration, the labels of *depression* and *bipolar* will be utilized

[24] Bentall, *Madness Explained*, 214.

[25] Marisa Toups, Thomas Carmody, Tracy Greer, Chad Rethorst, Bruce Grannemann, and Madhukar H. Trivedi, "Exercise Is an Effective Treatment for Positive Valence Symptoms in Major Depression," *Journal of Affective Disorders* 209 (Feb 2017): 188-94.

throughout this book for discussion's sake. But know that they are useless in understanding our human condition, in representing a validated theory, or in discovering a proved remedy to the common human problems that the labels comprise.

What may also be helpful is to recognize that leading secular theorists regularly refer to depression as a "syndrome" rather than calling it a disease or illness. For example, Charles Nemeroff, chairman of the department of psychiatry and behavioral science at the University of Miami states,

> Depression is this terrible syndrome. Its cornerstone is the inability to experience pleasure. If you think about the worst day of your life, loss of a loved one, lost your job, breakup of a relationship, think about feeling that way every day and not knowing why.[26]

Syndromes are collections of symptoms which correlate enough to be combined together into a social construct or into a theorized disease. The theory in psychiatry/abnormal psychology is that constructing a syndrome makes it easier to attempt explaining common struggles or impairments. The term comes from the Greek word *syndromos* meaning "the place where many roads run together." However, the syndrome is not the real problem: the symptoms are.

In contrast, diseases/illnesses are biological conditions which have a measurable pathology (underlying physical cause) and biological markers which are typically diagnostic tools (physical characteristics; e.g., cancer has identifiable cancer cells). Valid diseases also have symptoms, but the true nature of the disease does not depend on the list of symptoms. Depression has no

---

[26] Charles Nemeroff interviewed by David Carreon and Jessica Gold, "Depression: A Killing Disease," *Psychiatric Times Online* (April 30, 2018): http://www.psychiatrictimes.com/ major-depressive-disorder/depression-killing-disease.

known physical cause (though speculative theories abound and are claimed to be true) and has no biological markers such as lipomas, neurological tangles, or abrasions, etc.

The construct of depression consists of a group of features of normal human nature which are impairing and distressful. Psychiatrists at the University of Amsterdam explain,

> Depression is often viewed as a common medical disorder like measles — one either has it or one doesn't. As a result, diagnosis is generally followed by assigning specific treatment options. But unlike physical disorders where blood tests or other objective tests enable a reliable diagnosis, there are no such measures to determine whether someone is depressed. Instead, researchers and clinicians query patients about symptoms that are indicative of depression, such as sadness, suicidal ideation and sleep problems. If a person has many depression symptoms, she is considered depressed.[27]

Similarly, in his address to the World Psychiatric Association, published in *World Psychiatry*, David Goldberg expresses his same concerns about the construct of depression's sustaining false perspective:

> At present major depression has become a monolith [a political or social construct], with the assumption that the diagnosis can be made merely on the number of depressive symptoms present, with an associated disability. It may be politically important to utter such simplifications to doctors in a general medical setting, *but it is a convenient fiction* [emphasis added].[28]

The idea of depression being an objective disease concept is not valid despite the APA's and Big Pharma's insistence that it is well-founded. In accordance, psychiatrist Peter Breggin remarks,

[27] University of Amsterdam (UVA), "The Heterogeneous Nature of Depression," *Science Daily Online*, October 24, 2016, https://www.science daily.com/releases/2016/10/161024131122.htm.

[28] David Goldberg, "The Heterogeneity of 'Major Depression,'" *World Psychiatry (WPA)* 10, no. 3 (2011): 226.

Depression is never defined by an objective physical finding, such as a blood test or brain scan. It is defined by the individual's personal suffering and especially by the depressed thoughts and feelings that a person expresses. In other words, if a person has depressed thoughts and feelings, the diagnosis of depression is made. Based on that alone, it makes little sense to view depressed feelings, or the emotional state of depression, as a disease or disorder. The severity of a person's depression should not mislead one into thinking it is a genuine physical disease like diabetes or pneumonia. Depression is always defined by its subjective emotional quality.[29]

Even so, while depression is a social construct, the criteria the construct or syndrome seeks to explain are very real and distressing.

But the list of criteria or symptoms contained in the *DSM-5* is not exhaustive as it fails to acknowledge other prevalent symptoms of human suffering that many diagnosed with depression experience (e.g., anxiety and crying).[30] Many professional psychologists and psychiatrists acknowledge this reality:

The context-free diagnoses outlined by *DSM* may not provide enough information to represent the heterogeneity observed in depressed patients . . . . The *Diagnostic and Statistical Manual of Mental Disorders – Fifth Edition (DSM-5;* American Psychiatric Association (APA), 2013) organizes depressive psychopathology based on symptom count and course (i.e., MDD and Persistent Depressive Disorder, formerly Dysthymic Disorder in *DSM-IV* (APA, 2000)). However, this non-etiological approach assumes that depressive psychopathology is homogenous, does not explain factors associated with mild or severe presentations, and largely

---

[29] Breggin, *Anti-Depressant Fact Book*, 18.

[30] "Many depressions are likely to be accompanied by anxious symptoms" (Goldberg, "Heterogeneity of 'Major Depression'").

ignores the context in which the symptoms of depression manifest.[31]

As this group of clinicians note, the *DSM-5* labeling system does not consider a person's life context (e.g., history and relationships), include all of the symptoms, or offer a helpful explanation.

To complicate matters further, many of the *DSM-5* somatic symptoms contradict other symptoms within the same construct. Dr. Goldberg remarks:

> The *DSM* diagnosis of major depression is made when a patient has any 5 out of 9 symptoms, several of which are opposites. Thus, a patient who has psychomotor retardation, hypersomnia and gaining weight is scored as having identical symptoms as another who is agitated, sleeping badly and has weight loss. This causes real problems with research designs.[32]

The secular construct of depression does not describe, let alone explain, the human condition well. Other biological psychiatrists, such as Chris Aiken, recognize that the labels exclude the possibility of considering that not everyone suffers in the exact same way as the *DSM-5* maintains within its limited structure and labeling system.[33] But such is the nature of a subjective construct or syndrome versus a valid disease entity. When a person is diagnosed with depression, physicians/clinicians/therapists are not discovering or identifying a disease,

---

[31] Sarah Simon, Nicole M. Cain, Lisa Wallner Samstag, Kevin B. Meehan, and J. Christopher Muran, "Assessing Interpersonal Subtypes in Depression," *Journal of Personality Assessment* 97, *no.* 4 (2015): 364-73.

[32] Goldberg, "The Heterogeneity of 'Major Depression.'"

[33] Chris Aiken, "Two Categories of Bipolar Disorder That Can Change Treatment," *Psychiatric Times Online* 35, no. 5 (May 7, 2018): http://www.psychiatrictimes.com/bipolar-disorder/two-categories-bipolar-disorder-can-change-treatment.

but assigning a label to a group of common features of human nature which regularly appear together.

To better understand how depression is a syndrome or social construct, one only needs to look at the diagnostic process. In order to diagnose depression, no medical training, no knowledge of biology, and very little familiarity with the diagnostic criteria asserted in the *DSM-5* is required. All a person needs is to be able to observe and interpret revealed mindsets, emotions, and behaviors according to the philosophical approach of the APA and assign their established labels. This reality exposes that the sustained belief that depression is a physical disease is due in large part to the construct being listed as a "mental illness" in an allegedly medical book by people who believe in the medical model.

Adding to this belief is both secularists' ongoing assertion that depression is an illness without any empirical evidence to support their claims as well as their regular insistence that psychotropic drugs be accepted as medicines framed as "antidepressants." Unfortunately, the *DSM-5* and its labeling system has gained such acceptance in America that many people prefer to interpret almost every impairing or distressful mindset, emotion, and behavior from this moral perceptive, and thus they believe the psychiatric labels/constructs to be real diseases.

But several psychiatrists, such as Allen Frances — whom many considered to be the most powerful and influential psychiatrist in America at the turn of the century and presided as chair of the *DSM-IV* task force — insists in his book *Saving Normal* that the *DSM* is not a catalog of diseases and sadness does not equal sickness:

> We saw *DSM-IV* as a guidebook, not a bible — *a collection of temporarily useful diagnostic constructs, not a catalog of "real" diseases* [emphasis added] . . . . Sadness should not be synonymous with sickness. There is no diagnosis for every disappointment or a pill for

every problem. Life's difficulties — divorce, illness, job loss, financial troubles, interpersonal conflicts — can't be legislated away. And our natural reactions to them — sadness, dissatisfaction, and discouragement — shouldn't all be medicalized as mental disorder or treated with a pill.[34]

Others, such as former director of the National Institute of Mental Health (NIMH), Thomas Insel, boldly stated in 2013 in anticipation of the *DSM-5's* release,

> While *DSM* has been described as a 'Bible' for the field, it is, at best, a dictionary, creating a set of labels and defining each. . . . The weakness [of the *DSM*] is its lack of validity. Unlike our definitions of ischemic heart disease, lymphoma, or AIDS, the *DSM* diagnoses are based on a consensus about clusters of clinical symptoms, not any objective laboratory measure.[35]

Similarly, former professor of psychiatry at Johns Hopkins, University of Maryland, and George Mason University, and full-time consultant for the NIMH Peter Breggin affirms that depression is not a disease:

> It is a mistake to view depressed feelings or even severely depressed feelings as a 'disease.' Depression, remember, is an emotional response to life. It is a feeling of unhappiness — a particular kind of unhappiness that involves helpless self-blame and guilt, a sense of not deserving happiness, and a loss of interest in life.[36]

Depression is a secular construct or syndrome — an anthropology, which simply recognizes, describes, and lists common impairing features of human nature from a humanistic vantage point. Despite these prominent psychiatrists' (and many

[34] Allen Frances, *Saving Normal: An Insider's Revolt against Out-of-Control Psychiatric Diagnosis, DSM-5, Big Pharma, and the Medicalization of Ordinary Life* (New York: HarperCollins, 2013), 73; 155.

[35] Thomas Insel, "Transforming Diagnosis," http://www.nimh.nih.gov/about/director/2013/transforming - diagnosis.shtml.

[36] Breggin, Anti-Depressant Fact Book, 14.

others') public transparency about the *DSM-5* and its ever-expanding psychiatric constructs, many people still believe that constructs like depression are primarily medical issues and valid diagnoses instead of merely subjective, descriptive, humanistic labels.[37]

People who have accepted the psychiatric labels have, in one way or another, accepted by faith the American Psychiatric Association's theory and interpretation of human nature. Many people have understandably placed their faith in the psychiatric concept of depression simply because it lists and describes their exact struggles. By identifying with the created label and disease construct, people begin to assume that to deny the label and construct is to deny the underlying problems and subsequently any potential remedy.

But denying the psychiatric constructs are not in any way denying the very real struggles. Instead, dismissing psychiatric labels frees us to examine the cluster of symptoms and observe them through a different philosophical lens. What then emerges is a discovery that these same criteria, which compose the construct of depression, are explained in detail from a different perspective than that of the APA and its *DSM-5*.

It may be surprising to learn that the Bible presents and explains thoroughly the same criteria that psychiatrists utilize from the list of constructs of depressive disorders and bipolar disorders in the *DSM-5*. Of course, Scripture approaches these criteria with a different worldview from the humanistic vantage point and interprets, classifies, and names them differently than the *DSM-5* does. Likewise, the Bible does not limit human struggles to

[37] For further study on the *DSM-5* and the American Psychiatric Association's claims of its authority and reliability, see Daniel R. Berger, *Mental Illness: The Necessity for Faith and Authority* (Taylors, SC: Alethia International Publications, 2016).

social constructs. Nonetheless, God's written Word talks at length about these features of human nature and regularly presents them in clusters. While both the Bible and the *DSM-5* acknowledge the destructive nature of the criteria, these two approaches represent opposing beliefs about our human nature and its subsequent remediation.

Having two opposing interpretations, approaches, and explanations of the same criteria from which to choose determines that one or the other be granted authority; everyone must decide upon a presuppositional faith. In fact, Wilhelm Wundt, considered by many to be the "father of modern psychology" and the "father of experimental psychology" [38] said the same in regard to studies/approaches to human nature — what he called "psychology": "All psychological investigation extrapolates from metaphysical [spiritual] presuppositions."[39] Truly, as Wundt acknowledged, the presuppositional beliefs or apologetics that you or I choose are foundational to any attempt to study, explain, interpret, classify, and remedy every aspect of our human nature. With this truth in mind, we must not only examine the features of depression, but also the underlying philosophies that sustain the current beliefs and approaches.

For the Christian, the two prominent and available presuppositional faiths options are: (1) faith in the constantly changing human wisdom of the APA and its *DSM*, or (2) faith in

---

[38] Saul McLeod, "Wilhelm Wundt," *Simply Psychology Online*, 2008, https://www.simplypsychology.org/wundt.html. Both Sigmund Freud and Emil Kraepelin studied under Wundt's teaching, and both formed their own psychological paradigm by which to explain human nature. Today, the Kraepelinian theory is the predominant medical model of mental illness in America.

[39] Wundt: *System der Philosophie* 1 (1919), preface ix.

the fixed wisdom of Christ as offered in Scripture. As we will see, these presuppositional lenses are antithetical. Whether you place your faith in the Word of God or in the APA's *DSM-5* to describe and approach your struggles, you must accept a moral authority — a presuppositional faith — by which to interpret and attempt to remedy your own mindsets and behaviors as well as to discern those of others around you.

AN OVERVIEW OF THE MAJOR CRITERIA

While there are numerous features or criteria listed in the *DSM-5*, there are three major features of depression which both Scripture and the *DSM-5* discuss at length and which are well-recognized as depression. We will focus our discussion on these three primary features to gain a broad understanding, and thereafter, we will examine each of the three major features of depression more in depth as well as the secondary criteria. Understanding and discussing these very real struggles versus simply identifying with a label that attempts to combine the struggles into a syndrome will be key to interpreting and remedying them.

It is also important to understand that although the *DSM-5* lists numerous alleged types of depression,[40] the APA admits that each of these various sub-constructs share the same core problems. In the *DSM-5*, these allegedly different disorders are primarily listed under "depressive disorders" (unipolar depression) and "bipolar disorders" (bipolar depression). While the APA suggests that these constructs represent different types

---

[40] "Disruptive mood dysregulation disorder, major depressive disorder, persistent depressive disorder (dysthymia), premenstrual dysphoric disorder, substance/medication-induced depressive disorder, depressive disorder due to another medical condition, other specified depressive disorder, and unspecified depressive disorder. Unlike in *DSM-IV*, this chapter 'Depressive Disorders' has been separated from the previous chapter 'Bipolar and Related Disorders'" (APA, *DSM-5*, 155).

of depression, it admits that these various labels merely describe differences in time and speculated causes ("etiologies").[41] In fact, the APA states this reality precisely in the *DSM-5* introduction to depressive disorders and makes it clear that all of these different psychiatric labels share the same common problems:

> The common feature of all of these [depressive] disorders is the presence of sad, empty, or irritable mood, accompanied by somatic and cognitive changes that significantly affect the individual's capacity to function. What differs among them are issues of duration, timing, or presumed etiology.[42]

According to the APA the differences between alleged types of depression are found in what it speculates as (1) the causes of depression, (2) the time it seems to first surface in a person's life, and (3) the duration of its episodes. But at their core, the criteria are the same throughout all the unipolar and bipolar constructs.[43]

Because these psychiatric labels share the same underlying problems, there is no need to address each one individually or accept the APA's numerous labels. As even the APA acknowledges in its own publication, "The classification of depression disorders has long been controversial."[44] Again, the genuine problem is the "common features" and not the various subjective and ever-changing psychiatric labels or categories of

---

[41] None of the APA's presumed causes of depressive disorders have been proven. Correlations do not equal causation.

[42] APA, *DSM-5*, 155.

[43] As will be seen in chapter 4, even the manic pole in the construct of bipolar is a common feature in the depressive disorders.

[44] Gordon Parker, "Classifying Depression: Should Paradigms Lost be Regained?" *American Psychiatric Association Online* (August 1, 2000): https://doi.org/10.1176/appi.ajp. 157.8.1195.

classification. Looking at the three major criteria will yield the most benefit, provide much needed clarity, and lead to genuine hope so desperately needed.

A DETAILED VIEW OF THE THREE CRITERIA

People whom clinicians diagnose as having unipolar depression or manic depression (now called bipolar depression by the APA) struggle with one of or a combination of three core criteria. The *DSM-5* lists three major criteria for depressive disorders: (1) deep impairing sorrow ("feels sad" and "empty"[45]), (2) a sense of being "hopeless"[46], and (3) guilt or shame ("feelings of worthlessness or excessive or inappropriate guilt"[47]) as the three major criteria for depressive disorders.[48]

Deep sorrow or sadness stands out in the list of symptoms, as it is likely the most recognized feature of depression, and many times, deep sadness is the only observable feature necessary for a person to be diagnosed as depressed. Though persistent or enduring sorrow is viewed by psychiatrists as an abnormality, most secular theorists admit that sorrow is an unfortunate aspect of everyone's life experience and not just some people. During our lives we may lose loved ones, be rejected by others, fight with our children or our parents, be betrayed, be fired from our job, contract a serious disease, struggle with sin, be unsatisfied with our life's pursuits, lose an important game, go through a divorce, be falsely accused, be cheated on, have a terminal illness, be abandoned by our biological parents, or have our

[45] APA, *DSM-5*, 160.

[46] Ibid.

[47] Ibid., 161.

[48] Ibid., 160-61.

plans fall through after great sacrifice and effort. Life is full of experiences and realities that multiply sorrows.

There are three important features of the nature of sorrow, hopelessness, and guilt that need to be identified and better understood: they are (1) naturally not desired, (2) metaphysical or spiritual, and (3) most of the time, an accurate or honest assessment of life. These are the true nature of the major features of depression.

They are Impairing

By nature, sorrow or sadness, hopelessness, and guilt are all impairing/distressful mental states. No one lives his/her life looking for sorrow, hopelessness, or making decisions according to what will incur the most sadness or guilt. People normally pursue help in attempt to assuage or eliminate them. Sorrow, hopelessness, and guilt are so impairing that they can negatively affect the body, producing negative biological changes such as tears, catatonia, atrophied brains, and insomnia to name a few.

As with sorrow, hopelessness is a mental state one experiences in respect to his/her faith and in relation to one's own condition and future. Hopelessness is not a criterion that is secondary to sorrow in the construct of depression, though; it is the major tenet. Hopelessness is so relevant to our discussion that humanistic psychologist Rollo May once offered this definition: "Depression is the inability to construct a future."[49]

The distressful and impairing nature of hopelessness, as with sorrow, often negatively alters and impairs the physical body and leads to death. In fact, it is widely understood that without some form of hope, death is inevitable. In 2005, the American Psychology Association reviewed and assessed large numbers of

---

[49] Rollo May, *Love and Will*, (New York: W.W. Norton, 1969), 243.

studies conducted to determine what causes people to change in counseling. One of the most powerful negative change agents that they discovered was hopelessness. They explain,

> Data analyses revealed a dramatic dose-response relationship between hopelessness and mortality. . . . Hopelessness is an independent and powerful predictor of morbidity and mortality.[50]

Hopelessness is so impairing that it can kill a person.

A great example of how hopelessness can negatively affect the body — even leading to death — is found in what many have come to call "Give-Up-Itis":

> Some individuals who are exposed to extreme trauma, including prisoners of war and survivors of shipwrecks and air crashes, develop a syndrome that has been labeled "give-up-itis" (GUI). It is characterized by progressively severe demotivation that can end in inexplicable death.[51]

One psychiatrist states in the article that the remedy to GUI is "instilling hope."[52] Hopelessness is a central feature of depression, and it (as with hope) has a major impact on the human body.

Guilt is the third major criteria in the psychiatric constructs of depression, and it is likely the least acknowledged factor. In an

---

[50] Mark Hubble, Barry Duncan, and Scott Miller, *The Heart and Soul of Change: What Works in Therapy* (Washington, D.C.: American Psychological Association, 1999), 268.

[51] Pauline Anderson, "Psychogenic Death: Why Do Healthy People Give Up on Life?" *Medscape Medical News Online*, October 16, 2018, https://www.medscape.com/viewarticle/903507?nlid=125620_2051&src=WNL_mdplsnews_181019_mscpedit_psyc&uac=264124BV&spon=12&impID=1774566&faf=1.

[52] Ibid.

article published on *Psychcentral*, Margarita Tartakovsky discusses the correlation of guilt and depression:

> If you also have depression, you, too, probably have a list. And you, too, probably can relate to the gnawing, stubborn and heavy weight of guilt. It's guilt that can lead to self-doubt or even self-harm. . . . Guilt sparks insecurity, indecision and even poor decisions.[53]

Sadly, the article goes on to suggest humanistic ways to "chip away at your guilt." Other physicians, such as Andy Belden, note similarly,

> To date, one of the most consistent and robust correlates of [childhood] depression has been the tendency for pathological guilt. This includes both the experience of excessive guilt and infrequent or chronic maladaptive attempts to repair, amend, or correct wrongdoings (real or imagined) from which a sense of guilt emerged.[54]

From every perspective, guilt (real or false) is understood to be a factor of depression.

As with sorrow and hopelessness, guilt is a burden of the human soul which everyone wishes to escape. In quoting Peter Marin, West Point psychologist Dave Grossman discusses the normal social perspective of guilt as an impairing "pathology" (medical issue):

> "As a society, we seem unable to deal with moral pain or guilt. Instead it is treated as a neurosis or a pathology, something to

---

[53] Margarita Tartakovsky, "Overcoming Guilt in Depression," March 3, 2013, www.psychcentral.com/blog/ archives/2013/03/31/overcoming-guilt-in-depression.

[54] Andy Belden et al., "Anterior Insula Volume and Guilt: Neurobehavioral Markers of Recurrence after Early Childhood Major Depressive Disorder" *JAMA Psychiatry* vol. 72 (1) (2015): 40-8.

escape rather than something to learn from, a disease rather than . . .
an appropriate if painful response to the past."[55]

Guilt is impairing and thus we rightly desire to escape it, but as Grossman points out, guilt has positive meaning and purpose. So while valid guilt is distressful, it is also appropriate, and when guilt is resolved appropriately, the person is bettered.

Leading secular researchers now recognize that struggling with guilt is an indicator of future mental struggles and psychiatric diagnoses:

> Excessive guilt is a known symptom of adult depression, but a new study finds that such feelings in the childhood can predict future mental illness, including depression, anxiety, obsessive-compulsive disorder and bipolar disorder.[56]

One must seriously consider what causes guilt, how it leads to deeper mental struggles, and how to remedy it since it is at the core of depression.

They are Honest

Most people think of sorrow, hopelessness, and guilt as impairments but not as an honest assessment of life. Yet, at their core, sorrow and hopelessness are mindsets that always relate to one's perception of reality and his/her own spiritual heart. We might say, then, that sorrow is a reaction to the fallen nature of life and our heart's desires, or that sadness is simply being honest about the vanity, emptiness, trauma, and tragedy of this

---

[55] Peter Marin quoted by Dave Grossman, *On Killing: The Psychological Cost of Learning to Kill in War and Society*, rev. ed. (New York: Back Bay Books, 2009), 95.

[56] Belden, et al., "Anterior Insula Volume and Guilt." See also "Feelings of Guilt during Childhood Linked to Mental Illness," http://www.huffington post.com/ 2015/01/07/guilt-mentalhealth_n_6423434.html? cps=gravity_ 2692_-3767883313446572831.

present age. In a similar fashion, hopelessness is the honest realization of one's current physical or spiritual state and the acknowledgement that deliverance is either not available or is not obtainable in the future.

If life in general is happy, then sadness should be viewed as an abnormality. But if life is generally sorrowful and fallen, then sorrow should be expected and understood — no matter how deep, enduring, or impairing — as a normal honest assessment of and reaction to life. This reality might be why the APA chose "manic-depressive reaction" and "depressive reaction" as their first constructs published in the *DSM-I* used to describe the mindsets, emotions, and behaviors now framed as depressive and bipolar disorders.[57] Sadness is simply the right and expected reaction to the broken reality of this life and our own unfulfilled desires after the fall of Adam and Eve. Likewise, most people who are struggling with hopelessness have had their hopes crushed and are in an honest state of despair as they acknowledge their true condition.

The same is true with guilt. Guilt is the natural mental process which results as one mentally/consciously relates to a moral law. Guilt that is valid — that is, it directly relates to God's moral law to love God and love others — is natural. But valid guilt does also multiply sorrow and hopelessness, since all people naturally fail to perfectly uphold God's moral law and must inevitably and consequently face death and judgment. One might say, then, that guilt is an honest evaluation of one's reality as he or she relates to God's moral law and to God Himself as the perfect judge, his or her own conscience, and social law that surrounds him or her. Biblically, guilt and God's justice are directly related, and justification is the only means of appeasing valid guilt.

[57] Bentall, *Madness Explained*, 58.

Because guilt indicates how one relates to the law (whether God ordained or man-made), legalistic relationships and mindsets regularly create an environment for guilt, sorrow, and hopelessness to flourish. It is no wonder, then, that many people who grow up in legalistic religious families, where the law is stressed and a moral standard apart from grace (which is impossible to meet) is established, end up being diagnosed within the psychiatric system as depressed. Some also end up taking their own lives because of their guilt/false guilt and apparently hopeless condition. In a number of homes where an established social law is emphasized over a loving relationship with Christ and others (the true law), depression is prevalent. Wherever guilt cannot be assuaged, hopelessness and deep sorrow are inevitable.

Both true and false guilt are features of the construct of depression.[58] True guilt is determined by God — the true and perfect judge, and it is based upon His perfect moral law and judgment. In contrast, false guilt is established upon a false judge in accordance with a false law, and is regularly experienced because of both the deceived nature of our spiritual hearts as well as the judging nature of our own conscience.

They are Metaphysical

Sorrow, hopelessness, and guilt are also immaterial/metaphysical/spiritual — that is, these features have no physical quality. Sorrow, hopelessness, guilt cannot be observed with the physical eye or neuroimaging, and they cannot be measured with scientific instruments or approached with the scientific process. Of course, the physical effects of sadness, hopelessness,

[58] Secularists who deny God's moral law and humanity's culpability believe that all guilt is false guilt. See National Institute of Mental Health, "Depression," *NIMH* (2018): https://www.nimh.nih.gov/health/topics /depression/index.shtml.

and guilt (e.g., catatonia, apathy, associated behaviors, and effects on the nervous system) can be observed and measured, but there is no scientific means to measure or observe actual sorrow, hopelessness, or guilt. This reality is why the Bible states with full assurance that "faith [not material] is the substance of things hoped for the evidence of things not seen" (Hebrews 11:1). Romans 8:24b affirms this truth, "Now hope that is seen is not hope. For who hopes for what he sees?" Hopelessness is the metaphysical condition of the soul that longs for deliverance. The nature of both hope and hopelessness are always metaphysical and relate to a person's faith.

Sorrow, hopelessness and guilt then, are spiritual realities of human nature that often produces symptoms which can be observed in the physical realm, but no one can see or touch sorrow or guilt, and science cannot measure or approach hopelessness using the scientific method. The only way that researchers, clinicians, and counselors can know that someone feels guilty is by the counselee's own testimony, the testimony of others, and the knowledge of a person's life circumstances.

Sorrow, hopelessness, and guilt all relate and are born out of the spiritual heart. As one's desires meet the inevitable disappointments and unsatisfying realities of fallen nature and the fallen world, sorrow is realized. As one naturally attempts to establish hope after failed hope and comes to realize the futility in such human endeavor, hopelessness is realized, and as one acknowledges their inability to perfectly keep God's moral law written on their spiritual heart or fails at their own created moral law apart from God, guilt is realized. These spiritual mindsets all reflect the spiritual heart's true impaired condition.

A BIBLICAL UNDERSTANDING OF THE THREE CRITERIA

The Bible speaks extensively about sorrow, hopelessness, and guilt and often clusters them together. That Scripture discusses these metaphysical features of human nature at length should make Christians question why they are viewed as medical conditions or foundationally as biological problems. More importantly, however, Christians must seek to understand God's perspective on sorrow, hopelessness, and guilt.

The Core Elements

It is imperative as one decides how to interpret these common but impairing mindsets that he or she examines carefully how the Bible describes the core elements. Such understanding will provide clarity that leads to healing.

It is also important that we recognize how Scripture utilizes different words from modern secularists to describe the same mindsets and behaviors listed in the psychiatric construct of depression. For example, the Hebrew presentation of what we today call sadness or sorrow in English is presented as "spiritual pain" (e.g., Isaiah 53 – Christ was a man of spiritual pain; "a man of sorrows"). This perspective makes sense when we understand that sorrow is metaphysical pain that cannot be seen or approached with science; it occurs in the soul and manifests in the physical realm. Psychiatrist Allen Frances notes that "our capacity to feel emotional [spiritual] pain has great adaptive value equivalent in its purpose to physical pain—a signal that something has gone wrong [or was wrong from the start]."[59] Scripture also uses words such as *lament* to describe the heavy burden of sorrow that people must mentally and physically bear in life.

---

[59] Frances, *Saving Normal*, 155.

In a similar fashion, the English versions of Scripture do not use the word *hopelessness*. Instead, the majority of English versions utilize the phrase "a crushed spirit" to describe the Hebrew understanding of hopelessness and being humbled. The biblical idea of a crushed spirit conveys the reality that people are by their own nature unable to bear the harsh realities of this life. For instance, in Proverbs 18:14 the Bible contrasts physical sickness with the soul's crushing or depression: "A man's spirit will endure sickness, but a crushed spirit who can bear?" The biblical commentator Bruce Waltke states of this Scripture that "when the spirit is gone, a person is as good as dead. Therefore, psychological depression is worse than physical affliction."[60]

Whereas, the word *depression* has the idea of pushing down or being weighted down, the phrase "a crushed spirit" is far more violent and better reflects what occurs in the soul/psyche. When people are hopeless, it is not merely that they are weighted down. Rather, their identity, desires, aspirations in life, and sense of purpose and value (the spiritual heart) have been crushed or even destroyed. Unlike the biblical phrase "a crushed spirit," however, the secular term *depression* lacks clarity in describing what exactly is being depressed or crushed within a person. The crushing nature of deep sorrow and hopelessness exposes the truth that human nature is fragile rather than strong.

Vexation is another important word found throughout Scripture that encompasses a very wide range of internal turmoil and stress/distress (e.g., fear or anxiety [Psalm 2:5], terror [Isaiah 28:19], trauma [Nehemiah 9:27], sorrow [Psalm 31:9; Ecclesiastes 1:14, 17-18; 2:11], anguish [Isaiah 9:1], distress [Deuteronomy 2:9], guilt and shame [Proverbs 12:16; 27:3], etc.). Often English

---

[60] Bruce Waltke, *The Book of Proverbs: Chapters 16-31* (Grand Rapids, MI: Eerdmans, 2005), 81.

versions of Scripture convey the meaning as "vexation of spirit" (Ecclesiastes 2:17) or "vexation of heart" (Ecclesiastes 2:22) to highlight the true nature and source of the internal struggle. Any spiritual pain, distress, or struggle which is a result from humanity's fallen condition fits under the broad umbrella term of *vexations.*

The core elements of sorrow, guilt, and hopelessness in the psychiatric construct of depression are not just topics that the Bible discusses; they are also three specific aspects of human nature for which Christ came to die and to provide the divine remedy. Sorrow, hopelessness, and guilt are fundamental components of human nature and primary concerns that the gospel of Jesus Christ addresses. Continuing forward in this study, it is essential to realize just how intertwined these very real human struggles are within God's plan to save His people from both their fragility and depravity.

Sorrow, hopelessness, vexation, and guilt — along with sin — are major considerations in the Bible's teaching on why people need an intimate covenant relationship with God. Isaiah 53 explains specifically how Christ took upon himself our sorrow and guilt in order to provide hope and deliver humanity from its fallen condition:

> He is despised and rejected of men; a man of sorrows, and acquainted with grief: and we hid as it were our faces from him; he was despised, and we esteemed him not. Surely he hath borne our griefs, and carried our sorrows: yet we did esteem him stricken, smitten of God, and afflicted. But he was wounded for our transgressions, he was bruised for our iniquities: the chastisement of our peace was upon him; and with his stripes we are healed. . . . Yet it pleased the LORD to bruise Him; He hath put him to grief: when though shalt make his soul an offering for sin, he shall see his seed, he shall prolong his days, and the pleasure of the LORD shall prosper in his hand. He shall see of the travail of his soul, and shall be satisfied: by his knowledge shall my righteous servant justify many; for he shall bear their iniquities (3-12).

Christ became our only hope by bearing our sorrows and providing a guilt offering to pay for our sins on the cross of Calvary that none other could. God considers those who receive Christ and His atoning work on the cross to be guiltless and fully accepted despite their depraved, undeserving nature. Scripture states that attempting to remedy guilt apart from Christ is foolish and futile, as there is no other way for mankind to make peace with God: "Fools mock at the guilt offering, but the upright enjoy acceptance" (Proverbs 14:9).

The Secondary Elements

Although the core elements of depression can be easily observed in passages like Genesis 3 and Isaiah 53, the secondary criteria of depression may not be as easily recognized in Scripture. Consider, for instance, the idea of *catatonia*. The *DSM-5* defines catatonia as the negative bodily changes or impairments. These secondary physical symptoms include inability to move (mental paralysis), nervous twitches,[61] insomnia, fatigue, weight loss, restlessness,[62] and even death.[63] But these criteria are all symptoms of the three core criteria.

Psalm 77:1-15 is one of many passages that shows how the body can be impaired as the direct result of the mental distress of sorrow and hopelessness, and it reveals that the physical negative effects are normal indicators of a soul in need of comfort. The passages states,

> I cry aloud to God, aloud to God, and he will hear me. In the day of my trouble I seek the Lord; in the night my hand is stretched out without wearying; *my soul refuses to be comforted. When I remember*

[61] APA, *DSM-5*, 119.

[62] Ibid., 160.

[63] Nemeroff, "Depression: A Killing Disease."

God, I moan; when I meditate, my spirit faints. Selah You hold my eyelids
open; I am so troubled that I cannot speak [emphasis added]. I
consider the days of old, the years long ago. I said, "Let me
remember my song in the night; let me meditate in my heart." Then
my spirit made a diligent search: "Will the Lord spurn forever, and
never again be favorable? Has his steadfast love forever ceased? Are
his promises at an end for all time? Has God forgotten to be
gracious? Has he in anger shut up his compassion?" Selah

The hopeless condition of perceiving God to be far off and
seemingly forgetting the soul that is suffering leads to the spirit
fainting (apathetic to life, unmotivated, unable to experience
pleasure) and the body shutting down (catatonia). Job attests to
the same reality in Job 17:7: "My eye has also grown dim because
of grief, and all my members are as a shadow." The negative
physical effects of sorrow, such as crying, atrophied brains, and
insomnia are not causative; rather, the physical features are
effects of the spirit's fainting and the soul's need of comfort.

As a person struggles with his/her own sorrow, hopeless
thinking, and guilt (whether valid or not), one must realize that
these struggles are not primarily physical illnesses or caused by
physical malady or dysfunction. Instead, each person must begin
to realize that his/her struggle — though distressful and
impairing — is a normal spiritual reality with significant
meaning. While it is human nature to want to escape painful
realities of one's own life, these seasons have purpose according
to God's plan and can yield incredible fruit despite their
crushing nature. Silver lining aside, however, the symptoms of
depression must be addressed, and this book is intended to
show that genuine hope is available for all people struggling
with deep impairing sorrow, hopelessness, and guilt.

CHAPTER 3

ESTABLISHING NORMALCY

"We are more apt to feel depressed by the perpetually smiling
individual than the one who is honestly sad. If we admit our
depression openly and freely, those around us get from it an
experience of freedom rather than the depression itself."[64] – Rollo
May, father of existential psychotherapy

In 2018, Americans faced the far-too-common news that some
beloved celebrities and public figures had given in to despair
and had taken their own lives. One of these who had even
acknowledged his struggle publicly was the well-known chef
and TV personality Anthony Bourdain. Ironically and tragically,
Bourdain kept on his nightstand a saying by Graham Greene —
considered by many to be one of the greatest writers of the
twentieth century — which exposes the historic view of deep
impairing sorrow prior to the acceptance of psychiatric theory:

> Sometimes I wonder how all those who do not write, compose or
> paint can manage to escape the madness, the melancholia, the panic
> fear which is inherent to the human condition.[65]

[64] Rollo May, *Paulus: Reminiscences of a Friendship* 1st ed. (New York: Harper
& Row, 1973), 77.

[65] Graham Greene quoted by Belinda Luscombe, "Mental Health: A New
Understanding," *Time Magazine* Special Edition (November 2018), 26.

Are depression and madness (deceit)[66] inherent to the human condition as once perceived, or are these common human mindsets, emotions, and behaviors an abnormality or an illness to be treated within the field of medicine?

Most people believe — whether directly stated or implied by the acceptance of depression as a disease entity — that those who struggle with deep impairing sorrow, hopelessness, and guilt are abnormal or disordered. Some go as far as to state that these mindsets are caused by diseases, are themselves illnesses, or are at least physical abnormalities such as genetic variances, chemical imbalances, or brain dysfunctions. It is a common belief that people are normally happy, full of hope, and do not struggle with valid and false guilt for lengths of time. But what if being normal is to struggle throughout one's life with deep impairing sorrow and guilt, having been born into a hopeless condition? These are certainly important questions that need to be answered.

The Psychiatric View

The *DSM-5* specifically states that human weaknesses, distresses, impairments, and maladaptive behaviors which persist or endure should be considered as abnormalities/disorders.[67] Sadness, hopelessness, and guilt are not exceptions to this perspective, and this viewpoint is why the construct of depression exists as an alleged syndrome or mental illness within psychiatric thinking.

[66] For further study on the historical and modern concepts of madness and their normalcy, see Daniel Berger, *The Insanity of Madness: Defining Mental Illness* (Taylors, SC: Alethia International Publications, 2018).

[67] APA, *DSM-5*, 20.

Individual Degenerationism

Undergirding the theory that most people are not naturally depressed is the philosophy of *individual degenerationism*. Individual degenerationism is the belief that when something is mentally, emotionally, or behaviorally wrong with a person and that impairment or distress persists, then the problem occurred apart from normal human nature and became defective at a point in a person's history or within the person's biological makeup.

Throughout psychiatry's short existence, the belief in individual degenerationism has been a central doctrine to psychiatric theory and abnormal psychology.[68] Biological psychiatrists and psychologists, for example, believe that a malfunction or dysfunction in the body causes mental struggles (nature); whereas, romantic psychiatrists, humanistic psychologists, and secular therapists believe that environments and trauma cause dysfunction and mental disorder (nurture). Nonetheless, both types of clinicians and those who combine the two approaches view human fragility and depravity as abnormal or as a disorder when it is impairing or distressful and persists.

Since the APA lists enduring negative symptoms as defining the syndrome of depression, then sorrow, hopelessness, guilt, and many other spiritual vexations are conceptualized as abnormalities. Psychiatric epidemiologist Allan Horwitz and professor of sociology Jerome Wakefield explain,

> The fact that these symptom-based definitions are the foundation of the entire mental health research and treatment enterprise makes their validity critically important. Psychiatric research and treatment are like an upside-down pyramid, and the *DSM* definitions of mental disorders that determine who is counted as disordered are

[68] Thomson Gale, "Degeneration," 2006, https://www.encyclopedia.com /history/encyclopedias-almanacs-transcripts-and-maps/degeneration.

the one small point on which the soundness of the entire pyramid rests.[69]

In other words, individual degenerationism is the very small foundation of all the constructed psychiatric disorders, including depression. Psychiatrists must maintain a distinction between normal and abnormal for their so-called treatments to continue being perceived as falling within the medical realm. Psychologist Philip Hickey remarks,

> Physicians are trained in the medical disease-centered model. This approach, which is extraordinarily *effective* in the treatment of real illness, is proportionately *harmful* when applied to problems of thinking, feeling, and behaving. The critical difference here is that real illnesses have a very large degree of homogeneity with regards to their origins, etiology, course, outcome, and appropriate treatment. By contrast, the kinds of life problems that psychiatry purports to address do *not* have this homogeneous core. Pneumonia is caused by germs in the lungs and the treatment consists essentially of eliminating those germs. The causes of depression and other forms of "psychiatric" distress, however, are as varied as the individuals who experience them. The notion that one can develop guidelines for the "treatment" of human distress analogous to those for real illnesses is a fundamental error. Shoe-horning the vast complexity of human problems into psychiatry's invalid and unreliable "diagnoses," and using these labels to justify widespread drugging and electric shocks, is arguably the most destructive hoax in human history. And *as long as the illness thesis is retained, there is no possibility of reform.* But if the central thesis is abandoned, then psychiatry loses the reason for its existence, and psychiatrists will have to find honest work. And that is the critical issue: *for psychiatry this is a death-struggle.*[70]

[69] Allan Horwitz and Jerome Wakefield, *The Loss of Sadness: How Psychiatry Transformed Normal Sorrow into Depressive Disorder* (New York: Oxford, 2007), 7-8.

[70] Philip Hickey, "Robert Whitaker Refutes Jeffrey Lieberman; But Is Psychiatry Reformable?" *Mad in America Online,* June 22, 2017, https://www.madinamerica.com/2017/06/robert-whitaker-refutes-jeffrey-lieberman-but-is-psychiatry-reformable/.

The "medical disease-centered model "or "illness thesis" of the soul is built upon the philosophy of individual degenerationism and is vitally necessary to sustain psychiatry.

There are two primary philosophies which rely heavily on individual degenerationism and which undergird the current psychiatric paradigm. These beliefs are shamanism and humanism.

Shamanism

Individual degenerationism guided the very first psychiatrists- previously called shamans or witchdoctors. This truth may surprise some, as shamanism is primarily a religion that uses magical potions and divinations to construct ideas about and to approach problems in human nature. *Meriam Webster's Dictionary* defines shamanism as:

> a religion practiced by indigenous peoples of far northern Europe and Siberia that is characterized by belief in an unseen world of gods, demons, and ancestral spirits responsive only to the shamans.[71]

Psychiatrist Allen Frances explains this important but overlooked fact of psychiatric history:

> Psychiatry seems like a young profession, barely two hundred years old but you could fairly say it is the oldest. Diagnosing and ministering to the mentally ill was part of the job description of the shaman, or medicine man. . . . The shaman got to stay home doing sick calls, *using his magic to assess the causes and apply the cures for mental and physical symptoms.* . . . Doing psychiatry was always a big part of a shaman's practice [emphasis added].[72]

---

[71] "Shamanism," January 4, 2019, https://www.merriam-webster.com /dictionary/shamanism.

[72] Frances, *Saving Normal*, 36-37.

Frances further highlights the shaman's/psychiatrist's reliance upon individual degenerationism:

> *Abnormal behavior* constitutes a threat not only to the individual; it is also a clear and present danger to the future of the tribe. Psychiatric emergencies must be quickly labeled, understood, treated, and cured. *The shaman had all the tools to define and deal with abnormality. He could diagnose mental disorder, explain its origin, and make it better. . . . The shaman had great authority and healing power.* Magical belief and suggestion can go a long way. But beyond the hocus-pocus, he had practical common sense, *wisdom about human nature, and medicinal plants.* Cures were expensive, and the shaman was the richest person in the tribe [emphases added].[73]

Psychiatrists, like their predecessors, base their approaches and practices upon their "wisdom about human nature" and their subsequent subjective beliefs about what constitutes mental/ spiritual abnormalities. As Frances notes, psychiatry is primarily rooted in the religion of shamanism.

At the end of 2018, the Group for the Advancement of Psychiatry published an article in the *Psychiatric Times,* affirming once again psychiatry's origins in shamanism/sorcery:

> When did psychiatry begin? Was it with the discovery of the unconscious? Or was it the discovery of neurotransmitters? As it turns out, *healers* have been treating mental disorders for thousands of years. Modern psychiatry reflects some, but not all, *the values and concepts* held by early civilizations. Early civilizations relied on shamans, sorcerers, magicians, mystics, priests, and other approved healers to treat illnesses. Using rituals, incantations, and offerings, sickness could be prevented or healed. . . . Shamans entered into trances or altered states of consciousness, enabling their souls to journey into spirit worlds, sometimes into the underworld. During the journey, shamans connected to souls of the dead and to living *souls that had strayed or been stolen. Interacting with demons and lost*

---

[73] Ibid., 37.

*souls without losing their own souls, they brought about cures. The
shaman acted as both priest and healer* [emphasis added].[74]

Entering the spirit world and interacting with demons as a
means of "rescuing strayed souls," discovering cures for
perceived spiritual abnormalities, and obtaining new knowledge
is what Scripture calls *divinations*. The similarities between
societal healers of the mind who were once called shamans and
societal healers of the mind who are now called psychiatrists are
not coincidental. As these groups of influential psychiatrists
admit, psychiatry ("the medical treatment of the soul") is neo-
shamanism.

Both the ancient shaman and the modern psychiatrist rely on a
created diagnostic system of alleged abnormalities — based upon
their wisdom or knowledge about human nature — as well as
relying on psychoactive substances to achieve enlightenment
and transcendence:

> Western psychotherapy and indigenous shamanic healing systems
> have both used psychoactive drugs or plants for healing and
> obtaining knowledge (called "diagnosis" or "divination"
> respectively).[75]

If normal human nature relating to our psyche/soul which is
impairing or distressful can be framed as an abnormality —
especially as a biological issue, then sorcery can be viewed as
legitimate medicine instead of what it truly is.

---

[74] Kenneth J. Weiss on behalf of the Group for the Advancement of
Psychiatry, "Psychiatry's Ancient Origins," *Psychiatric Times Online* 35, no. 11
(November 29, 2018): http://www. psychiatrictimes.com/cultural-psychiatry/
psychiatrys-ancient-origins?rememberme=1&elq_mid= 4523&elq_cid=893295.

[75] Ralph Metzner, "Hallucinogenic Drugs and Plants in Psychotherapy and
Shamanism," *Journal of Psychoactive Drugs* 30, no. 4 (September 6, 2011):
Abstract. http://dx.doi.org/10.1080/ 02791072.1998.10399709.

The humanistic philosophy of individual degenerationism enables the ancient shaman and the modern psychiatrist alike to construct "healing systems" that control whom society views as normal and whom they consider to be degenerated or disordered. Of course, in today's neo-shaman system there are differences: (1) the metaphysical soul or psyche has theoretically been replaced with biological explanations, (2) modern magic potions are manufactured by pharmaceutical companies rather than by the individual shaman, (3) so-called scientific piety is claimed and championed over previously claimed spiritual superiority (shamans claimed only they could heal or rescue the soul),[76] and (4) the role of shaman has been professionalized, standardized, and granted authority in determining normalcy.

It may seem as though the modern psychiatric theory is free from obtaining knowledge from supernatural sources ("divinations"), but this notion is far from true. In his book, *Shrinks: The Untold Story of Psychiatry*, immediate past president-elect of the APA who presided over the publication of the *DSM-5* and is current head of psychiatry at Columbia University, Jeffrey Lieberman, writes about psychiatrists' common usage of mind-altering drugs. In his words, he admits that through his own consumption of LSD he began to accept psychopharmacology as a legitimate and ethical way to treat the mind/soul:

> Along with many other psychiatrists from my generation [like Bob Spitzer] — many of whom also experimented with psychedelic drugs — I became receptive to the unexpected new role of psychiatrists as psychopharmacologists, as empathic prescribers of medicine.[77]

[76] "Shamanism," January 4, 2019, https://www.merriam-webster.com/dictionary/shamanism.

[77] Jeffrey A. Lieberman, *Shrinks: the Untold Story of Psychiatry* (New York: Little, Brown and Company, 2015), 191-92.

Lieberman has been one of the most influential and powerful psychiatrists who continues to ardently promote and defend the medical model of mental illness and psychopharmacology as a legitimate remedy. Lieberman later expounds upon his own experience of divination and explains with clarity why he became receptive and supportive of psychotropic drugs:

> Until then, the effects of the LSD had been mostly perceptual. Now a new experience emerged that was far more intense and mind-bending — in fact, I often recall this portion of my trip when I work with psychotic patients. As I gazed upon the religious accouterments of the church, *I was filled with an overwhelming spiritual awareness, as if God was communicating His secret and divine meaning to me. A cascade of insights tumbled through my consciousness, seeming to touch my soul and thrilling me with their profundity.* And then in the midst of this revelatory reverie, *a disembodied voice whispered,* "and no one will ever know," which seemed to signify to me that *this was where the real truths lie, in these secret interstices of consciousness which most human beings never accessed* — or if they did, they were unable to retain these precious encounters in their memory . . . We later realized that our individual experiences [on LSD] were entirely separate and often absurdly different. *As my mind soared through metaphysical realms of empyrean* [heavenly] *knowledge,* [my girlfriend] spent most of her trip reflecting on her relationship with her father [emphases added].[78]

Lieberman — who continues to receive large sums of money from big pharma for his support and advocacy of mind-altering drugs as treatments for the soul[79] — goes on to describe the knowledge he obtained from the "disembodied voice" in the metaphysical realm:

> My trip did produce one lasting insight, though — one that I remain grateful for to this day. Though my LSD-fueled reverie dissipated with the light of the morning, I marveled at the fact that such an incredibly minute amount of a chemical — 50 to 100 micrograms, a fraction of a grain of salt — could so profoundly affect my perceptions and emotions. It struck me that if LSD could so

[78] Ibid., 191-92.

[79] Hickey, "Robert Whitaker Refutes Jeffrey Lieberman."

dramatically alter my cognition, the chemistry of the brain must be susceptible to pharmacologic manipulation in other ways, including ways that could be therapeutic. . . . My psychedelic experiment opened me up to an alternative way of thinking about mental pathologies beyond psychodynamics — as something concrete and biochemical in the cellular coils of the brain . . . . The psychopharmacologists didn't just voice a *new and radical philosophy about mental illness*; they behaved in forbidden ways [emphasis added].[80]

Lieberman has been at the front line in establishing the medical model of mental illness and psychopharmacology as legitimate ways to view and approach human nature since his "spiritual enlightenment." Receiving new knowledge about human nature and possible remedies for its struggles through mind-altering substances, as with the shamans of old, is foundational to psychiatry's medical model of mental illness.[81] This "new and radical philosophy about mental illness" was partially born out of sorcery, which the Bible condemns. While secularists who support the biomedical model regularly criticize Christians who place their faith in divine revelation, the beliefs that sustain the construct of mental illness are sourced in the faith of past and present shamans.

Humanism

Along with the traditions of shamanism, the presuppositional belief of humanism demands that individual degenerationism be upheld. A core teaching of the philosophy of humanism is that people are by nature progressing in a positive direction and evolving within their own strength — "the capacity for self-realization through reason."[82] Humanists also deny the reality of

[80] Ibid., 192-94.

[81] Oliver Sacks, *Hallucinations* (New York: Random House, 2012), 106.

[82] "Humanism," January 4, 2019, https://www.merriam-webster.com/dictionary/humanism.

a Creator God and eternity and believe that only people can save themselves from their problems. The Humanist Society of Western New York describes this common position:

> Humanism is: A joyous alternative to religions that believe in a supernatural god and life in a hereafter. Humanists believe that this is the only life of which we have certain knowledge and that we owe it to ourselves and others to make it the best life possible for ourselves and all with whom we share this fragile planet. *A belief that when people are free to think for themselves, using reason and knowledge as their tools, they are best able to solve this world's problems* [emphasis added].[83]

The American Humanist Association, which holds as their celebrated motto "Good without a God," agrees:

> Humanism is a progressive philosophy of life that, without theism or other supernatural beliefs, affirms our ability and responsibility to lead ethical lives of personal fulfillment that aspire to the greater good.[84]

Humanism is faith and hope in mankind's wisdom, abilities, and perceived goodness.

When mental impairment or distress endures and is unresolved from within a person or from within his/her community — people are unable to save themselves, the secular theory of humanism is undermined. The only way to sustain the false theory that humanity is able to fully deliver itself from deep impairment and distress is to classify people who struggle mentally, emotionally, and behaviorally in a persistent way as degenerates or as disordered. Dr. Allen Frances provides a good example of one who holds to this position:

---

[83] American Humanist Association, "Definition of Humanism," *American Humanist Association Online* (December 2018): https://american humanist.org/what-is-humanism/definition-of-humanism/.

[84] Ibid.

> We are *usually resilient, lick our wounds, mobilize our resources, and our friends, and get on with it.* Our capacity to feel emotional pain has great adaptive value equivalent in its purpose to physical pain—a signal that something has gone wrong. We can't convert all emotional pain into mental disorder *without radically changing who we are* [emphases added].[85]

As Frances rightly notes, one's view of normalcy is vitally important to his/her view of abnormality. If we understand that it all went wrong in Genesis 3 for everyone—that no one is "usually resilient" or morally good, then how we perceive who we are and others around us radically changes.

Humanists must frame sorrow, guilt, and hopelessness which cannot be resolved by one's own will-power, self-actualization, and/or self-esteem as an abnormality known as depression. Since most humanists also believe in the philosophy of materialism,[86] these speculated abnormalities are explained as biological diseases. Framing these common features of human fragility as an alleged disease makes them seem bearable and denies the truth that Scripture establishes, which is that a person's spirit is crushed and cannot bear the weight of his/her own reality. Still, many psychotherapies seek to establish higher self-esteem and greater self-actualization in the counselee as an attempt to remedy depression. Celebrated humanistic psychologist, Rollo May explains,

> Therapy isn't curing somebody of something; it is a means of helping a person explore himself, his life, his consciousness. My purpose as a therapist is to find out what it means to be human.[87]

---

[85] Frances, *Saving Normal*, 155.

[86] See chapter 5 for further discussion on the philosophy of materialism.

[87] Rollo May quoted by James E. De Burger, "Problem, Issues, and Alternatives," *Marriage Today* (1977): 444.

Secularists' underlying belief about human nature is that it can be saved from its condition by turning inward and empowering or transcending the human spirit (e.g. psychotherapy and psychopharmacology). But such theory has clearly failed over the last century. Ironically, some secular psychiatrists even describe depression as "a morbid preoccupation with 'me'"[88] or as those who have "their minds turned agonizingly inward."[89]

Professor of psychiatry and researcher at Yale Medical School, Anna Yusim also exemplifies the modern psychiatric perspective. As with shamans of old, Yusim found her own so called deliverance and purpose in life from seeking out traditional shamans and embracing humanistic philosophy taught to her in school. In an interview conducted by fellow psychiatrist Drew Ramsey at the end of 2018 for *Medscape Psychiatry*, Yusim describes her own journey:

> Spirituality entered my clinical work when it entered my own life because I found a spiritual path to be quite transformative. I had my own dark night of the soul that led me to soul searching. That search took me to ashrams in India, learning meditation in Thailand, working with shamans in South Africa and South America, and eventually studying Kabbalah here in New York City.[90]

Yusim's teaching is not a fringe approach to psychiatry, and she has won numerous awards from the NIMH, the World Psychiatric Association, and various other prominent psychiatric

[88] Ronald Pies and Cynthia Geppert, "'Clinical Depression' or 'Life Sorrows'? Distinguishing between Grief and Depression in Pastoral Care," *Ministry Magazine* (May 2015) 8-9.

[89] William Styron, *Darkness Visible: A Memoir of Madness* (New York: Vintage, 1992), 47.

[90] Yusim Ramsey interviewed by Drew Ramsey, "How Can Spirituality Be used in Clinical Practice?" *Medscape Psychiatry Online* (December 27, 2018): https://www.medscape.com/viewarticle/9065 28?nlid=126876_424&src= WNL_mdplsfeat_190102_mscpedit_psyc&uac=264124BV&spon=12&impID=18 50427&faf=1.

institutions and medical societies for her research and teaching on the importance of spiritual rituals and spirituality (humanism) within psychiatric practice. In her book, *Fulfilled: How the Science of Spirituality Can Help You Live a Happier, More Meaningful Life*,[91] Yusim teaches that people must turn inward for meaning and fulfillment:

> As people start to connect to that [spiritual] part of themselves, they rely less on external ways of starting to fill their inner voids. They start to look for fulfillment more internally — within their own hearts.[92]

Yusim also defines the soul according to her humanistic and spiritualistic beliefs:

> The soul is the blueprint we bring into this world of how we are meant to grow, change, evolve, transform and meaningfully contribute to humankind over the course of our lives. . . . Once we learn to hear our soul's whispers and uncover its deepest longings, it will guide us to a life of meaning and fulfillment.[93]

In the humanistic perspective, the soul or self is the empowering agent that delivers and guides people through their lives. When the soul/psyche is unable to do so successfully, the person is viewed as dysfunctional, and a psychiatrist, therapist, or shaman must step in to reconnect the disconnected or degenerate soul. Yusim maintains that

> a *disconnection from one's soul* may present in many ways: anxiety, depression, obsessions, excessive worrying, suicidal thoughts, self-harm behaviors, psychosis, mania, addictions, and phobias, among

[91] Anna Yusim, *Fulfilled: How the Science of Spirituality Can Help You Live a Happier, More Meaningful Life* (New York: Grand Central Life and Style, 2017).

[92] Ramsey, "How Can Spirituality Be used in Clinical Practice?"

[93] Anna Yusim interviewed by Eric R. Maisel, "Anna Yusim on Humanistic Psychiatry," *Psychology Today Online* (February 15, 2016): https://www.psychologytoday.com/us/blog/rethinking-mental-health/201602/anna-yusim-humanistic-psychiatry.

many other presentations I may see in my medical office . . . . Although medications can treat the symptoms resulting from a disconnection from one's soul, they rarely treat the underlying etiology, which is the disconnection itself. *Only by looking inside oneself and aligning with the deepest part of yourself can you address the root cause of the problem instead of the effect* [emphasis added].[94]

Most modern psychiatrists do not frame mental disorders as "a disconnection from one's soul" — a traditional shamanic view; instead, they choose to view problems of human fragility and depravity as "biological disorders" and maintain the appearance that they practice valid science and medicine. The World Psychiatric Association, however, realizes that to continue insisting that people with persistent mental problems are degenerates or disordered requires that objective standards of normalcy first be established.

To establish that a condition is a *disorder in* the sense of Wakefield's analysis, we would have to establish, or at least have a consensus about, whether it arose because of or at least involved *"failure of a natural mental or behavioural mechanism to function as designed in evolution."* But as opposed to what? Behavioural scientists working in an evolutionary theoretic framework have suggested that *failure of function* in Wakefield's sense as a pathway to harmful conditions can be contrasted with, for instance, evolutionary design/current environment mismatch, or maladaptive learning. If these are the kinds of intended contrasts, we need to wait until the science has been done to establish which types or sub-types of problems are "genuine disorders" in the sense of Wakefield's analysis, and which are not. And in the meantime, during what might be a long wait, we would need *another name for* the problems, not *disorder* (which in this scenario we are interpreting in Wakefield's sense), but perhaps, for instance, *mental health problems,* the criteria for which would have to be reliable enough for us to do meaningful, generalizable research [their own emphasis].[95]

[94] Ibid.

[95] Derek Bolton, "The Usefulness of Wakefield's Definition for the Diagnostic Manuals," *World Psychiatry (WPA)* 6, no. 3 (2007): 164-65.

As the World Psychiatric Association indicates by its published contemplations, the theory of mental disorder rests on the subjective evolutionary theory and philosophy of individual degenerationism. Within an evolutionary framework, normalcy has never been objectively established. One must consider, then, why anyone is considered to be a deviant.[96] In truth, individual degenerationism exists, not because it is scientifically sound or because it helps explain human nature, but because it is a necessary belief to sustain the false anthropology of humanism.

Individual degenerationism is an important tenet of humanistic thinking and the reason why the APA considers ongoing mental distress and impairment to be mental illnesses/disorders in the *DSM-5* and why shamans considered mental distress and impairment to be a spiritual abnormality. Additionally, individual degenerationism provides a philosophy whereby people can create systems in which the weak and defective (e.g., the theory of eugenics) are identified and controlled as they were in historical insane asylums and during the Holocaust.[97] To believe that deep and persistent sorrow, hopelessness, distress, anxiety, guilt (depression), and other spiritual vexations represent human disorder rather than normal human nature is to accept the humanistic philosophy of individual degenerationism.

Claimed Differentials

To be clear, most psychiatrists and clinicians do acknowledge that sadness, hopelessness, and guilt are all normal aspects of human nature. But they attempt to establish a line of

[96] For further study on normalcy, see Berger, *Mental Illness: The Necessity for Faith and Authority*, 30-44.

[97] For further study on the history of psychiatry as a social control, see Daniel Berger, *Mental Illness: The Reality of the Spiritual Nature*.

demarcation by differentiating between normalcy and alleged disorders in order to maintain their theory of individual degenerationism. Thus, a significant question that must be answered is: if normal people struggle with sorrow, hopelessness, and guilt, what objective factor(s) would cause humanists to diagnose someone as being depressed and disordered? In other words, what objectively differentiates between normal sorrow (e.g., grief), guilt, and hopelessness with that of alleged abnormalities?

If no objective difference between normalcy and alleged abnormality exists, then individual degenerationism — thereby considering any type of depression to be a disorder — is exposed to be a failing belief system maintained only by subjective and speculative theory. The medical model that governs today's theory of mental illness and specifically the idea that depression is a disorder (something apart from normal) rests on the philosophy of individual degenerationism. It is beneficial, then, for us to explore specifically how the construct of depression is based upon individual degenerationism as well as to discover the APA's subjective means of determining normalcy and abnormality.

In order to maintain the belief that deep impairing sorrow and hopelessness are abnormalities, the APA must create a differential between normal sadness and hopelessness and alleged disorders. The *DSM-5* represents this attempt to establish a line of demarcation — a clinical standard. *Diagnoses* — which "simply means 'discernment' or 'knowing the difference between' one thing and another"[98] — of depressive disorders is less about discerning between constructs and more about

[98] Ronald Pies, "Positivism, Humanism, and the Case for Psychiatric Diagnosis," *Psychiatric Times Online* 31, no. 7 (July 1, 2014): http://www. psychiatrictimes.com/couch-crisis/positivism-humanism-and-case-psychiatric-diagnosis/page/0/1.

attempting to tell if someone is normal or abnormal. When someone is diagnosed as mentally ill, he/she has been discerned, according to humanistic belief, to be a disordered soul.

The *DSM-5* lists three specific criteria under the construct of depression which the APA asserts delineates between normal and disordered people. It is on these three axioms that the APA promotes and maintains its belief in individual degenerationism and continues to assert its relevance. The *DSM-5* specifically states about major depression,

> Periods of sadness are inherent aspects of the human experience. These periods should not be diagnosed as a major depressive episode unless criteria are met for [1] severity, [2] duration [a two-week period for major depression], and [3] clinically significant distress or impairment. The diagnosis *other specified depressive disorder* [emphasis added] may be appropriate for presentations of depressed mood with clinically significant impairment that do not meet criteria for duration or severity.[99]

As highlighted in the above statement, the American Psychiatric Association recognizes that sadness is inherent to human nature, and this group of psychiatrists has come to agree upon and established three standards or axioms as an attempt to differentiate between what they consider to be healthy from mental illness. But are their standards objective, and do they reliably delineate between normal and abnormal?

The Severity Axiom

The first criterion the APA offers is a psychiatrist's or other clinician's judgment on how deep or severe a person's sorrow is. Since there is no objective standard of severity, all clinicians must base the level of dysfunctional sorrow on their own subjective opinions.

---

[99] APA, *DSM-5*, 168.

This axiom also assumes that "normal sadness" is not deep or severe and is not impairing. As previously addressed, though, sorrow is by nature impairing and distressful, and even what some call grief is not a pleasant or desirable state. The pain of losing a loved one, the hurt and false guilt a child experiences over his/her parents' divorce, the agony of being cheated on or betrayed by a spouse, or the sorrow and distress of desiring to find a spouse without any apparent hope are examples of how deep sorrow can stay with people their entire lives. Normal people find all degrees of sorrow, hopelessness, and guilt to be distressful and impairing.

The APA asserts in the *DSM-5* that a person must have 5 of the 9 listed symptoms in order for the severity qualifier to be met.[100] But this requirement is also subjective and fails to distinguish normalcy from abnormality.

Despite its severity axiom, the APA does rightly acknowledge in the *DSM-5* that if an alleged psychiatric disorder such as depression lacks biological markers and physical ways to empirically measure severity, then discerning whether someone is normal or abnormal is not a legitimate practice:

> In the absence of clear biological markers or clinically useful measurements of severity for many mental disorders, it has not been possible to completely separate normal and pathological symptom expressions [alleged abnormalities] contained in the diagnostic criteria.[101]

Since depression is a syndrome (based upon proposed "pathological symptom expressions"), it becomes impossible for clinicians to measure the severity of symptoms in an objective and useful way. There also do not exist biological markers that

[100] Ibid., 160.

[101] Ibid., 21.

are diagnostic for depression. As the APA rightly admits, the severity axiom offers no objective distinction between normalcy and what it asserts to be an abnormality.

The Time Axiom

The second criteria or axiom which the APA claims separates alleged normal sorrow from depression is the *time* or *duration axiom*. This axiom is typically stated as a specific period of time in which a person is sorrowful and feels hopeless. In the major depression construct, for example, the sorrow and hopelessness must persist "most of the day, nearly every day for at least 2 weeks."[102] Two weeks is a subjective time frame that the appointed leaders of the APA *DSM-5* task force have agreed upon. This criterion assumes that deep sorrow does not normally last for lengthy periods of time (e.g., past two weeks). But who decides how long sorrow should normally last, and is there no room for individuals to sorrow differently over similar circumstances?

The Distress Axiom

The APA suggests a third axiom, which it refers to as "clinically significant distress or impairment," and this axiom is sometimes called "clinically significant disturbance."[103] This criterion can be referred to as the *distress axiom* or *impairment axiom*, and it is found in every alleged disorder in the *DSM-5*. In fact, the *DSM-5* states at its beginning: "Mental disorders are usually associated with significant distress or disability."[104] Therefore, if a person is thinking or behaving in a way that impairs his/her life or an individual feels distressed or is judged by others to be distressed

[102] Ibid., 168.

[103] Ibid., 20.

[104] Ibid.

in an ongoing way, then that person will be viewed as mentally ill by modern psychiatrists.

As with the severity axiom and the time axiom, the distress axiom is based upon a clinician's subjective concept of what constitutes impairment, which is why many clinicians refer to the distress axiom as "subjective distress."[105] In the view of most psychiatrists as represented in the *DSM-5*, people should regard various types of ongoing/persistent mental impairment or distress as abnormalities and not as a natural part of being human.

The subjective position asserted in the distress and severity axioms ensures that everyone who seeks help from a professional already qualifies as disordered and abnormal. "Clinically significant distress" translates into the reality that if a person goes to a clinician who holds to individual degenerationism to seek help for significant distress, then he/she will likely be leaving with a clinical diagnosis and be categorized as a degenerate — one who is disordered. Horwitz and Wakefield comment on how the subjective nature of depression makes the construct pliable and fluid and allows the APA to assert authority over concepts of human nature.

> In effect, these *DSM* definitions have become the authoritative arbiter of what is and is not considered mental disorder throughout our society. . . . In modern psychiatry, definitions move the treatment and research firmament, and modern clinicians with an invalidly broad definition can move diagnosed disorder to virtually whatever level they desire, especially when they deal with a disorder such as depression that features such symptoms as sadness, insomnia, and fatigue, which are widespread among non-disordered people.[106]

---

[105] Lieberman, *Shrinks*, 136.

[106] Horwitz and Wakefield, *Loss of Sadness*, 8.

In the medical model of mental illness, who is normal and who is degenerate depends entirely upon the subjective definition the APA chooses.

The astute reader will realize that there exist serious problems with trying to differentiate between normal and abnormal people by applying any or all of these psychiatric axioms; they are all rooted in the philosophy of individual degenerationism, and they are all subjective. Despite this fact, the APA has convinced society to consider all human impairment and distress that is not resolved in a short time frame from a person's own resources to be a mental disorder requiring medical attention. Take for example the widespread attempt to frame grief as normal and persistent sorrow as abnormal:

> The death of a loved one, loss of a job or the ending of a relationship are difficult experiences for a person to endure. It is normal for feelings of sadness or grief to develop in response to such situations. Those experiencing loss often might describe themselves as being "depressed." But being sad is not the same as having depression. The grieving process is natural and unique to each individual and shares some of the same features of depression. Both grief and depression may involve intense sadness and withdrawal from usual activities. They are also different in important ways:[107]

The APA attempts to differentiate between the two by offering these two alleged differences:

> [1] In grief, painful feelings come in waves, often intermixed with positive memories of the deceased. In major depression, mood and/or interest (pleasure) are decreased for most of two weeks. [2] In grief, self-esteem is usually maintained. In major depression, feelings of worthlessness and self-loathing are common. For some people, the death of a loved one can bring on major depression. Losing a job or being a victim of a physical assault or a major

---

[107] APA, "What is Depression?" *The American Psychiatric Association Online* (December 2018): https://www.psychiatry.org/patients-families/depression/what-is-depression.

disaster can lead to depression for some people. When grief and depression co-exist, the grief is more severe and lasts longer than grief without depression. Despite some overlap between grief and depression, they are different. Distinguishing between them can help people get the help, support or treatment they need.[108]

The American Psychiatric Association assumes that people are normal when faced with grief if they are not devastated by the loss of their loved one, can overcome grief in less than two weeks, and maintain a normal or high level of self-esteem — whatever that non-existent standard of normal self-esteem might be. Otherwise, in the APA's subjective opinion, people are depressed. Dr. Allen Frances comments,

> A lot of what passes for major depressive disorder [MDD] is not really "major," is not really "depressive," and is not really "disorder." Loose diagnosis has created a false epidemic of MDD, with fifteen million Americans now qualifying at any given time. The transformation of expectable sadness into clinical depression has turned us into an overmedicated, pill-popping population.[109]

While Frances attributes the growing number of diagnoses to the APA's loose redefining of their subjective constructs, the people being diagnosed as depressed have real struggles and desire genuine help. Frances later concedes that no objective line of demarcation exists between alleged normalcy and abnormality:

> There is no way to demarcate a clean boundary between the milder forms of clinical depression and severer forms of ordinary, normal sadness [emphasis added]. If we try to diagnose everyone who really has major depression, inevitably we will misdiagnose many people who are simply having a rough patch in their lives.[110]

Assigning two different words (e.g., *grief* versus *depression*) with subjective qualifiers in attempt to delineate between alleged

[108] Ibid.

[109] Frances, *Saving Normal*, 154.

[110] Ibid.

normal and abnormal sorrow does not validate the theory of abnormality; it merely sustains belief in the subjective philosophy of individual degenerationism.

In the *DSM-5*, the APA admits that what they believe to separate normal sorrow from allegedly abnormal sadness rests entirely in the "clinical judgment" of the evaluator in reference to cultural norms:

> Responses to a significant loss (e.g., bereavement, financial ruin, losses from a natural disaster, a serious medical illness or disability) may include the feelings of intense sadness, rumination about the loss, insomnia, poor appetite, and weight loss noted in Criterion A, *which may resemble a depressive episode*. Although such symptoms may be understandable or considered appropriate to the loss, the presence of a major depressive episode in addition to the normal response to a significant loss should also be carefully considered. *This decision inevitably requires the exercise of clinical judgment* based on the individual's history and the cultural norms for the expression of distress in the context of loss [emphasis added].[111]

If "normal responses" can "resemble a depressive episode," then on what objective basis are depressive episodes determined to not be normal responses? The truth is that no objective standard or clinical test exists; psychiatrists must make diagnoses according to their "clinical judgment" and established "social norms." In truth, mental health clinicians make their decisions based upon their presuppositional philosophies rather than objective medicine. Individuals whom secular clinicians perceive to lack faith in self to overcome sorrow within a short timeframe qualify as disordered within the current paradigm.

The psychiatric axioms of severity, time, and impairment are not objective or legitimate ways to distinguish normalcy from alleged abnormalities. While most psychiatrists admit that the criteria (e.g., sadness, hopelessness, and guilt) found in their

---

[111] APA, *DSM-5*, 161.

construct of depression are all a part of normal human nature, they have convinced much of society to accept their framework of perceiving deep and enduring sadness and hopelessness as a disorder without any objective or scientific evidence. This psychiatric perspective (the biomedical narrative) allows people to believe that depression is not only a disorder (something a degenerate has) but also is within the domain of medicine.[112]

Realizing that the psychiatric construct of depression is based upon false beliefs and subjective concepts in no way dismisses the very real struggles that people have or their need of deliverance. What this discovery does provide is the opportunity for those who are in distress to realize that they are not abnormal or disordered simply because they are hurting and struggling in a persistent way and are unable to save themselves. Genuine healing can only begin as the person created in the image of God begins to view his/herself as God sees him/her and not as mankind theorizes. When people are stigmatized as abnormal, they are further isolated, and any remnant of hope often fades away. Dr. Frances comments on this common occurrence,

> Having a mental disorder label "marks" someone in ways that can cause much secondary harm. . . . A great deal of the trouble comes from a change in how you see yourself — the sense of being damaged goods, feeling not normal or worthy, not a full-fledged member of the group. . . . Labels can also create self-fulling prophecies. If you are told you are sick, you feel and act sick, and other treat you as if you are sick. . . . The sick role can be extremely destructive when it

---

[112] This assertion is the same perspective that was utilized by the ancient shaman, recycled by Francis Galton in his theory of eugenics in the mid-1800s, reframed as mental illness (the medical model) by Emil Kraepelin in the late 1800s, and acted upon by Kraepelin's premier student and the Father of Nazi eugenics under Hitler's leadership, psychiatrist Ernst Rudin (Berger, *Insanity of Madness*, 125-27.). Sadly, the Kraepelinian theory of mental illness, which governs today's mental health system in America (including the *DSM-5*) and made popular by men like Jeffrey Lieberman, is constructed upon faith in humanism, individual degenerationism, materialism, and genetic determinism.

reduces expectations, truncates ambitions, and results in a loss of personal responsibility [emphasis added]."[113]

Labeling people as abnormal within the medical model when they are not stigmatizes them and does great damage.

Though the APA has failed to provide a standard of normal human hopelessness, sorrow, and guilt, it still insists in the *DSM-5* that ongoing sadness, prevalent hopelessness, and drastic changes in mood constitute abnormalities or deviances, derived from a non-existent standard. This speculative claim enables psychiatrists to assert an alleged abnormality though none exists. To be sure, the idea that depression is an abnormality or disorder (let alone a medical disorder) is an entirely subjective belief founded upon the wide acceptance of individual degenerationism, humanism, and evolutionary thinking; it is conjecture and not scientifically based.

The Biblical View

What if deep sorrow, hopelessness, guilt and the numerous other vexations of soul are all features of normalcy, instead of indications of abnormality? If we are all burdened with the reality of this fallen world and the subsequent impairments and distresses, then how we approach those who have come to realize or be transparent about their true impaired and naturally hopeless condition will look far different from approaching them as abnormal. If we believe the scriptural teaching of *universal degenerationism* (including both depravity and fragility) that occurred in the Garden of Eden as a direct result of Adam and Eve's sin rather than accepting the philosophy of *individual degenerationism*, then we will also realize that all people need a renewed mind and deliverance. In truth, we are all pursuing happiness, hope, joy, and peace—not just some of us.

---

[113] Frances, *Saving Normal*, 109.

Degenerationism is one of the fundamental philosophies that undergirds every view of human fragility and depravity and especially what is today referred to as depression. Whereas individual degenerationism suggests that everything is normally okay with people and that something goes wrong only with degenerates, the Bible teaches that everyone is degenerate and in need of *regeneration* (lit. the spiritual rebirth or new birth) and mental renewal. Universal degenerationism does not speculate about what causes things to go wrong, what produces distress, or what creates mental and behavioral impairment. Instead, the biblical philosophy teaches that the normal human state is universally weak and depraved; we are all degenerates from the start of our lives.

In Genesis 3, we discover the historical account of humanity's universal degeneration — often referred to in the field of theology as the Fall. It is not surprising that this Bible passage includes the three main criteria for a psychiatric diagnosis of depression.[114] This passage, as well as others, presents sorrow, hopelessness, and guilt as being a part of every person's true nature after the Fall.

Genesis 3 is foundational to understanding and accepting human nature, the gospel of Jesus Christ, and the true issues framed within the psychiatric construct of depression. If a person cannot or will not accept the bad news about his/her own soul's common condition and the fallen world in which all live, then it is impossible to accept the good news (the gospel) or find answers to one's own guilt, sorrow, and hopelessness. All that is available to people who dismiss the gospel of Christ are temporal and false hopes that when they fail, bring worse pain to the soul (Proverbs 13:12).

---

[114] Genesis is a theological seed passage of Scripture; it introduces theological truths but does not explain them in their full revelation.

In regards to the conditions psychiatrists and psychologists have framed as depression, all agree that sorrow, hopelessness, and guilt must be remedied. But God's and man's wisdom are antithetical when it comes to how deliverance occurs. The Bible teaches that regeneration (Titus 3:5; a spiritual rebirth) along with sanctification (a progressive spiritual and behavioral transformation/restoration to God's original design) are the answers to degenerationism. Whereas, psychiatry teaches that believing in oneself, enlightenment, chemicals, electric shock, and the accumulation of numerous other false hopes provide the answer. Nonetheless, each of us must interpret, approach, and attempt to remedy our sorrow, hopelessness, and guilt according to either individual or universal degenerationism.

A Closer Look

So, what does Scripture specifically say about sorrow, hopelessness, and guilt, and are these mindsets normal? Genesis 3 provides us with key foundational answers.

Sorrow

In Genesis 3:16-19, the Bible offers two examples of the normalcy and universality of sorrow as a direct result of the Fall. Keep in mind that these two examples do not convey God's full revelation of what makes people sorrowful; they are, though, theological seeds of how all people must face sorrow because of the historic fall of Adam and Eve. Thereafter, the Bible develops the normalcy of sorrow more in depth throughout its pages.

One example of these two sorrowful experiences is addressed to women and the other is addressed to men. In verse 16, it is the woman who first hears of her expected struggle with sorrow:

> Unto the woman he said, I will greatly multiply thy *sorrow* and thy conception; in *sorrow* thou shalt bring forth children; and thy desire shall be to thy husband, and he shall rule over thee [KJV].

As previously stated, the Hebrew word for sorrow or sadness found in Scripture is *pain*, and many English versions of the Bible translate these words as *pain* instead of *sorrow*. Regardless of which English word the translators utilized, deep sorrow (spiritual pain) is an expected result of the child-bearing process even from a secular perspective[115] — what many call "postpartum depression."[116] The connection of sorrow with pregnancy is so common that

> in May 2015, the American College of Obstetricians and Gynecologists has recommended that all pregnant and postpartum women be screened at least once during the perinatal period (pregnancy and 12 months postpartum) for depression and anxiety.[117]

It is not merely the perinatal period of childbirth, however, that brings women sorrow; it is the entire process. From monthly menstrual cycles and common miscarriages to menopause and everywhere in between, women are burdened with sorrow because of the fall of Adam and Eve.

Secular theorists recognize the normalcy of sorrow in the child birthing process, but they attempt to establish severe or troubling behavior associated with this struggle as being an

[115] See WHO, "Depression is Common After Childbirth," video, World Health Day (April 7, 2017): https://youtu.be/1Fx FU_xfAzQ.

[116] "Postpartum depression is a mood disorder that can affect women after childbirth" (National Institute of Mental Health, "Postpartum depression Facts: https://www.nimh.nih.gov/ health/publications/postpartum-depression-facts/index.shtml).

[117] Joanna E. Chambers, "Perinatal Psychiatry: Where Psychoanalytic Theory, Neuroscience, and Integrated Clinical Psychiatry Meet," *Psychiatric Times Online* 34, no. 3 (March 24, 2017): http://www.psychiatrictimes.com/depression/perinatal-psychiatry-where-psychoanalytic-theory-neuroscience-and-integrated-clinical-psychiatry.

abnormality. "Baby blues" is the term they have created and popularized, which psychiatrists say identifies the normal sorrowful process most women experience. Whereas, psychiatrists have created *postpartum depression* as an alleged disorder if a woman's sorrow and impairment are severe, persist, and are associated with bad or antisocial behavior. They have applied the same theory to a woman's menstrual cycle and menopause: *premenstrual dysphoric disorder* and *perimenopause disorder* respectably:

> Several forms of depression are unique to women because of their apparent association with changes in gonadal hormones, which in turn modulate neuroregulatory systems associated with mood and behavior. This review examines the evaluation and treatment of depression that occurs premenstrually, postpartum, or in the perimenopause on the basis of current literature.[118]

Even from the secular perspective, it can readily be observed that the entire process of childbirth women face in their life brings them much sorrow. But this sorrow is normal after the Fall and not a disease or an abnormality, and just as with alleged major depressive disorder, there is no objective difference between baby blues and postpartum depression.

Throughout Scripture, child birth and sorrow are consistently correlated. For example, Jesus utilizes the normalcy of sorrow in the child birthing process as an illustration to reveal the normalcy of sorrow in this life for those who trust in Christ. In John 16:20-21, Christ comforts His disciples by telling them to expect sorrow but anticipate the joy that is to come:

> Truly, truly, I say to you, you will weep and lament, but the world will rejoice. You will be sorrowful, but your sorrow will turn into joy. When a woman is giving birth, she has sorrow because her hour

[118] Ellen W. Freeman, "Treatment of Depression Associated with the Menstrual Cycle: Premenstrual Dysphoria, Postpartum Depression, and the Perimenopause," *Dialogues in Clinical Neuroscience* 4, no. 2 (2002): 177.

has come, but when she has delivered the baby, she no longer remembers the anguish, for joy that a human being has been born into the world.

The more people see life as God sees it and accept the human condition as it truly is, the more they will be able to accept and endure the sorrows of this life and the joy that is to come.

As with women, sorrow is also a part of men's nature and common experience. In Genesis 3:17-19, God explains to Adam one of the ways in which men will realize their sorrowful condition:

> And unto Adam he said, Because thou hast hearkened unto the voice of thy wife, and hast eaten of the tree, of which I commanded thee, saying, Thou shalt not eat of it: cursed is the ground for thy sake; *in sorrow* shalt thou eat of it all the days of thy life; Thorns also and thistles shall it bring forth to thee; and thou shalt eat the herb of the field; In the sweat of thy face shalt thou eat bread, till thou return unto the ground; for out of it wast thou taken: for dust thou art, and unto dust shalt thou return (*KJV*).

Both men and women suffer spiritual pain (sorrow or sadness) because of the Fall. It is important to reiterate that not all experiences of sorrow are listed here in Genesis 3. These verses introduce sorrow as a normal part of human nature after the Fall and offer tangible illustrations that all people can recognize and with which to experientially identify.

As we discern what constitutes normalcy from Scripture, it is also helpful to consider why God gave us the Scripture and why so much of it deals with sorrow. For example, the book of Lamentations ("a passionate expression of sorrow) (1) reveals the one true God, (2) reveals humanity's true nature after the Fall, (3) reveals God's redemptive/gracious plan to restore humanity back to His own likeness and for His glory (His will), and (4) provides a presuppositional faith from which to interpret the natural world and one's own experiences (Hebrews 11:1-4).

King David and Asaph experienced great sorrow as reflected in their numerous laments (40 percent of the psalms are laments). Unlike many men today, though, David and Asaph did not hesitate to reveal their brokenness. They did not suppress tears or deny their sorrow, but openly cried out to God on numerous occasions.

It is also beneficial for us to examine how Scripture develops and illuminates the nature of sorrow first proposed in Genesis 3. Many passages in Scripture directly state humanity's condition to be characterized by deep impairing sorrow. Proverbs 14:13 says, "Even in laughter the heart aches, and the end of joy is grief." Most biblical commentators note that this verse reveals humanity's true nature to be sadness, and moments of joy and laughter allow only a temporal escape. The biblical commentator Tremper Longman, for example, states that "sorrow better reflects reality than joy."[119] Other passages are more explicit in their statements. Ecclesiastes 2:23, for one, declares,

> For all [man's] days are full of sorrow, and his work is a vexation.
> Even in the night his heart does not rest. This also is vanity.

Here, Solomon references the curse from Genesis 3 by restating that life is full of sorrow and that work is a vexation (lit. "a cause of internal trouble or turmoil"; mental distress). Jeremiah 20:17-18 shares the same Genesis 3 perspective on sorrow:

> Because he did not kill me in the womb: so my mother would have been my grave and her womb forever great. Why did I come out from the womb to see toil and sorrow, and spend my days in shame?

Struggle, sorrow, and guilt/shame are all aspects of our human condition; the Bible makes this point clear.

---

[119] Tremper Longman III, *Proverbs* (Grand Rapids, MI: Baker Academic, 2006), 301.

Unlike the modern psychiatric perspective, the Bible does not differentiate between alleged abnormal sorrow and normalcy. Rather, Scripture sees all people as sorrowful, and it understands that life itself is a "vexation" or to use contemporary vernacular: life is depressing, internally distressing, and a constant struggle.

At its very end, in fact, the Bible declares precisely when sorrow will no longer be a part of normalcy for those who place their faith in Jesus Christ. Revelation 21:4 states,

> And I heard a loud voice from the throne saying, "Behold, the dwelling place of God is with man. He will dwell with them, and they will be his people, and God himself will be with them as their God. He will wipe away every tear from their eyes, and death shall be no more, neither shall there be mourning [lament or sorrow], nor crying, nor pain anymore, for the former things have passed away."

From the beginning of human existence (Genesis 3) until the end of this age (Revelation 21), sorrow is the norm. Admitting sorrow is simply being honest about one's own and others' true fallen condition; all are degenerates when compared to Christ and God's original design. In the biblical perspective, to deny or attempt to dissociate from one's own sorrowful condition in this life is delusional thinking.

But many renowned psychiatrists within humanism, such as Peter Breggin, have also come to believe that depression is normal to human nature:

> Depression is a natural or normal human response to emotional injury and loss. Even when depressed feelings become extreme or unrelenting, these reactions usually have obvious causes, such as the breakup of a marriage, the inability to leave an unhappy marriage, the death of a loved one, failure to work, an inability to achieve one's fondest hopes in life, ill health, or a lonely old age. A human

emotional or psychological state – basically, a feeling – should not be considered a "disease" simply because it becomes extreme.[120]

Allan Horwitz, psychiatric epidemiologist, and Jerome Wakefield, who the World Psychiatric Association asserts "has done more in the last decade or so to clarify and analyze the concept of mental disorder"[121] than any other person, note that to deny depression as an abnormality or the depressed as a sick degenerate is to accept an ugly truth about human nature that must be resolved:

> Sadness is an inherent part of the human condition, not a mental disorder. Thus, to confront psychiatry's invalid definition of depressive disorder is also to consider a painful but important part of our humanity that we have tended to shunt aside in the modern medicalization of human problems.[122]

The well-known successor to Sigmund Freud, Carl Jung, also realized the normalcy and necessity of sadness:

> Even a happy life cannot be without a measure of darkness, and the word happy would lose its meaning if it were not balanced by sadness. It is far better to take things as they come along with patience and equanimity.[123]

Sorrow – though distressful, impairing, and undesirable – is a normal feature of human nature that has meaning and purpose, and even how people reference and define happiness is never apart from their reality of sorrow.

---

[120] Breggin, *Anti-Depressant Fact Book*, 14.

[121] Bolton, "Wakefield's Definition," 164.

[122] Horwitz and Wakefield, *Loss of Sadness*, 225.

[123] Carl Jung, quoted by Can Akdeniz, *7 Values of Highly Effective People* (Bodendorf, Germany, Best Business Books, 2014), 22.

Hopelessness

As with sorrow, Genesis 3 also places humanity in a hopeless condition apart from a relationship with God. Hopelessness is not a mindset that people fall into; it is the genuine reality of our fallen state whether acknowledged or not. Genesis 3:22-24 relates,

> Then the LORD God said, "Behold, the man has become like one of us in knowing good and evil. Now, lest he reach out his hand and take also of the tree of life and eat, and live forever — " therefore the LORD God sent him out from the garden of Eden to work the ground from which he was taken. He drove out the man, and at the east of the garden of Eden he placed the cherubim and a flaming sword that turned every way to guard the way to the tree of life.

At this point in history, all humanity became hopeless — faced with the reality that everyone is dying, falling short of the moral law of God, and facing the prospect of eternal judgment for their sins and separation from the Holy Creator God for all eternity.

The hopeless condition of humanity and, consequently, the genuine hope found in Christ alone are fundamental truths to the gospel message found in the Word of God. For example, Jeremiah 29:11 reflects on God's goodness and plans to bring hope to the hopeless, "For I know the plans I have for you, declares the Lord, plans for welfare and not for evil, to give you a future and a hope." In the New Testament, the same hope is extended to every nation. Romans 15:12-13 states,

> The Root of Jesse will come, even he who arises to rule the Gentiles; in him will the Gentiles hope. May the God of hope fill you with all joy and peace in believing, so that by the power of the Holy Spirit you may abound in hope.

Here, hope not only is shown to be a common human need, but also is revealed to be received supernaturally through the ministry of the Holy Spirit. This revelation is significant as it exposes that hopelessness is a normal, natural, and right human mindset — albeit undesirable and impairing. To view hopelessness as a sin or as a sickness is to view hopelessness as something apart from normalcy. In the same manner, to view hopelessness as a sin or sickness is to accept individual degenerationism over universal degenerationism and to set aside the biblical truth that genuine lasting hope is supernaturally given through the power of the Holy Spirit and realized apart from human ability or efforts.

Although people are by nature hopeless, all are skilled at creating temporal and false hopes. But temporal and false hopes fail. People do not possess genuine hope which resolves guilt and hopelessness and which extends beyond this life. On the other hand, genuine hope provides stability to the naturally unstable soul. Hebrews 6:17-20 (13-20) explains,

> So when God desired to show more convincingly to the heirs of the promise the unchangeable character of his purpose, he guaranteed it with an oath, so that by two unchangeable things, in which it is impossible for God to lie, *we who have fled for refuge might have a strong encouragement to hold fast to the hope set before us. We have this as a sure and steadfast anchor of the soul,* a hope that enters into the inner place hind the curtain where Jesus has gone as a forerunner on our behalf [emphasis added].

God's providing hope to remedy our hopeless condition is based upon the fulfilled promise of Jesus Christ and His death, burial, and resurrection to guarantee death's defeat. Because Jesus overcame His death, then we have eternal hope and our psyche has stability despite life's storms. It is Jesus who came to accomplish God the Father's purpose of regenerating and restoring degenerates through a covenant relationship based upon God's mercy and grace. It is no wonder that the Bible speaks at length about finding hope in Jesus.

We are all seeking for lasting and healing hope, but the object of our hope determines our mental stability. Simply having hope does not cure our crushed spirit, and accumulating false hopes — though it may help for a time — will inevitably worsen and destroy our souls (a point developed further in the chapters to come).

Guilt

Genesis 3 not only provides the first accounts of sorrow and hopelessness, but also the passage (Genesis 3:6-9) reveals the first human experiences of guilt, shame, and anxiety:[124]

> So when the woman saw that the tree was good for food, and that it was a delight to the eyes, and that the tree was to be desired to make one wise, she took of its fruit and ate, and she also gave some to her husband who was with her, and he ate. Then the eyes of both were opened, and they knew that they were naked. And they sewed fig leaves together and made themselves loincloths. And they heard the sound of the Lord God walking in the garden in the cool of the day, and the man and his wife hid themselves from the presence of the Lord God among the trees of the garden. But the Lord God called to the man and said to him, "Where are you?"

It was at this point in time that Adam and Eve became conscious of their moral state — knowing good and evil, and as a result, all humanity thereafter would need to resolve their personal guilt for both their legitimate and falsely perceived failures.

As previously noted, guilt is the spiritual/mental awareness of wrong doing; it is clear evidence that the law is written on each of our hearts and that no one perfectly keeps God's moral law. Romans 2:15 explains how even those who deny God's moral law still conscientiously know its reality and, therefore, must still deal with their guilt:

124 Anxiety is our normal honest assessment that life and many of its situations are out of our control: Humanistic psychologist Rollo May states, "Anxiety is an even better teacher than reality, for one can temporarily evade reality by avoiding the distasteful situation; but anxiety is a source of education always present because one carries it within" (Rollo May, *The Meaning of Anxiety* [New York: W.W. Norton & Company, 1950], 45).

> They show that the work of the law is written on their hearts, while their conscience also bears witness, and their conflicting thoughts accuse or even excuse them.

In this way, one's conscience is the constant internal judge that knows the law well, and guilt—whether true or false—is the constant reminder of every person's inescapable death sentence. Guilt is like an emergency siren that serves to remind people that they are morally and relationally imperfect and have need to be restored and justified or face death and punishment handed down by God—the only perfect judge.

But the Bible is not alone in showing that guilt is not disconnected from our conscience, our identity, an established law, or our mental stability. Secular psychiatrist Peter Breggin remarks on his understanding of guilt: "In depression and guilt, blame is directed toward oneself as evil, bad, harmful to others, and deserving of punishment."[125] He later notes,

> In discussing depression we found that guilt focuses on our feelings of being bad—our power to do harm and even evil to others. Feelings of blame are directed toward ourselves rather than toward others, and anger is directed inward rather than outward. We look within for any sign that we are evil.[126]

Prominent humanistic psychiatrist, Dr. William Sadler also agrees with this understanding: "A clear conscience is a great step toward barricading the mind against neuroticism [moodiness that relates to reality]."[127] Whether from a Christian

---

[125] Peter R. Breggin, *Toxic Psychiatry* (New York: St. Martin's Press, 1991), 128.

[126] Ibid.

[127] William Sadler, *Practice of Psychiatry* (St. Louis: C.V. Mosby Co., 1953), 1012. Psychiatrists called moodiness that related to reality *neuroticism,* and they referred to moodiness that denied or seemed out of touch with reality as *psychosis.*

or secular perspective, the concept of guilt includes one's perception of self as he/she relates to a moral law, and guilt and sorrow are regular correlates.

Though every person has God's moral law written on his/her heart and incurs guilt when morally failing to keep that law, sometimes we can also falsely impose another's guilt upon ourselves or impose a moral law upon ourselves that is not based on God's truth. Survivors of rape, for example, regularly assume that they are at fault for the wrong done to them. Many soldiers who return from war struggle with what is commonly referred to as survivor's remorse/guilt,[128] and they falsely take personal responsibility for everything evil that occurred in the theatre of war.[129] In the same way, children who endure their parents' divorce regularly struggle with the false guilt that they are somehow responsible for their parents' separation.

Because human nature is so deceived, false guilt is a common struggle for survivors of traumatic experiences. Kirk Brower, professor of psychiatry at the University of Michigan, in his address to congressional staffers on December 14, 2016, said this of his own experience of losing his brother to suicide:

> As I descended the stairs, I knew he was dead. I had no warning, but I knew. I don't know how. I only know that other survivors of suicide with whom I have talked have had similar experiences. Still, I was not prepared for the sight of him hanging by a rope. Silently still and lifeless with tongue protruding. I was shocked, horrified, and panicked. I screamed. Within a day, the guilt rushes in. If only I had done this or only did that. Also the blame, "Why didn't the psychiatrist prevent this?" But such is magical thinking, as if the event could have been undone . . . . In addition to guilt and shame, I

---

[128] Berger, *Influence of Nurture*, 479.

[129] Dave Grossman, *On Killing*, 74. Grossman writes that "you don't even have to personally kill to experience these response stages and the interaction between the exhilaration and remorse stages" (246).

and other survivors are likely at times to feel anger at or abandoned by our loved one for dying by suicide, to feel fear during our own down moments that we may succumb to suicidal depression, relief that their suffering is over, and the most painful feeling of all — that which all the others are designed to defend against — profound painful grief and sadness.[130]

False guilt, hopelessness, a "profound painful grief and sadness," and suicidal ideation are regularly multiplied at the loss of a loved one — especially if it is as traumatic as suicide. So, while guilt is a necessary mental struggle that exposes one's moral condition as it relates to God's perfect law and the need for regeneration, false guilt is one way in which a person's moral nature is exposed to be deceived — another destructive feature of normal human nature observed in Genesis 3.

A Distinction Made

As with the secular construct of depression, Scripture associates hopelessness, guilt, and sorrow as seen in Genesis 3. Yet, the Bible also shows that these three aspects of human nature can be experienced independently of each other and are a part of a much bigger problem than the limited idea of depression conveys. Consider, for instance, how a person can experience sorrow without being hopeless, and can be hopeless without experiencing a sense of guilt.

Not only do many secularists label some people to be depressed who are merely in a state of sorrow but are not hopeless, but they also view depression as an abstract idea that is different for everyone and without any real objective criteria. In fact, more and more secular theorists and pharmaceutical companies promote this position and regularly refer to the "heterogeneity

---

[130] Kirk J. Brower, "The Legacy of Suicide," *Psychiatric Times Online* 34, no. 2 (February 17, 2017): http://www. psychiatric times.com/suicide/legacy-suicide?rememberme=1&elq_mid= 4656&elq_cid=893295.

of depression" (a diverse set of characteristics rather than limited to the *DSM-5* list of symptoms):

> Depression is generally considered to be a specific and consistent disorder characterized by a fixed set of symptoms and often treated with a combination of psychotherapy and medication. However, the standard rating scales used by healthcare professionals and researchers to diagnose this disease often differ in the symptoms they list.[131]

The NIMH concurs that the construct of depression is an abstract or subjective idea:

> Not everyone who is depressed experiences every symptom. Some people experience only a few symptoms while others may experience many. Several persistent symptoms in addition to low mood [sorrow] are required for a diagnosis of major depression, but people with only a few – but distressing – symptoms may benefit from treatment of their "subsyndromal" depression.[132]

In this common view of depression, sorrow or loss of desire is the essential feature – the only struggle a person must have.[133] If a person is in deep sorrow, then he/she qualifies for depression regardless of the other symptoms. *Subsyndromal* is a fancy way to say that a person really does not need to meet the *DSM* criteria – to have any of the listed symptoms – in order to be diagnosed with depression. In fact, the APA included in the *DSM-5* the "Other Specified Depressive Disorder" as a catch-all for people who are impaired because of their sorrow but not according to the requirements for any of the official depressive labels:

[131] University of Amsterdam (UVA), "The Heterogeneous Nature of Depression," *Science Daily Online* (October 24, 2016): https://www.sciencedaily .com/releases /2016/10/161024131122.htm.

[132] National Institute of Mental Health, "Depression," *NIMH* (2018): https://www.nimh.nih.gov/health/topics/depression/ index.shtml.

[133] APA, *DSM-5*, 160.

This category applies to presentations in which *symptoms characteristic of a depressive disorder* that cause *clinically significant distress or impairment* in social occupational, or other important areas of functioning predominate *but do not meet the full criteria* for any of the disorders in the depressive disorders diagnostic class [emphases added].[134]

To be labeled as depressed, one only needs to be in distress and his/her life impaired. The existence of the Other Specified Depressive Disorder and the fact that so many clinicians and theorists have thrown out the criteria as qualifying a person for a diagnosis of depression reveals just how subjective and speculative is the common but false belief that depression is a disease rather than a subjective secular construct seeking to explain human nature. In truth, depression is a secular "syndrome" (recognized by its list of symptoms) where the symptoms — other than sorrow and hopelessness — do not truly matter.

So, while hopelessness, sorrow, and guilt are regularly clustered together in both Scripture and psychiatric constructs as a part of human nature, they are also considered separately. In helping people through these struggles, counselors should never assume that a person labeled as depressed within the psychiatric system meets any or all of the necessary requirements. Within psychiatric theory, if a person is impaired or distressed and struggles to any degree with sorrow, he/she can be labeled as depressed.

Receiving Christ as the deliverer of one's soul does not mean that a Christian will escape sorrow in this world; it means that he/she gains hope that enables joy despite inevitable sorrows. Like anyone else, Christians regularly struggle with sadness though they do have a stabilizing hope. First Thessalonians 4:13 explains, "That you [believers] may not *sorrow* as others do who

[134] Ibid., 183.

have no hope." Having saving hope in Christ both changes one's understanding of the value of sorrow and his or her response to loss. In 2 Corinthians 6:10, the apostle Paul shares this supernatural mindset which he himself practiced: "As sorrowful, yet always rejoicing." Possessing genuine hope enables thankfulness and joy despite the sorrowful reality of this life.

The Bible presents the normal human condition after the Fall to be sorrowful, hopeless, and full of guilt. Those whom secularists consider to be depressed are simply responding in a normal manner to the fallen condition of both humanity and to the world in which they live. These are honest people who have come to realize the emptiness of false hopes, the sorrowful condition of life, their hopelessness apart from Christ, and the need to assuage their guilt.

While all people are in the same struggle, not everyone is honest about his/her true condition. Most people do not realize that they are allegedly depressed because of the false hopes they have accumulated and the idols they are pursuing. But false hopes and false gods always fail, and when they do, a person's true condition is revealed.

Individual degenerationism and *universal degenerationism* are opposing presuppositional philosophies. Individual degenerationism, the idea that normal people can overcome distress and impairment from their own internal resources and those who cannot are degenerates, is a major tenet of humanistic thinking, whereas universal degenerationism, the belief that all people are naturally weak and wicked, is a foundational teaching of Scripture and a major tenet of the gospel. To believe in the psychiatric construct of depression is also to accept the philosophy of individual degenerationism and view the construct of depression as an abnormality or disorder. To accept sorrow and hopelessness as normal human fragility and accept guilt as the result of universal human depravity is to accept the biblical view. How people choose to view these human experiences will determine their identity — whether they perceive themselves as normal or abnormal — and their attempted remedies. From the beginning of Genesis until the end of Revelation, faith in who a person is and who God is are the foundational issues when approaching what is normal and what is allegedly abnormal.

CHAPTER 4

RESPONDING TO SORROW

"Depression is a natural or normal human response to emotional injury and loss."[135] — Peter Breggin, former consultant for the NIMH

Unfulfilled desires are an inescapable part of life, but how we respond to the sorrow produced by these losses is pivotal. First Corinthians 7:9-11a states the biblical truth that there are only two primary responses and subsequent outcomes one can choose when faced with sorrow: (1) sorrow that produces deliverance or (2) sorrow that leads to spiritual death:

> As it is, I rejoice, not because you were grieved, but because you were grieved into repenting. For you felt a godly grief, so that you suffered no loss through us. For godly grief produces a repentance [that leads] to salvation without regret, whereas worldly grief produces death [separation from God]. For see what earnestness this godly grief has produced in you.

A person's response to sorrow will either better or worsen his/her soul. When sorrow is produced by destructive desires and mentally processed on human terms ("worldly grief"), he/she will naturally be directed toward spiritual separation

---

[135] Breggin, *Anti-Depressant Fact Book*, 14.

from God. It is normal that the non-physical pain in the very spirit of a person produces further separation from God and others. In contrast, spiritual pain produced in accordance with both a desire for God and acceptance of His supernatural plan of hope established in His Word produces deliverance,[136] which is irrevocable[137] (see Table A). Paul's profound claim is not merely counsel of right reactions; it is also a secure promise of hope and deliverance from the fallen state. The natural human bent

TABLE A

Available Reactions to Sorrow
2 Corinthians 7:9-11a

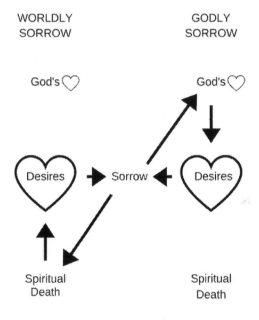

WORLDLY
SORROW

GODLY
SORROW

God's

God's

Desires

Sorrow

Desires

Spiritual
Death

Spiritual
Death

---

[136] σωτηρίαν; the rescue or salvation.

[137] ἀμεταμέλητον is also the word used in Romans 11:29: "For the gifts and the calling of God are irrevocable."

toward the soul's destruction can only be resolved through the supernatural work of God.

Everyone must choose — according to the moral nature of his/her heart — whether to respond to sorrow in God's will or react to it according to the world's expectation. Accepting God's plan leads to deliverance, whereas one's natural inclination leads to destruction and ultimately to spiritual death.

Destructive Responses

There are two basic destructive responses to sorrow that come naturally to us: (1) seeking out false hopes for deliverance or (2) giving up entirely on pursuing other hopes and becoming inattentive, catatonic, unmotivated, apathetic, and to the extreme, suicidal.

The destructive/impairing and often persistent nature of these two responses (false hopes and abandoning hope altogether) have led secularists to frame these common reactions as various disorders in the *DSM-5*. In other words, to be diagnosed with unipolar or bipolar depression often depends upon one's prominent destructive reaction within a specific time frame. Though, as we observed in chapter 2, depression is a subjective syndrome, and a person's simply admitting that he/she is sorrowful is enough to receive a psychiatric diagnosis. But most people naturally fluctuate between the two options and yield the diagnostic categories of unipolar and bipolar depressions to be irrelevant and misleading.

By nature, people are hopeful, but they often do not realize that their hopes are unfounded until those hopes give way and fail. Proverbs 13:12 offers this insight: "When hope is deferred it makes the spiritual heart sick, but a desire fulfilled is a tree of life." Biblical commentator Bruce Waltke remarks:

Deferred does not imply a revised time schedule but a never-ending extension of time. That hopeless external situation debilitates the heart (*leb*), the center from which his physical, psychic, and spiritual energies flow to the rest of his body. . . . With his true longings never satisfied, he stumbles in resignation and despair to his death.[138]

The never-ending and never-fulfilled trust in false hopes always leads to destruction, but having one's heart changed toward righteousness transforms that person's desires and establishes a unique hope that brings healing and satisfaction. Waltke then explains the second portion of this verse:

By contrast, the fulfilled desires of the righteous are like eating the fruit of the tree of life (cf. 13:25). A desire denotes an aspiration rooted deep in one's personality that draws him along to a desired state. . . . The metaphor of a tree of life functions as the antithesis of sickness; he is transferred from the realm of sickness and death into the realm of health and life.[139]

There are both sorrows and hopes that lead to death and sorrow and hope that lead to life. Self-serving desires, hopelessness, death, and eternal condemnation are never truly separate issues.

The spiritual pain of deferred and false hopes regularly leads people in modern society to a diagnosis of some type of depression. Many others, however, pursue money, fame, fortune, experiences, and fulfilled desires of every kind in order not to deal with the genuine hopeless state of their souls. Much of the television advertisements seek to convince viewers that they cannot live without the product, service, or experience. In many ways, marketing capitalizes on people's need to hope and find happiness/fulfillment in something apart from themselves. In 1935, philosopher, writer, and commentator G.K. Chesterton aptly described the world's philosophy of marketing as

[138] Waltke, *Proverbs: Chapters 1-15*, 563.

[139] Ibid.

the utterly un-philosophical philosophy of blind buying and selling; of bullying people into purchasing what they do not want; of making it badly so that they may break it and imagine they want it again; of keeping rubbish in rapid circulation like a dust-storm in a desert; *and pretending that you are teaching men to hope, because you do not leave them one intelligent instant in which to despair* [emphasis added].[140]

The world's system and our own human depravity are both bent toward creating false hopes that leave people unaware of their true despair and fatal condition apart from Christ. Sadly, people continue returning to the broken "rubbish" of false hopes which keep most from the only genuine hope that can rescue them from hopelessness, guilt, sorrow, and the many vexations of the soul. These false hopes do not merely obstruct humanity's true nature and genuine deliverance; they also lead further toward destruction and spiritual death.

Mania

One of the most troubling responses to sorrow is known in the psychiatric constructs of bipolar as *mania*. Mania is simply the false belief that people can pick themselves up by their own bootstraps by exerting great effort, experiencing extravagant pleasure, pursuing knowledge, and denying their reality. Humanist and clinical psychologist Richard Bentall understands mania to be a reaction to sorrow and hopelessness:

People tend to react to being depressed in [different] ways. Some people ruminate about their feelings, others launch into attempts to solve the problems that they believe have led to their depression, some try to distract themselves and a few indulge in dangerous activities.[141]

---

[140] G. K. Chesterton, *The Well and the Shallows* (London: Aziloth Books, [1935] published in 2012), 127.

[141] Bentall, *Madness Explained*, 290.

A person's attempt to escape sorrow through his/her own efforts establishes self as the greatest source of hope. But as the constant cycle of attempting to rescue oneself and then returning to hopelessness continues, so too does greater despair. As Dr. Breggin notes, "It can become nearly impossible to rise out of depression by one's own – to 'pull yourself up by your bootstraps.'"[142]

Mania is Normal:

Before examining this common, destructive, and worldly response to sorrow, it is helpful to understand that the manic response is a part of normal human nature and not an abnormal or unique state. All people naturally trust in their own understanding, pursue their own pleasure, and think more highly of themselves than they ought to. In other words, everyone naturally establishes self as the best possibility to escape the fallen condition. Mania is the delusion that *I am my best or only hope for deliverance from sorrow and guilt – the captain of my soul*.[143]

The APA defines a common feature ("one that is typically present") of mania in the *DSM-5* as "inflated self-esteem" or "grandiosity,"[144] and later it asserts that

> inflated self-esteem is typically present, ranging from uncritical self-confidence to marked grandiosity, and may reach delusional proportions (Criterion B1). Despite lack of any particular experience or talent, the individual may embark on complex tasks such as writing a novel or seeking publicity for some impractical invention.

[142] Breggin, *Anti-Depressant Fact Book*, 25.

[143] This reality is precisely why the construct of bipolar was first called "affective psychosis" (the deceived emotional response of the soul) by the German psychiatrist Emil Kraepelin (Berger, *Insanity of Madness*, 49-52).

[144] APA, *DSM-5*, 124.

Grandiose delusions (e.g., of having a special relationship to a famous person) *are common* [emphasis added].[145]

Though psychiatrists may not perceive some inflated self-esteem or uncritical self-confidence (what scripture calls pride) to be false beliefs, a person's false lofty opinion of himself/herself — no matter the degree — is delusional. Pride is humanity's greatest and most destructive delusion, and as with the other features of depression, pride is first observed as a common destructive characteristic of normal human nature in Genesis 3.

Some psychiatrists also realize that so-called normal passionate pursuits are virtually the same as described in the psychiatric concept of mania. In a *Psychiatric Times* article published at the end of 2018 by psychiatrist James Phelps (whom many consider to be a leading expert on bipolar), a comparison of fanaticism and mania are admitted to be so similar that they are hard to distinguish:

> Do you sometimes have trouble continuing your daily work, under the shadow of looming climate change? Wonder about chucking your practice and working exclusively on ending our reliance on fossil fuels? Is someone who devotes his life to arresting climate change a fanatic — or maybe even manic? . . . What is the difference? The literature on this question is surprisingly small: there are no references on *PubMed* for a search of fanatic manic, or fanatic bipolar, for example. A more substantial work has examined the boundary of religious and delusional beliefs. . . . Whatever the etiology, some fanaticism comes very close to the behaviors of bipolar mania: energized devotion to an idea. Sex and money are frequent foci, but also political ideas: see, for example, the complex patterns of "bipolar-like" behaviors in world leaders, examined by Nassir Ghaemi in his book *A First-Rate Madness* (narcissism is just the beginning). *In this territory of highly uncertain boundaries between passion and determination and mental illness* [emphasis added] lies the story of a diagnosis of bipolar mania in a man for his insistence that

---

[145] Ibid., 128.

humankind itself is insane for continuing to mine and burn fossil fuels. It's an interesting twist, no?[146]

Passionately seeking pleasure and euphoric experiences, pursuing knowledge and enlightenment, being determined to escape sorrow and find happiness at high energetic levels, and attempting to ease guilt or forget one's history are all normal tendencies of human nature. These human behaviors are also not medical issues and require no medical training or knowledge of biology to diagnose. Dr. Frances remarks,

> Manic episodes are unmistakable and unforgettable. The person is supercharged in thought and deed; racing around; talking under pressure; spouting grandiose ideas, heightened creativity, a wild succession of totally impossible schemes; joking nonstop; floating on an elevated mood, but irritable if crossed; spending money like a drunken sailor; feeling boundless energy; acting inappropriately and impulsively; being intrusively sexual; and needing little sleep. Your Aunt Tillie could make the diagnosis of classic mania in a minute.[147]

Those who look to themselves for hope and exert great effort to escape their distress are most often trying to escape the sorrows and horrors of trauma[148] and/or tragedy or the haunting guilt of their own past behavior. While psychiatrists frame mania as an abnormality, it is, in fact, the natural bent of each person to trust in himself/herself and lean unto his/her own understanding in order to get through life (Proverbs 3:5-6).

[146] James Phelps, "Bipolar Disorder or Fanaticism?" *Psychiatric Times Online* (October 15, 2018): http://www. psychiatrictimes.com/bipolar-disorder/bipolar-disorder-or-fanaticism/page/0/1.

[147] Frances, *Saving Normal*, 150.

[148] "Bipolar disorder has been linked to traumatic childhood experience and to the potential for violence," (Allison M. R. Lee, Igor I. Galynker, Irina Kopeykina, Hae-Joon Kim, and Tasnia Khatun, "Violence in Bipolar Disorder," *Psychiatric Times Online* [December 16, 2014]: http://www.psychiatrictimes. com/bipolar-disorder/violence-bipolar-disorder?GUID=31158D64-F01A-4DEA-AC1A-D3CE843FC9BC&rememberme=1&ts= 21042017).

Mania is a Response:

The American Psychiatric Association chose "manic-depressive reaction" in the *DSM-I*[149] as a forerunner to the label of "bipolar disorder." The title of manic-depressive reaction reflects the reality that mania is another way to describe the emotionally-charged-self-dependent and destructive reaction to sorrow, hopelessness, and guilt that is an unfortunate part of human nature. While mania (trusting in one's self and one's efforts) always fails, the false hope that one can finally escape sorrow, hopelessness, and guilt persists. Psychiatrist Peter Breggin relates how many choose mania as "a great escape,"

> Often mania seems like nothing more than the flip side of depression. In mania the individual feels like the most wonderful person in the world. The businessman who was disappointed in himself now gets high on himself and all his projects and feels invulnerable to failure. He's filled with ideas and projects and spills them out in a rush of words. *Mania is a great escape, a shortcut to pscyhospiritual heaven on earth* [emphasis added]. As already noted, it often attempts to deny and overcome grave feelings of guilt and depression. It declares, "I'm not feeling low, I'm feeling high!" but it also can be driven by extreme humiliation or worthlessness.[150]

Breggin notes several of the key features: escape, guilt, deceit, self-focus, reaction to deep sorrow, and self-reliance. Renowned clinical psychologist Richard Bentall also comments on how depression and mania are related to guilt, deceit, and belief:

> Psychotically depressed people, for example, often *believe* that they are inadequate, or guilty of imaginary misdeeds. Manic patients, in contrast, often *feel that they are superior to others*, and are capable of achievements that will amaze the world [emphasis added].[151]

---

[149] Bentall, *Madness Explained*, 58.

[150] Breggin, *Toxic Psychiatry*, 137.

[151] Bentall, *Madness Explained*, 204.

"Psychotically depressed people" describes those who have false beliefs (sometimes they are accurate) about themselves which bring them low, whereas those who are "manic" have false beliefs about who they are (and their abilities) which sets them on a high. As Bentall notes, however, both groups are struggling with deceit — another feature of normal human nature described in the Genesis 3 account.

By attempting to resolve guilt and sorrow, people look to themselves to be their own hope. When that hope is empty and cannot deliver, people return to their original state of sorrow, having accumulated new behaviors and experiences which regularly incur more guilt, deeper sorrow, and highlight hopelessness further. Thus, the cycle ensues from the depressive pole to the manic pole and back again to the depressive pole.

As related in the previous chapter, depression is the normal state, and fleeting moments of merriment are normal human experiences. Proverbs 14:13 states, "Even in laughter the heart is sorrowful; and the end of that mirth is heaviness" (KJV). The New Living Translation renders the verse this way: "Laughter can conceal a heavy heart, but when the laughter ends, the grief remains." Though the APA suggests that extreme emotional changes from joy to sadness constitutes a physical sickness,[152] Scripture understands that our true fallen nature is a state of sadness and that both genuine merriment and forced attempts to escape sorrow are also part of the human experience. When people are happy, society in general does not view them as abnormal. But when people who are struggling with "inflated self-esteem or grandiosity"[153] do all they can (even taking dangerous risks) to escape sorrow, society as a whole has chosen

[152] http://www.nimh.nih.gov/health/publications/bipolar-disorder-in-adults/index.shtml.

[153] APA, DSM-5, 124.

to view these self-centered and highly motived people as abnormal. One might say, then, that the psychiatric construct of mania is a forced and delusional attempt to be happy despite a person's true reality of sorrow. This explanation is why the APA insists that

> the essential feature of a manic episode is a distinct period during which there is an abnormally, persistently elevated, expansive, or irritable mood and persistently increased activity or energy. . . . Mood in a manic episode is often described as euphoric, excessively cheerful, high, or 'feeling on top of the world.'[154]

The "euphoric" or "excessively cheerful" mood is not genuine, and represents a delusional attempt to escape sorrow rather than an abnormality. Commentator Bruce Waltke comments on Proverbs 14:13:

> In addition to the catchword "the end of it," this proverb continues the theme that present appearances are deceptive and the true reality is manifest in its outcome. Outward merriment may mask heartache, but in the end grief will manifest itself. . . . Sorrow forms the unchanging background of the occasional, distracting moments of merriment.[155]

Through people's own mental and physical efforts, they may experience or attempt to create a fleeting moment of laughter, joy, excitement, accomplishment, or a high or pleasure, but that relief from sorrow is temporary. King Solomon realized, that though he had everything he could wish for, he himself had "turned about and given [his] heart up to despair over all the toil of [his] labors under the sun" (Ecclesiastes 2:20). The National Institute of Mental Health (NIMH) explains this common reaction:

> People with bipolar disorder experience unusually intense emotional states that occur in distinct periods called 'mood

[154] Ibid., 127.

[155] Waltke, *Proverbs: Chapters 1-15*, 592.

episodes.' An overly joyful or overexcited state is called a manic episode, and an extremely sad or hopeless state is called a depressive episode. [156]

Human effort is a false hope in self, which people naturally depend upon in an attempt to escape from sorrow, hopelessness, and guilt. When these destructive mindsets and behaviors persist, they regularly become habits or lifestyles. An abnormal psychology textbook describes the normal but impairing response of mania becoming a pattern:

> [People] become disturbed because they are unable to accept their own nature and the world as it is, and thus cannot shape their aims according to their assets. Failing in the achievement of their unrealistic goals, they develop feelings of inferiority, apprehensiveness, and other faulty emotional attitudes which lead to the use of neurotic defensive measures. These nonadjustive attitudes and responses gradually develop into habitual reaction patterns [emphases added].[157]

"Habitual reaction patterns" to sorrow, deceit, and the many vexations of the soul defines well the psychiatric concept of mania. As depression (a crushed spirit) is discerned biblically and logically to be normal human nature, mania is also clearly understood as an expected but delusional attempt to assuage guilt and escape sorrow through natural but destructive self-reliance.

Mania is a Subjective Concept

Although the Bible has always depicted human efforts to escape sorrow and the soul's vexation as normal, many secularists only now are beginning to honestly assess and expose the serious

---

[156] Http://www.nimh.nih.gov/health/publications/bipolar-disorder-in-adults/index.shtml.

[157] Walter Coville, Timothy Costello, and Fabian Rouke, *Abnormal Psychology: Mental Illness Types, Causes, and Treatment* (New York: Barnes and Noble, 1960), 40.

problems with their separate constructs of unipolar and bipolar depression. Not only have attempts to establish objective criteria that distinguish normal from abnormal failed, but so also has the attempt to objectively delineate between unipolar and bipolar depressions. What secular researchers and clinicians alike have come to realize is that mania is a normal but destructive response to sorrow, guilt, and hopelessness.

The APA asserts within their *DSM-5* classification system that not everyone who is labeled as depressed enters into mania. In their minds, mania is the distinguishing feature between the bipolar and unipolar constructs of depression.[158] The APA insists in the *DSM-5* that in order to meet the criteria of "major depressive disorder" the person being diagnosed must attest that "there has never been a manic episode or a hypomanic episode."[159] Having a manic or hypomanic episode, according to the secular belief, uniquely qualifies a person as having bipolar rather than unipolar depression. But numerous studies expose that many people whom secularists diagnose as having depressive disorders actually do experience manic episodes: "Manic symptoms during unipolar depression are more common than thought."[160]

From its first conception, depression was not viewed as two separate diseases. When Emil Kraepelin constructed his theory of mental illness (the *medical model* or *biological perspective*), he first categorized only one manic-depressive group rather than seeing passionate attempts to escape depression (what theorists

---

[158] APA, *DSM-5*, 155.

[159] Ibid., 161.

[160] G.H. Vázquez, M. Lolich, C. Cabrera, et al. "Mixed Symptoms in Major Depressive and Bipolar Disorders: A Systematic Review," *Journal of Affective Disorders* 225 (2018): 756-60.

now call bipolar) as a separate theorized disease from unipolar depression:

> When Emil Kraepelin published his diagnostic texts, he put these patients into his manic-depressive group. This diagnostic category also included patients who suffered from depression or mania only (as opposed to both), and Kraepelin reasoned that these varied emotional states all arose from the same underlying disease. The splitting of manic-depressive disorder into separate unipolar and bipolar factions got its start in 1957, when a German psychiatrist, Karl Leonhard, determined that the manic form of the illness seemed to run more in families than the depressive form did [the eugenics theory of mental illness]. He called the manic patients "bipolar," and other researchers then identified additional differences between the unipolar and bipolar forms of manic-depressive illness.[161]

The idea that mania is a disease and different from depression arose out of the eugenics theory and not from valid scientific or medical discovery.

The *DSM-IV* also combined unipolar and bipolar depression into one larger syndrome—a point that the APA acknowledges in the *DSM-5*.[162] Though they are often considered separately today, many psychiatrists recognize there is no objective difference between the two constructs. Psychiatrist John Miller remarks,

> As we have become more sophisticated in our ability to diagnose psychiatric disorders, a large hurdle remains: the ability to differentiate between a primary bipolar I disorder (BDI) major depressive episode versus a unipolar major depressive episode in a newly presenting patient that meets clear diagnostic criteria for a *DSM-5* major depressive episode. Significantly, as has been the case

---

[161] Robert Whitaker, *Anatomy of an Epidemic: Magic Bullets, Psychiatric Drugs, and the Astonishing Rise of Mental Illness in America* (New York: Broadway Books, 2015), 178.

[162] "Unlike the *DSM-IV*, this chapter 'Depressive Disorders' has been separated from the previous chapter 'Bipolar and Related Disorders'" (APA, *DSM-5*, 155).

with previous editions of the psychiatric *Diagnostic and Statistical Manual of Mental Disorders, the DSM-5 criteria for a major depressive episode is identical for both a unipolar depression and a bipolar depression* [emphasis added].[163]

In other words, depression is depression no matter how psychiatrists attempt to fit the normal human condition into various social constructs or label various reactions. David Goldberg, professor of psychiatry at the prestigious King's College London, concurs: "The depressed phase of bipolar illness may be difficult or impossible to distinguish from unipolar depression."[164] Dr. Frances also remarks on the difficulty of objectively distinguishing between the two alleged disorders:

> Perhaps the most important distinction in all of psychiatry is unfortunately often the most difficult. Does the patient have bipolar mood swings (with cyclical lows alternating with highs) or is this just a straight unipolar depression (recurrent lows with no highs?) . . . . *The tough question is how to draw the diagnostic line between bipolar and unipolar* to balance the risks of taking versus the risks of not taking the mood-stabilizing medication [emphasis added].[165]

However, it is not just difficult to subjectively determine in a clinical setting or in published lists; leading psychiatrists, such as Boadie Dunlop who specializes in alleged mood disorders and Helen Mayberg, renowned neuroscientist at Icahn School of Medicine at Mount Sinai New York, have concluded from years of clinical research and in neuroscience that neuroimaging does not distinguish between alleged normal and abnormal brains or between alleged unipolar and bipolar depression:

---

[163] John J. Miller, "Major Depressive Episode: Is It Bipolar I or Unipolar Depression?" *Psychiatric Times Online* 35, no. 7 (July 31, 2018): http://www.psychiatrictimes.com/special-reports/major-depressive-episode-it-bipolar-i-or-unipolar-depression?rememberme=1&elq_mid=3608&elq_cid= 893295.

[164] Goldberg, "Heterogeneity of 'Major Depression,'" 226.

[165] Frances, *Saving Normal*, 149-50.

> Despite its failure to distinguish the healthy from the depressed, neuroimaging may have value in defining subtypes of depression . . . . Although these methods have identified differences at the group level, *their inability to clearly distinguish individuals with bipolar disorder from those with major depressive disorder may indicate that these illnesses represent points on a spectrum, rather than distinct biological entities.* Given the difficulty in generating markers that can reliably sort major depression and bipolar depression, it may seem unlikely that neuroimaging will achieve clinically relevant subtyping within major depression alone [emphasis added].[166]

From every angle, there simply does not exist objective differences between what secularists theorize to be unipolar and bipolar depression.

In fact, Dr. Frances acknowledges in his book *Saving Normal* that he and his *DSM-IV* task force constructed bipolar II as an attempt to resolve their serious problem of lacking an objective-distinguishable mark between alleged unipolar and bipolar depressions:

> Patients who have alternating periods of depression and hypomania are at the crucial boundary separating bipolar and unipolar depression. They could have been classified in either camp. If we classify them as bipolar, they will receive mood-stabilizing medication that may prevent rapid cycling, but they might be exposed to unnecessary mood-stabilizing medication that could be quite harmful. If we classify them as unipolar, they will receive only antidepressant medication, and this may trigger a manic episode. Faced with these ambiguous cards, we chose to add a new category, bipolar II, to describe patients who have depression and hypomanic episodes.[167]

Bipolar II is not a new disease entity; it is another created theory in attempt to sustain the medical model apart from any science.

---

[166] Boadie W. Dunlop and Helen S. Mayberg, "Neuroimaging Advances for Depression," *Cerebrum: The Dana Forum on Brain Science* vol. 16-17. (Nov. 1, 2017): https://www.ncbi.nlm.nih.gov/pmc/articles/PMC6132047/.

[167] Frances, *Saving Normal*, 150-51.

Secular theorists have also tried to distinguish between mania, hypomania, and allegedly normal feelings of euphoria, excitement, and effort:

> Hypomanic episodes have the same symptoms as manic episodes with two important differences: the mood usually isn't severe enough to cause problems with the person working or socializing with others (e.g., they don't have to take time off work during the episode), or to require hospitalization; and there are never any psychotic features [deceitful thinking] present during the episode.[168]

The APA created Bipolar II not only as an attempt to differentiate unipolar and bipolar depression, but also because humanists fail to see that all attempts to escape sorrow by human efforts are destructive. In creating the idea of *hypomania*, psychiatrists minimize the time, severity, and distress axioms, which as discussed in chapter 3, allegedly differentiate between normal sorrow and abnormal sorrow (e.g., "baby blues" versus "postpartum depression disorder"). In accordance with this thinking, if exaggerated attempts to escape sorrow do not impair one's life, are not considered severely impairing, or include false ways of thinking (e.g., delusions of grandeur or false guilt; psychotic features), then psychiatrists view these behaviors as hypomanic episodes rather than manic episodes. But this newly attempted distinction has created a new problem for the APA, as Dr. Frances acknowledges:

> There is no clear boundary between hypomania and simply feeling good — so [pharmaceutical] advertisements began suggesting that even slight shifts upward in mood or passing irritability might be a subtle sign of bipolar disorder.[169]

---

[168] Steve Bressert, "Hypomanic Episode Symptoms," *PsychCentral* (September 8, 2018): https://psychcentral.com/disorders/hypomanic-episode-symptoms/.

[169] Frances, *Saving Normal*, 150-51.

Now, if after receiving a diagnosis of depression a person starts to feel good or begins a grand adventure in order to escape sorrow that is not too impairing, psychiatrists can view that individual as having bipolar II. Such reality is also the reason that some psychiatrists now see fanaticism as resembling or equal to the constructs of bipolar,[170] and why the number of people being diagnosed as allegedly having a bipolar disorder has increased dramatically. There is no significant objective difference between normal sorrow and alleged abnormal sorrow, between unipolar and bipolar, between mania and hypomania, or between hypomania and feeling good and enjoying pleasurable experiences in order to be happy. There are simply moments of laughter and pleasure in this life, but in the end, everyone returns to sorrow in this life (Proverbs 14:13). The simple truth is that normal people who are honest about their hopeless, sorrowful, and guilty condition — no matter how psychiatrists attempt to label and categorize them or what terms they create to sustain their paradigm — will try anything to escape, including turning to their own efforts, dangerous chemicals, and naturally leaning unto their own understanding.

Since humanists assert that self-esteem and self-actualization are of the upmost importance to human advancement and deliverance from their problems, the true underlying theme of unipolar and bipolar depression relates to people's self-perception — their identity. Psychiatrists assert depression as "too low of self-esteem,"[171] and they view mania as "inflated self-esteem."[172] A person's perceived level of self-esteem, then, is

[170] Phelps, "Bipolar Disorder or Fanaticism?"

[171] APA, "What is Depression?" *American Psychiatric Association Online* (December 2018): https://www.psychiatry. org/patients-families/depression/what-is-depression.

[172] APA, *DSM-5*, 124.

the only significant difference between alleged unipolar and bipolar depressions. Yet, this judgment is also subjective as no standard of healthy self-esteem exists. What is revealed in these psychiatric constructs, however, is that turning to self in any way is destructive rather than healing. In the humanistic perspective, those who deviate one way or another from a hypothetical standard of normal self-esteem are degenerates.

The labels of bipolar and unipolar depression are insignificant, misleading, and merely reflect theories of destructive and normal human responses to the fallen condition. Yet, for many, the psychiatric labels create a far more damaging delusion that regularly becomes their identity and fuels their dependence upon false hopes. Mania is best understood as a person's turning to self for hope to remedy the sorrow, hopelessness, deceit, guilt, and vexations of the soul. Mania is a common destructive reaction to our fallen state and not an abnormality or a disease.

Mania is Biblically Discerned

In order to better understand both the normalcy of mania and how Scripture clearly explains this common reaction to sorrow, it is beneficial to carefully examine the mindsets, emotions, and behaviors which secularists have constructed into psychiatric diseases. What may surprise some is just how precise Scripture is in describing the APA's concept of mania within their psychiatric construct of bipolar I.

In Ecclesiastes 1-2, Solomon records his own personal attempts to escape his fallen/vexed condition. In verses 2:1-11, the text states,

> I said in my heart, "Come now, I will test you with pleasure; enjoy yourself." But behold, this also was vanity. I said of laughter, "It is mad," and of pleasure, "What use is it?" I searched with my heart how to cheer my body with wine—my heart still guiding me with wisdom—and how to lay hold on folly, till I might see what was good for the children of man to do under heaven during the few

days of their life. I made great works. I built houses and planted vineyards for myself. I made myself gardens and parks, and planted in them all kinds of fruit trees. I made myself pools from which to water the forest of growing trees. I bought male and female slaves, and had slaves who were born in my house. I had also great possessions of herds and flocks, more than any who had been before me in Jerusalem. I also gathered for myself silver and gold and the treasure of kings and provinces. I got singers, both men and women, and many concubines, the delight of the sons of man. So I became great and surpassed all who were before me in Jerusalem. Also my wisdom remained with me. And whatever my eyes desired I did not keep from them. I kept my heart from no pleasure, for my heart found pleasure in all my toil, and this was my reward for all my toil. Then I considered all that my hands had done and the toil I had expended in doing it, and behold, all was vanity and a striving after wind, and there was nothing to be gained under the sun.

This text is a detailed description of the vanity of self-indulgence, self-dependence, and self-effort that begins in and is guided by the spiritual heart. It is also a list of the precise criteria the APA insists are diagnostic features of mania within the bipolar construct it has created. It appears as if secular theorists took Solomon's description of his own mindsets, emotional responses, and failed efforts to remedy human nature and constructed the current bipolar disorders. Pleasure, laughter, mind-altering substances, grand projects, promiscuity, lack of self-control, indulgence, adventures, and pride (or high self-esteem) all characterize what secularists call bipolar disorder, but what Scripture presents in this text as humanity's normal but failing pursuit of vanity and a cure for the soul's vexation (see Table B for comparison). Stated differently, what secularists call bipolar, the Bible presents as a normal but failed attempt to escape humanity's true fallen condition. The criteria listed in the *DSM-5* as a "manic episode" in the construct of bipolar and thought to be an abnormality within humanistic thinking is presented in Ecclesiastes 1-2 as normal human nature and expected destructive responses to the fallen condition of all people.

TABLE B

A comparison of Ecclesiastes 2:1-11 and the *DSM-5* criteria for mania listed in the construct of Bipolar I	
ECCLESIASTES 2	***DSM-5* – BIPOLAR I**
vs. 9 – "So I became great and surpassed all who were before me in Jerusalem."	p. 124 – "Inflated self-esteem or grandiosity."
vs. 4-8 – "I made great works. I built houses and planted vineyards for myself. I made myself gardens and parks . . . I made myself pools from which to water the forest of growing trees. I bought male and female slaves, and had slaves who were born in my house. . . ." vs. 10 – "And whatever my eyes desired I did not keep from them. I kept my heart from no pleasure."	p. 124 – "Increase in goal-directed activity." p. 128 – "During the manic episode, the individual may engage in multiple overlapping new projects . . . nothing seems out of the individual's reach."
vs. 8 – "I got . . . many concubines, the delight of the sons of man."	p. 128 – "Increased sexual drive, fantasies, and behavior are often present." p. 129 – "Sexual behavior may include infidelity or indiscriminate sexual encounters with strangers."
vs. 3a – "I searched with my heart how to cheer my body with wine."	p. 131 – "There may be substantial overlap in view of the tendency for individuals with bipolar I disorder to overuse substances during an episode."

ECCLESIASTES 2	*DSM-5* – BIPOLAR I
vs. 3b – "My heart still guiding me with wisdom— and *how to lay hold on folly* [emphasis added], till I might see what was good for the children of man to do under heaven during the few days of their life." (See Proverbs on the fool and his mouth).	p. 129 – "Gambling and antisocial behaviors may accompany the manic episode." p. 128 – "Speech can be rapid, pressured, loud, and difficult to interrupt. Individuals may talk continuously and without regard for other's wishes."
vs. 7-8 – "I had also great possessions of herds and flocks, more than any who had been before me in Jerusalem. I also gathered for myself silver and gold and the treasure of kings and provinces."	p. 130 – "Bipolar disorder is more common in high-income than in low-income countries."
vs. 20 – "So I turned about and gave my heart up to despair."	p. 123-27 – "extreme mood changes"
vs. 17 – "So I hated life, because what is done under the sun was grievous to me."	p. 131 – "The lifetime risk of suicide in individuals with bipolar disorder is estimated to be at least 15 times that of the general population. In fact, bipolar disorder may account for one-quarter of all completed suicides."

Solomon also offers (in Ecclesiastes 1:16-2:26) three categories of human effort as attempts to escape sorrow—essentially making one's self to be the agent of hope (1:17; 2:1-3; 2:12): people can turn to (1) *wisdom* (the pursuit of knowledge and enlightenment apart from God; vs. 13 — "I applied my heart to seek and to search out by wisdom all that is done under heaven. It is an unhappy business that God has given to the children of man to be busy with"), (2) *madness* or *mania* (the delusional pursuit of pleasure and happiness; vs. 2:1-2 — "I said in my heart, 'Come now, I will test you with pleasure; enjoy yourself.' But behold, this also was vanity. I said of laughter, 'it is mad,' and of pleasure, 'What use is it?'), and (3) *folly* (mindsets and behavior that reflect the true empty, deceptive, and destructive desires of the heart; "how to lay hold on folly" — vs. 2:4-11).[173] While not everyone chooses the same destructive responses to the many vexations of the soul, everyone who lives apart from hope in Christ must choose at least one of these attempts as their hope. In Ecclesiastes 2:12, Solomon declares this truth: "For what can the man do who comes after the king? Only what has already been done." What makes Solomon's confession even more sobering is the fact that he speaks from the position of one who was wise beyond any other mortal, privileged beyond any other human, and pleasured beyond any other being. King Solomon, with all of his unlimited resources, knowledge, adventures, and pleasures, had tried every possible human effort apart from Christ to remedy his broken spirit (vs. 4-11). Yet, these false hopes of the heart, which Solomon offers, are empty promises and always return the soul to its broken state. The will of the flesh cannot regenerate (new birth) degenerates (John 1:13) and deliver them from their fragility and depravity; only God can.

Solomon's self-dependence and high self-esteem are not abnormal, and his experience explains why the *DSM-5* acknowledges that the more privileged a person or country, the higher rate of manic attempts to escape sorrow.[174] It is often

---

[173] See Daniel R. Berger II, *The Truth About ADHD: Genuine Hope and Biblical Answers* (Taylors, SC: Alethia International Publications, 2015), 126-47.

[174] APA, *DSM-5*, 130.

difficult for the affluent to trust in God because of humanity's natural self-dependence (Matthew 19:23-24),[175] and even wealthy Christians must be careful not to be proud and let riches become a false hope:

> As for the rich in this present age, charge them not to be haughty, nor to set their hopes on the uncertainty of riches, but on God, who richly provides us with everything to enjoy (1 Timothy 6:17).

False hopes, no matter how grand and promising and how well-funded they might be, always return people to their deep sorrow (reality).

In Ecclesiastes 1-2, Solomon puts the three categories of human effort to escape his depraved nature and sorrow to the test only to discover that they are worthless. One might say, then, that Solomon in all his knowledge, wisdom, and resources was one of the first to research the human condition and record the empirical evidence and results.

Solomon first tests the pursuit of knowledge (e.g., human philosophy, false religion, scientism). But this human effort, instead of producing happiness, produces further vexation and sorrow (vs. 17-18):

> And I applied my heart to know wisdom and to know madness and folly. I perceived that this also is but a striving after wind. For in much wisdom is much vexation [internal struggle or distress], and he who increases knowledge increases sorrow.

The more we understand our true moral nature, the fallen condition of the natural world, and the emptiness of obtaining knowledge apart from God, the more sorrow and agony we also realize. This reality also explains why adolescents and collegians

---

[175] Depression is most often diagnosed among the poor, whereas bipolar is most often diagnosed among the rich. The more resources people have, the more tendency they have to turn to their own devices and display their pride.

are now struggling with anxiety, sorrow, hopelessness, anger, fear, etc. to the extent not previously seen in our nation. Psychologist Gregg Henriques writes,

> It is neither an exaggeration nor is it alarmist to claim that there is a mental health crisis today facing America's college students. Evidence suggests that this group has greater levels of stress and psychopathology than any time in the nation's history.[176]

As the pressure to pursue science, knowledge, and enlightenment increases, so too does vexation and sorrow. The false hope that science will provide answers and deliverance is faith in scientism, and such faith is destroying lives, not saving them.

Sadly, though, leading secular theorists still insist that "enlightenment" brings about happiness. Editor in Chief Emeritus of the prestigious psychiatric journal, *The Psychiatric Times*, Ronald Pies wrote an editorial in 2018 where he discussed Harvard professor of psychology Steven Pinker's book, *Enlightenment Now*. In the book, Pinker addresses the clear unhappy state of Americans and asserts that enlightenment is the remedy. In Pies' review of Pinker's chapter on how unhappy Americans are despite their privilege, Pies disagrees with Pinker as to why Americans are unhappy, but agrees with him on the proposed remedy to the human condition:

> I am in broad sympathy with Prof. Pinker's larger aims in the book, which are founded on the belief that knowledge and reason can enhance human flourishing. What humanistically inclined psychiatrist could argue with that?[177]

---

[176] Gregg Henriques, "The College Student Mental Health Crisis, *Psychology Today Online* (February 15, 2014): https://www.psychologytoday. com/us/blog/theory-knowledge/201402/the-college-student-mental-health-crisis.

[177] Ronald W. Pies, "Should Americans Be Happier Than They Are?" *Psychiatric Times Online* (April 5, 2018): http://www.psychiatrictimes.com/

According to popular secular thinking today, the answer to the fallen human condition is to gain knowledge and to be educated despite its emptiness. But if the wisest of men could not find an escape from his sorrow and hopeless condition through obtaining human wisdom, then neither can we today.

In Ecclesiastes 2:1-11, Solomon, after realizing the futility of trusting in human wisdom, then turns to his other available choices of madness and folly. While still pursuing knowledge (vs. 3), he chooses to also pursue pleasurable experiences/ temporal satisfaction — what he calls madness or laughter. After going on adventures, pursuing countless encounters with women, turning to mind-altering substances, accomplishing great human feats, accumulating wealth, and completing grand projects (1-9), he responds to the pursuit of pleasure (vs. 10-11):

> And whatever my eyes *desired* I did not keep from them. *I kept my heart from no pleasure, for my heart found pleasure* in all my toil, and this was my reward for all my toil. Then I considered all that my hands had done and the toil I had expended in doing it, and behold, all was vanity and a striving after wind, and there was nothing to be gained under the sun [emphasis added].

The pursuit of happiness through life experiences is an empty promise — a vanity or false hope — that cannot genuinely deliver people from their depravity and fragility.

Pursuing pleasure or a fantasy life as Solomon did in order to deny or escape one's reality falls into the definition of psychosis or delusional thinking within the *DSM-5* definition. Delusions are false beliefs that are regularly used in attempt to dissociate from trauma, distress, guilt, human nature, and moral failure. It is not surprising then, to learn that many psychiatrists observe a common reaction to sorrow: turning to deceitful beliefs and perceptions rather than turning to pleasure. Both are madness in

couch-crisis/should-americans-be-happier-they-are-steven-pinker-thinks-so-i-have-my-doubts.

that they seek to replace truth with deceit or fantasy. Many psychiatrists refer to this response as "psychotic depression" and consider it to be a subtype of major depression,[178] while other clinicians frame specific denials of reality as new subtypes of depression (e.g., "smiling depression"):

> With their mask on, everything looks great, even at times perfect. However, underneath the mask they are suffering from sadness, panic attacks, low self-esteem, insomnia, and, in some cases, suicidal thoughts.[179]

Scripture does not use the word *psychosis* (which means the "condition of the soul") to describe the turning to deceit or someone who is given over to deceit. Instead, the English translations utilize the words *madness* and *mania*.[180] Nonetheless, the Bible fully understands and explains the normal human tendency to react to undesirable truths about life and human nature by turning to deceit. Ironically, to the deceived heart, madness seems like a logical escape from the reality of our fallen condition.

To complicate matters in regards to "psychotic depression," psychiatrists widely recognize that psychiatric drugs, illicit drugs, and alcohol use are known to increase hallucinations and delusional thinking—two key features of psychosis.[181] Alcohol

---

[178] Brian Miller, "Risk of Psychosis in Recurrent Episodes of Psychotic and Nonpsychotic Major Depressive Disorder," *Psychiatric Times Online* (September 24, 2018): http://www. psychiatrictimes.com/depression/risk-psychosis-major-depression.

[179] Rita Labeaune, "Smiling Depression," *Psychology Today* (November 12, 2014): https://www.psychologytoday.com/us/blog/the-guest-room/201411/smiling-depression.

[180] For further study on the concepts of psychosis, madness, insanity, delusions, and hallucinations, see Berger, *Insanity of Madness*.

[181] "Substance/Medication-Induced Depressive Disorder" (APA, *DSM-5*, 175).

and drugs, even prescription drugs, are commonly used to assuage depression or escape harsh or horrific circumstances. "Self-medicating" with these substances is a common feature of mania—an attempt to escape or assuage sorrow as Solomon also tried. One group of respected psychiatric researchers have concluded that

> mood disorders and alcohol dependence frequently co-occur. Etiologic theories concerning the comorbidity often focus on drinking to self-medicate or cope with affective symptoms.[182]

Turning to deceit and away from reality—however these reactions are named or the resulting behaviors categorized—is a common attempt to escape sorrow and hopelessness. To the natural man, knowledge, pleasure, and deceit seem to be the best remedies to sorrow.

In Ecclesiastes 2:12-13, Solomon again considers if wisdom, madness, or folly can remedy the human condition. This time, though, he examines whether folly is of any value, since pursuing human wisdom and pleasure have together failed:

> So I turned to consider wisdom and madness and folly. For what can the man do who comes after the king? Only what has already been done. Then I saw that there is more gain in wisdom than in folly, as there is more gain in light than in darkness. The wise person has his eyes in his head, but the fool walks in darkness. And yet I perceived that the same event happens to all of them. Then I said in my heart, "What happens to the fool will happen to me also. Why then have I been so very wise?" And I said in my heart that this also is vanity. For of the wise as of the fool there is no enduring remembrance, seeing that in the days to come all will have been long forgotten. How the wise dies just like the fool! *So I hated life, because what is done under the sun was grievous to me, for all is vanity and a striving after wind.* I hated all my toil in which I toil under the

[182] Rosa M. Crum, Ramin Mojtabai, and Samuel Lazareck, et. al., "A Prospective Assessment of Reports of Drinking to Self-Medicate Mood Symptoms With the Incidence and Persistence of Alcohol Dependence," *JAMA Psychiatry Online* (July 2013): doi:10.1001/jamapsychiatry.2013.1098.

sun, seeing that I must leave it to the man who will come after me, and who knows whether he will be wise or a fool? Yet he will be master of all for which I toiled and used my wisdom under the sun. This also is vanity. *So I turned about and gave my heart up to despair over all the toil of my labors under the sun,* because sometimes a person who has toiled with wisdom and knowledge and skill must leave everything to be enjoyed by someone who did not toil for it. This also is vanity and a great evil [emphasis added].

Solomon — the wisest, wealthiest, and most pleasured man to ever live — makes the truth abundantly clear that nothing in this world apart from Christ can remedy guilt, solve inevitable death, or bring lasting joy and satisfaction: "So I hated life, because what is done under the sun was grievous to me" (17). Deeper sadness and hating life are regularly the result of turning to self-dependence and vanities that promise what they cannot deliver. Suicide becomes an option only to the individual who has exhausted every other possible escape from the difficulties of the human condition and falsely asserts self to be the final hope. But as Solomon attests, nothing done under the sun by human hands can resolve sorrow, assuage guilt, or provide genuine hope that delivers humanity.

Solomon's conclusion of the matter — first proposed in Ecclesiastes 1:14-17[183] — highlights his assumption throughout the entire passage: humanity's true condition is sorrow and there is nothing a person can pursue apart from Christ that can bring about happiness or provide hope. He re-affirms this important anthropology in Ecclesiastes 2:22-23:

---

[183] Ecclesiastes 1:14-17: "I have seen everything that is done under the sun, and behold, all is vanity and a striving after wind. *What is crooked cannot be made straight, and what is lacking cannot be counted.* I said in my heart, 'I have acquired great wisdom, surpassing all who were over Jerusalem before me, and my heart has had great experience of wisdom and knowledge.' And I applied my heart to know wisdom and to know madness and folly. I perceived that this also is but a striving after wind."

What has a man from all the toil and striving of heart with which he toils beneath the sun? *For all his days are full of sorrow, and his work is a vexation. Even in the night his heart does not rest. This also is vanity* [emphasis added].

Sorrow, guilt, hopelessness and vexation of spirit represent the normal condition of the spiritual heart after the Fall. When human efforts to escape these realities fail (and they will), a person apart from Christ has only to turn about and give up his/her heart to despair: "So I turned about and gave my heart up to despair over all the toil of my labors under the sun," (20). These mood changes are not abnormalities, but expected responses to the brokenness of this life and the failed attempts to overcome it.

As previously noted, the constant cycling from sorrow to attempting to escape sorrow and back again are not tendencies unique to Solomon. In Ecclesiastes 9:3 (and in 7:25), Solomon reveals that everyone is naturally in the same struggle and distress.

This is an evil in all that is done under the sun, that the same event happens to all. Also, the hearts of the children of man are full of evil, and madness is in their hearts while they live, and after that they go to the dead.

Death, evil, madness, folly and wisdom are all direct references to the original sin of Adam and Eve found in Genesis 3:4-15:

But the Serpent said to the woman, "You will not surely die [death]. For God knows that when you eat of it your eyes will be opened, *and you will be like God, knowing good and evil.*" So when the woman saw that the tree was good for food [folly], and that it was a delight to the eyes [madness], *and that the tree was to be desired to make one wise* [wisdom], she took of its fruit and ate, and she also gave some to her husband who was with her, and he ate. Then the eyes of both were opened, and they knew that they were naked [guilt and shame].

All human effort to escape sorrow in this life — no matter how it is labeled or categorized — apart from God's grace is prideful, destructive, and does not bring about happiness or remedy guilt as promised. Instead, trusting in false hopes, including oneself, incurs more sorrow and brings the soul closer to death; self-reliance is futile and destructive.

Religion (Legalism; Phariseeism)

False religions are another prominent example of both how humanity shares the need to assuage guilt to find hope and how common false hopes are. Religions are largely based upon fulfilling a law and not breaking it, pursuing peace with a deity, finding transcendence (to be bettered beyond one's current state) and happiness, earning redemption and justification, discovering deliverance, and establishing security and meaning beyond this life. In essence, all religions are directly or indirectly seeking to remedy the common fallen human condition that some call depression.

But Scripture is unique in presenting the gospel of Christ as a covenant relationship and not primarily as a religion. John 17:2-3 states,

> Since you have given him authority over all flesh, to give eternal life to all whom you have given him. And this is eternal life, that they know you, the only true God, and Jesus Christ whom you have sent.

Every covenant relationship (e.g., marriage) has rules, of course, but the law is not the basis or focus of relationship with the one true God. This reality is precisely why legalism/Phariseeism — a common false hope — encourages sorrow, guilt, and hopelessness rather than healing the crushed spirit. The law cannot deliver a person from his/her own depravity nor provide peace between God and man, since Christ alone fulfilled the law and no one else can accomplish such perfection: "For by works of the law no human being will be justified in his sight, since through the law comes knowledge of sin" (Romans 3:20). The law does not save; instead, it exposes our sinful nature, teaches us our need for Christ's grace, and works in our conscience to produce guilt.

Attempting to resolve guilt on one's own, no matter how morally great the effort, results in a worse spiritual condition. Romans 4:3-8 both explains this reality and offers hope:

> For what does the Scripture say? "Abraham believed God, and it was counted to him as righteousness." *Now to the one who works, his wages are not counted as a gift but as his due* [emphasis added]. And to the one who does not work but believes in him who justifies the ungodly, his faith is counted as righteousness, just as David also speaks of the blessing of the one to whom God counts righteousness apart from works: "Blessed are those whose lawless deeds are forgiven, and whose sins are covered. Blessed is the man against whom the Lord will not count his sin."

In this text, Paul quotes from Psalm 32:1, in which David declares that *joy* (a "blessed" state of mind) comes to humanity through relationship with Christ and not through religious effort or temporal gain. When guilt is remedied by God's grace and peace with God is obtained through God's mercy, it brings about a supernatural joy that extends beyond this life. However, this transformation is not to say that one's fallen condition of sorrow has been entirely removed or that physical death has been eliminated. What has occurred is the acceptance of genuine hope that these destructive aspects of human nature will be entirely remedied when the covenant relationship with Christ is fully realized (Revelation 21:4). This guarantee of deliverance is the only hope that is able to save people from their soul's many struggles and provide joy despite sorrow.

In Matthew 7:21-23, Christ specifically states to those attempting to deliver themselves through the law and good works that they are lawless and condemned:

> Not everyone who says to me, 'Lord, Lord,' will enter the kingdom of heaven, but the one who does the will of my Father who is in heaven. And then will I declare to them, "On that day many will say to me, 'Lord, Lord, did we not prophesy in your name, and cast out demons in your name, and do many mighty works in your name?' 'I never knew you; depart from me, you workers of lawlessness.'

It is clear as one studies Scripture that a covenant relationship with Jesus Christ based upon His grace rather than human efforts delivers people from their hopeless condition and struggle with guilt. Religion apart from God's grace and plan of salvation only offers a false hope that inevitably fails (Galatians 3). Trusting in religion/legalism is a form of mania that turns to human wisdom, hopes in failing human nature, and believes in false gods as an attempt to find deliverance. Whereas, trusting in Christ is turning to His completed work on the Cross to remedy each person's fallen and condemned nature and to fulfill the law. Anyone's attempt to rid himself/herself of sorrow in this life apart from Jesus is to enter into mania, to inevitably remain in hopelessness on the pathway to spiritual death, and to miss God's good purposes for sorrow.

Godly Response

Sorrow is a depressing reality in all of our lives, and if we accept this unfortunate feature of human nature and submit to God's plan to restore people to his likeness, then the sorrow that is destructive within this world can, by God's grace, supernaturally lead to righteousness. When a person submits to God's will over his/her self-advancement, sorrow is used by God for that individual's good. This reality in no way diminishes or removes the distressful nature of sorrow. Instead, accepting sorrow and the goodness of God as necessary realities allows humanity as God's created beings to understand sorrow's meaning and to trust in God's redemptive and salvific work.

Many prominent secularists also realize that sorrow/depression has purpose and is not something to be considered apart from human nature. Evolutionary scientist, head of placebo studies at Harvard University, and administrator at Beth Israel Deaconess Medical Center, Ted Kaptchuk, comments from a reductionist point of view: "If we don't get depressed, we might not change our situation. If we don't have anxiety, we might miss important signals in the environment."[184] Secular psychiatrist Peter Breggin also shares this perspective:

> Most people who seek help for depression have no idea that their feelings of depression actually have a purpose in their lives. But when the meaning and purpose of depression are understood, the individual can actually benefit from the experience.[185]

While both Kaptchuk and Breggin remark from a secular perspective and from years of clinical experience, they both have come to realize that sorrow, hopelessness, and guilt must be understood as important to one's life rather than as something to escape or minimize.

It is helpful to again reflect on Paul's words in 2 Corinthians 7:8-10 as a reminder of the two choices: "For godly grief ["lit. according to God's will or purpose"] produces a repentance that leads to salvation without regret, whereas worldly grief produces death." All people will sorrow according to the purpose of God or according to the world's intent. Sorrow either drives an individual to Christ the Deliverer, or it drives that person to pursue false gods/hopes that cannot save anyone and which always lead to destruction.

The only right or biblical reaction to sorrow is to depend more fully on God and to seek to know Him more intimately. Therefore, in order to react to sorrow according to God's good intentions — in a way that is healing, people must fully trust in the Lord and gain a right theology of sorrow.

---

[184] Ted Kaptchuk, *New England Journal of Medicine* online Interview 4:30-4:48 (July 2, 2015): available from https://www. nejm.org/action/showMedia Player?doi=10.1056%2FNEJMdo00 2316&aid=10.1056%2FNEJMp1504023 &area=.

[185] Breggin, *Anti-Depressant Fact Book*, 25.

God Allows Sorrow

One of the first truths that must be accepted if people are to respond to sorrow as God intends is that God purposely/sovereignly allows sorrow. If God made the sinless Christ to be sorrow for us, then we must also consider whether or not He purposes in His goodness to sometimes allow and other times to withhold sorrow from us. Understanding and accepting these truths will enable us to view sorrow as an important part of His plan to prosper us and to give us hope. Biblical change, then, is first and foremost a change in thinking/perspective.

Although numerous books on Job have been written, it is important to understand that God not only allowed Satan to test Job, but also God knew that it would bring about sorrow and despair in Job's life. After going through incredible loss and being stricken with physical illness, Job's friends came to him while he lamented the loss of his family, and they "saw that his suffering was very great" (Job 2:13). In Job 6:2-4, Job describes just how severe his sorrow/suffering was:

> Oh that my grief were actually weighed and laid in the balances together with my calamity! "For then it would be heavier than the sand of the seas; therefore my words have been rash. "For the arrows of the Almighty are within me, their poison my spirit drinks; the terrors of God are arrayed against me (*NASB*).

In his crying, Job recognizes that God has allowed this deep impairing spiritual pain into his life. After at least a month of deep sorrow (Job 7:3), Job also attests that he had lost hope — not in God but in his temporal life (Job 7:6-7):

> My days are swifter than a weaver's shuttle, and come to an end without hope. "Remember that my life is but breath; My eye will not again see good" (*NASB*).

Job's suffering was severe to the point that he also experienced insomnia and night terrors. These dreams were so bad that he preferred death over this life (Job 7:13-16):

If I say, "My bed will comfort me. My couch will ease my complaint," then You frighten me with dreams and terrify me by visions [revelations]; So that my soul would choose suffocation, death rather than my pains. "I waste away; I will not live forever. Leave me alone, for my days are but a breath."

To further his suffering, Job and his counselors (so-called friends) constantly questioned his innocence and debated his guilt throughout the book of Job. Considering that his deep impairing sorrow lasted well beyond two weeks, that he was hopeless in his condition, and that his thoughts about himself and life were undoubtedly negative, it is easy to see that Job fits into the secular construct of major depressive disorder. But it was God who had allowed Job to realize his true depressed state in this life. Job's experience was not a disease or an abnormality, and it was not brought on by sin or idolatry. Rather, his experience was God's goodness at work in Job's life.

Job's story does not end in tragedy, as Job was delivered, accepted, and blessed by God. While Satan meant evil, God had plans to prosper Job and to give him hope. God knew that Job would rightly respond in sorrow to his losses, and thus He allowed Job's suffering to occur.

In fact, the history of Job is also a picture of the gospel of Jesus Christ. Without God's merciful restraint of evil and His offer of grace through His Word, surely sorrow, despair, and suffering would be unimaginable in our lives. Without Christ and His gracious revelation, all people, too, like Job, are full of sorrow and are hopeless in this world. If it were not for God's mercy and intervention of withholding Satan's work, crushing sorrow would be more fully experienced by every person in this life. Literally, everyone without exception would enter hell.

Lamentations 3 offers further insight into how those with a crushed spirit think and feel before placing their hope in God. In Lamentations 3 the Bible describes this broken state as a place of darkness, of imprisonment, of mocking and taunting, of bitterness of soul and of utter humility (physically and spiritually), and a place where the spiritual heart is without peace or happiness:

> I have become the laughingstock of all peoples, the object of their taunts all day long. He has filled me with bitterness; he has sated me with wormwood. He has made my teeth grind on gravel, and made me cower in ashes; my soul is bereft of peace; I have forgotten what happiness is. (3:14-17)

In verse 18 the mourner realizes that his own efforts and abilities are useless, and so he gives up hope — feeling the crushing of his soul:

> So I say, "My endurance has perished; so has my hope from the LORD." Remember my affliction and my wanderings, the wormwood and the gall! My soul continually remembers it and is bowed down within me."

The lamenter had come to a place of realizing that he could not bear his own sorrow as he was not an agent of hope. But in verse 21-25, he turns his attention from his circumstances and his own abilities to God's faithful loving character, and this change of mind — the right way of thinking — brings him into a place of hope:

> *But this I call to mind, and therefore I have hope*: the steadfast love of the LORD never ceases; his mercies never come to an end; they are new every morning; great is your faithfulness. "The LORD is my portion," says my soul, "therefore I will hope in him." The LORD is good to those who wait for him, to the soul who seeks him [emphasis added].

Genuine saving hope and mentally accepting God's goodness are never separate issues, though clearly in the next verse (26-33) sorrow and affliction where not removed from the one suffering despite his hope in the LORD:

> It is good that one should wait quietly for the salvation of the Lord. It is good for a man that he bear the yoke in his youth. Let him sit alone in silence when it is laid on him; let him put his mouth in the

dust—there may yet be hope; let him give his cheek to the one who strikes, and let him be filled with insults. For the LORD will not cast off forever, but, *though he cause grief* [emphasis added], he will have compassion according to the abundance of his steadfast love; for he does not willingly afflict or grieve the children of men [literally, the LORD's heart is not pleased when causing the sons of men to grieve].

Though God takes no pleasure grieving us, it is necessary that people understand their true condition in order to abandon hope in self and turn to hope in Him alone. It is in God's goodness that He causes sorrow. Responding to sorrow by mentally turning to God's goodness and discovering genuine hope in Him is of upmost importance.

God Withholds Sorrow

Responding to sorrow in a way that is restorative rather than destructive also means that Christians recognize God's sovereignty in perfectly withholding some sorrow. In Philippians 2:27, for example, the apostle Paul shares how God spared Epaphroditus from death and purposed in His mercy to withhold sorrow from Paul: "Indeed he was ill, near to death. But God had mercy on him, and not only on him but on me also, lest I should have sorrow upon sorrow."

Scripture also describes people of God who experienced deep sorrows and pleaded with God to graciously and mercifully help them through the many valleys of life. Some of these people questioned why God had created them to begin with or as Job, why they were born (Job 3:1-26). David is a great example of one who called out to God and expressed how his own deep sorrow had negatively affected his body: "Be gracious to me, O LORD, for I am in distress; my eye is wasted from grief; my soul and my body also" (Psalm 31:9). Christ Himself cried out to God the Father and asked for his own sorrow and suffering to be removed (Luke 22:41-43). But Christ's request to the Father was denied, since it was in God's plan of deliverance to allow Christ to suffer (Acts 3:18).

The desire to be delivered from sorrow is not sinful or unique to only some individuals. These passages teach that not only do godly people (also the Son of God) struggle with deep impairing sorrow, but that God knows in His sovereignty and according to His lovingkindness just how much sorrow each person needs to experience. In fact, as observed in the life of Job and Paul, it is only by God's mercy that anyone can enjoy moments of laughter and joy in this fallen world and possess life itself.

While God will not permanently remove sorrow until He ushers in His kingdom in full, He sovereignly and mercifully withholds some sorrow while allowing other tragic experiences to occur. One can be assured, when life's circumstances force people to realize their true sorrowful state, it is the loving and faithful God who has allowed it for their good.

God Uses Sorrow

Having a right theology of sorrow enables people to accept the human condition as sorrowful and trust in God's goodness as the only hope. Though sorrow is a result of the Fall, God masterfully uses what Satan means for evil and redeems it for the good of His people. Reacting to sorrow in a biblical way is turning to know and trust more fully in God.

Sorrow is Foundational to Salvation

Rightly responding to sorrow determines that we turn to Christ as our deliverer. Sorrow, hopelessness, and guilt are not merely consequences of the Fall; they are also the very real bad news about human nature that must be accepted if the good news of Christ (the gospel) is to be received. God purposes sorrow and hopelessness to deliver degenerates from their fallen state and to point them to the only one who provides true joy, genuine hope, and an efficacious payment to remedy guilt. Psalm 34:18 expresses how God desires to use sorrow and a "crushed spirit" (hopelessness):

> "The Lord is near to the brokenhearted [*shabar*; lit. the smashed, injured, or shattered of heart] and saves the crushed [*dakka'*; lit. hopeless, humbled (Psalm 57:15), or destroyed (Psalm 90:3)] in spirit."[186]

Until people come to a place of deep sorrow (brokenness) over the reality of their human nature and humbly accept their hopeless/broken condition — abandoning all other hopes, they will not be ready to respond to sorrow in a beneficial way by placing their hope in Christ alone. Depression, then, is the necessary spiritual condition of receiving salvation in Christ.

In Lamentations 3:29, the humbling of the soul (a crushed spirit) is also shown to be the necessary prerequisite to genuine hope: "Let him put his mouth in the dust — there may yet be hope." For Christ to be one's hope, he/she must first become hopeless — abandoning self-focus and self-reliance. Matthew 5:4 affirms the same truth as it relates to sorrow: "Blessed are those who mourn, for they shall be comforted." In Greek, the verse does not convey that people who sorrow will be happy in this life and sorrow will vanish. Rather, it states that those who are deeply sorrowful about their true nature will be "called near" or "invited" and blessed when God's redemptive plan is complete.[187] The *Beatitudes* of Matthew 5 are not a list of ways to find human happiness in this life — a prosperity gospel, but a means that humans, by God's mercy, can please God and be blessed in His

---

[186] See also Psalm 147:3.

[187] "Called near" (παρακληθήσονται) is future passive indicative in Greek, which is a reference to both immediate redemption and peace with God as well as to the future time when the believer will be fully glorified by God. Finding favor in God's economy will be fully realized when there is perfect peace with God in a sinless state.

eternal economy. Being at peace with God in covenant relationship brings about joy and thankfulness of heart that is unmatched and supernatural to the broken spirit even though sorrows will still abound in this life.

There are several other Scriptural references (e.g., James 4:7-9; Luke 6:21-25) which highlight the relationship between sorrow and salvation, but two need closer examination. Proverbs 15:13 and Ecclesiastes 7:3-4 are two passages which seem contradictory, but really these verses are texts which affirm Paul's same counsel in 2 Corinthians 7:8-10: there are only two possible human responses to and results of sorrow.

Proverbs 15:13 addresses the negative and normal reaction to sorrow, as it teaches that apart from Christ, sorrow will inevitably expose one's hopeless condition: "A glad heart makes a cheerful face, but by sorrow of heart the *spirit is crushed* [made hopeless, humbled, depressed]." Biblical commentator Bruce Waltke remarks,

> Verse 13 assumes that the heart affects both a person's outward appearance and his inward spirit. A joyful one denotes an enthusiastically glad or merry psyche, and its antithesis entails psychic [soul] pain . . . . But heartache denotes the pained and troubled psyche that comes from living in folly, not wisdom. It is equated with a broken spirit . . . and its adjectival derivative means "beaten, broken"; as a result, he falls into depression . . . . The imprecise antithesis assumes that the spiritual state of a person's inner being is manifested in the vitality, or the lack of it, in a person's eyes, genuine smile, and the like.[188]

Another biblical commentator Tremper Longman offers further insight,

> This proverb provides another insightful psychological comment. The point of the first colon is that one's internal well-being is reflected in one's appearance. Our emotions affect our demeanor.

---

[188] Waltke, *Proverbs: Chapters 1-15*, 624-25.

The second colon seems to go deeper in that it is not an internal influence on the external, but an internal influence on the internal. In other words, standing behind pained or troubled heart is a broken spirit.[189]

The natural heart becomes hopeless as it realizes its true sorrowful condition in accordance with its destructive desires and inability to escape within its own resources or efforts. This truth is precisely what Solomon concluded in Ecclesiastes 1-2.

But in Ecclesiastes 7:2-4, Solomon presents the other side of the coin: if a person accepts the sorrowful reality of human nature as God explains it rather than making laughter and parties the purpose of life, then sorrow becomes beneficial and leads to a glad heart:

It is better to go to the house of mourning than to go to the house of feasting, for this is the end of all mankind, and the living will lay it to heart. Sorrow is better than laughter, *for by sadness of face the heart is made glad* [emphasis added]. The heart of the wise is in the house of mourning [lit. at the place of death; a funeral], but the heart of fools is in the house of mirth [a party].

These three verses are packed with perspectives and values about sorrow that are vital to having a glad face. If people accept the genuine bad news about their broken, vexed, and condemned reality, they are in a place to receive the gospel (the good news) that transforms sad hearts and broken spirits into glad ones. Depending on how we accept sorrow (reliance upon self or dependence upon God) determines whether or not it crushes our spirits or gladdens our hearts.[190] Accepting this wise perspective is foundational to finding a remedy for hopelessness, sorrow, and guilt.

[189] Longman III, *Proverbs*, 317.

[190] The heart and face are not disconnected in Hebrew (e.g., Proverbs 15:13, "A glad heart makes a cheerful face, but by sorrow of heart the spirit is crushed").

It is difficult to accept the truth that in God's value system sorrow is better than merriment, since such a perspective opposes everyone's fallen way of viewing life. The wise — the one who has supernaturally by faith accepted God's perspective and way of viewing life — realizes and takes to heart that sorrow and death are his/her realities rather than his/her abnormalities. A desire to find purpose and meaning for sorrow will only start with having a right perspective of our own true human nature.

People become sorrowful because they are thinking honestly about their true condition and inevitable end even if they are unaware as to why they are sad. When people feel depressed without seemingly reasonable explanation, they are simply coming into a more honest view of this life and their own soul's condition. The realities that all will die and are hopelessly condemned for eternity apart from Christ are crushing, but these are realities that need to be taken to heart, genuinely accepted, and kept at the forefront of the mind.

The Apostle Paul shares his testimony of the value of sorrow, distress, and despair in his own life (2 Corinthians 1:8-10), and he offers an example of one who responded to sorrow according to God's goodness and sovereignty:

> For we were so utterly burdened beyond our strength that we despaired of life itself. Indeed, we felt that we had received the sentence of death. But that was to make us rely not on ourselves but on God who raises the dead.

Paul realized that he could not depend upon himself for deliverance and that the severity of his seemingly hopeless vexation was positive. Accepting these truths allowed him to depend upon Christ more fully and realize hope in God alone.

King David expressed this same perspective in Psalm 88:9: "My eye grows dim through sorrow. Every day I call upon you, O

LORD; I spread out my hands to you." When sorrow is inevitably realized, those who have Christ as LORD and their only hope react to deep impairing sorrow and distress by calling out to God as a child does to his/her mother.

For the Christian, sorrow is never separated from the realities of his/her fallen condition and the need to be restored to Christ-likeness and fellowship with God the Father. As with conversion, another aspect of salvation that has suffering and sorrow as its enablers is the theological concept of sanctification or, as Scripture calls it, discipline — the process of becoming a disciple. Hebrews 12:11 expresses that sorrow is necessary to become fruitful in Christ:

> All discipline for the moment seems not to be joyful, but sorrowful; yet to those who have been trained by it, afterwards it yields the peaceful fruit of righteousness.

God promises that the sorrows He allows in this life lead to positive changes and to righteousness in eternity for those who receive His good news. Christians both respond to sorrow and establish their hope based on the promises of God.

Likewise, these sure promises, given from the all-sufficient and entirely good Savior, enable Christians to be restored to God's original intent prior to Adam's fall and to gain victory over the power and destructive consequences of sinful desires (2 Peter 1:3-4ff.):

> His divine power has granted to us all things that pertain to life and godliness, through the knowledge of him who called us to his own glory and excellence, by which he has granted to us his precious and very great promises, so that through them you may become partakers of the divine nature, having escaped from the corruption that is in the world because of sinful desire.

Believers and non-believers alike must face sorrow, but how people respond to sorrow depends upon their relationship to God, their treasures and hopes, and their view of human nature—their identity. There is nothing new under the sun by which a person can remedy the many spiritual pains of the soul that has not already been tried and found to be futile. Only faith in Jesus can provide joy despite great sorrow, convert despair to hope, and permanently change bondage to freedom. Sorrow is the right and honest response to understanding the very bad news about human nature, which leads to accepting the very good news: the gospel of Jesus Christ.

CHAPTER 5

DISCERNING FALSE PERSPECTIVES

"Since Satan can't destroy the gospel, he has to often neutralize its usefulness by addition, subtraction, or substitution."[191] -J.C. Ryle

The Biological Perspective

In addition to individual degenerationism, another important tenet of humanism and the medical model of mental illness is the philosophy of materialism or as it is also called: scientism or reductionism. Materialism asserts that only that which can be approached using the scientific method (physical matter that can be observed and measured) is real, and all that is real can eventually be explained and approached through scientific enlightenment/the pursuit of human knowledge. Materialism, individual degenerationism, and biodeterminism are all philosophies founded upon humanism and require that psychiatric constructs, like depression, be created (see Table C). Any theory or approach to humanity's spiritual/metaphysical brokenness that is based upon one or more of these tenets of humanism is either a perversion of or an attempt to replace the gospel of Jesus Christ.

---

[191] J.C. Ryle quoted by Burk Parsons, "What Is the Gospel?" *Tabletalk Magazine* (January 2015): https://tabletalk magazine.com/article/2015/01/what-is-gospel/.

TABLE C

The Fundamentals of Secular Faith

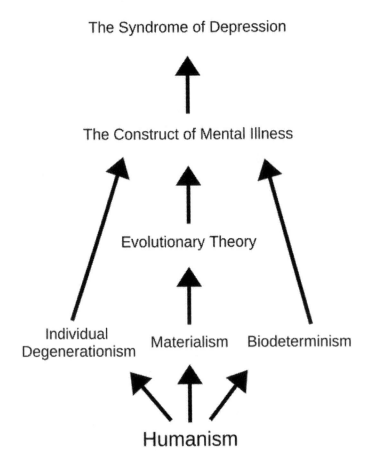

The Syndrome of Depression

The Construct of Mental Illness

Evolutionary Theory

Individual Degenerationism   Materialism   Biodeterminism

Humanism

Individual Degenerationism – views persistent mental impairment and distress (wickedness and weakness) as human abnormality rather than as normalcy.
Materialism – views humanity as only physical in nature.
Biodeterminism – views people as biologically predetermined, and denies personal responsibility for moral mindsets and behaviors.

When considering the syndrome of depression and all constructs of mental illness, materialists theorize that the metaphysical mind is only a product of the brain. Therefore, in secular thinking, the brain is responsible for all mindsets, emotions, and behavior. Professor of pediatric neurological surgery Michael Egnor admits,

> How does the mind relate to the brain? This question is central to my professional life. I thought I had it answered. Yet a century of research and 30 years of my own neurosurgical practice have challenged everything I thought I knew. The view [materialism] assumed by those who taught me is that the mind is wholly a product of the brain, which is itself understood as something like a machine.[192]

Dr. Egnor further reveals:

> Francis Crick, a neuroscientist and the Nobel laureate who was the co-discoverer of the structure of DNA, wrote that "a person's mental activities are entirely due to the behavior of nerve cells, glial cells, and the atoms, ions, and molecules that make them up and influence them." But as Francis Bacon's approach to understanding the world gained ascendency during the scientific enlightenment, it became fashionable to limit inquiry about the world to physical substances: to study the machine and ignore the ghost. Matter was tractable, and we studied it to obsession. The ghost was ignored, and then denied. This was what the logic of materialism demanded.[193]

In order to be a materialist, one must ignore or deny the human soul — the metaphysical reality of human nature — and its executive function.

---

[192] Michael Egnor, "More Than Material Minds," *Christianity Today Online* (September 14, 2018): https://www. christianitytoday.com/ct/2018/september-web-only/more-than-material-minds-neuroscience-souls.html.

[193] Ibid.

When physicians attempt to heal the body from valid diseases, they approach the person through the medical model, but when it comes to the soul/psyche/mind, the medical model excludes consideration of its spiritual nature and attempts to reduce every metaphysical feature to biological causes and explanations. Thus, psychiatrists and other humanists dogmatically view the syndrome of depression as a biological disease within materialism/scientism, though its true substance is metaphysical.

Materialism reduces all of human nature and especially the soul/mind into material causes or explanations. Psychiatrist Ronald Pies exemplifies this position:

> I don't like the term "mental disorder," because it makes it seem as if there's a huge distinction between the mind and the body — and most psychiatrists don't see it that way. I wrote about this recently, and used the term "brain-mind" to describe the unity of mind and body. So, for lack of a better term, I'll just refer to "psychiatric illnesses."[194]

Allen Frances shares the same perspective,

> The new biology of brain would explain behaviors previously considered to be within the abstract providences of the philosophers and the theologians. It might be impossible to plumb the depths of the human soul, but it should be possible to figure out the structural specification and electrical connections of the human brain.[195]

Within humanistic science and medicine today, there is no room to consider the metaphysical realities (such as the soul and emotions) of people as anything but products of the physical nature. Candace Pert, former chief of brain biochemistry at the

---

[194] Ronald W. Pies, et. al, "Doctor, Is My Mood Disorder Due to a Chemical Imbalance?" *Psychiatric Times Online* (August 12, 2011): http://www.psychiatri ctimes.com/blogs/doctor-my-mood-disorder-due-chemical-imbalance.

[195] Frances, *Saving Normal*, 125.

National Institutes of Health, explains where in history the soul and the body became separate studies:

> It was then that René Descartes, the philosopher and founding father of modern medicine, was forced to make a turf deal with the Pope in order to get the human bodies he needed for dissection. Descartes agreed he wouldn't have anything to do with the soul, the mind, or the emotions – those aspects of human experience under the virtually exclusive jurisdiction of the church at the time – if he could claim the physical realm as his own. Alas, this bargain set the tone and direction for the Western science over the next two centuries, dividing human experience into two distinct and separate spheres that could never overlap, creating the unbalanced situation that is mainstream science as we know it today. But much of that is now changing. A growing number of scientists recognize that we are in the midst of a scientific revolution, a major paradigm shift with tremendous implications for how we deal with health and disease.[196]

Understandably, materialists who wished to take control of society from Roman Catholicism and eliminate or minimize religion, philosophy, and morality eventually created social constructs to fit metaphysical truths into a scientific and medical framework.

Since Descartes' time, the conflict has been between materialism and dualism rather than between science and religion. Psychiatric belief and the Christian faith are in opposition to each other because they hold to opposing beliefs about human nature – namely over the understanding of the soul/psyche. Former president of the Royal College of Psychiatrists Andrew Sims acknowledges,

> The unhealthy situation in which psychiatry denies the significance, and even existence, of soul or spirit has led religious people to have

[196] Candace Pert, *Molecules of Emotion: The Science behind Mind-Body Medicine* (New York: Scribner, 1997), 18.

a profound distrust of psychiatry and been disastrous for all those involved.[197]

Christianity does not oppose valid scientific discovery; rather, it upholds both supernatural and natural truths. The Bible does not discard or ignore bodily changes when the spirit is crushed, it simply interprets and explains them according to a different presuppositional faith than humanism does.

In accordance with the guiding principle of reductionism, persistent mental struggles and distresses — what materialists call "mental illnesses" — are reduced to "brain dysfunction," "genetic variances," and or "chemical imbalances."[198] These popular theories are also common catch-phrases that expose the doctrine of materialism and promote belief in the biomedical or neo-Kraepelinian model ("mental illness"). As Dr. Frances notes, belief in reductionism is largely responsible for creating the current MDD epidemic:

> The "epidemic" of Major Depressive Disorder initiated by the loose *DSM* definitions was then driven by a combination of biological reductionism among physicians and fancy drug company marketing. Doctors brought the story line that all depression results from a chemical imbalance in the brain and therefore requires a chemical fix — the prescription of an antidepressant medication.[199]

The more people believe in materialism and individual degenerationism, the more they also see themselves through this philosophical lens.

---

[197] Andrew Sims, *Is Faith Delusion? Why Religion is Good for Your Health* (London: Continuum, 2009), 2.

[198] For further study on the disproven theory of chemical imbalances, see Berger, *Reality of the Physical Nature*, 46-51; Berger, *Influence of Nurture*, 140-43; Berger, *Necessity for Dependence*, 24-33.

[199] Frances, *Saving Normal*, 155.

Many humanists, though, understand that there exist serious problems with accepting materialism to approach and understand all of human nature. Clinical and forensic psychologist Stephen Diamond is one such individual who maintains that

> the medical model is a particular way of viewing human suffering, decay, dysfunction and, ultimately, death. *It is a paradigm, a lens through which physicians and others perceive certain abnormal or aberrant phenomena* like leukemia, diabetes, and now, depression and many other mental disorders [emphasis added]. But despite the immense contribution of the medical model in diagnosing and treating [valid] disease, its literal application to archetypal human experiences such as depression, psychosis, and anxiety is problematical.[200]

Highly respected psychiatrist and historian Edward Shorter also comments,

> Biological thinking gave psychiatry at the end of the twentieth century the capacity to be as science-driven as the rest of medicine. But this promise has remained unfulfilled, *a result to psychiatry's enmeshment in popular values, in corporate culture, and in a boggy swamp of diagnostic scientism* [emphasis added].[201]

Likewise, psychiatrist Peter Breggin directs attention toward how accepting the biological perspective and denying the spiritual nature to approach depression requires that people be viewed the same as machines:

> The biomythology of depression denies the obvious causes of depression in the lives of most people who become depressed. Biopsychiatrists dare not look their patients in the eye for fear of seeing the psychological truth; they cannot look into their patient's

---

[200] Stephen A. Diamond, "Is Depression a Disease?" *Psychology Today Online* (September 1, 2008): https://www. psychologytoday.com/us/blog/evil-deeds/200809/is-depression-disease.

[201] Edward Shorter, *A History of Psychiatry: From the Era of the Asylum to the Age of the Prozac* (New York: John Wiley & Sons, 1997), 288.

hearts for fear of empathizing with them. Ultimately, they must deny their own feelings in order to deny the feelings of others. To treat a depressed person as a biochemically defective mechanism, and to blunt or damage the brain of the suffering individual, many biopsychiatrists approach the patient with an especially dehumanizing view.[202]

One can clearly see by Breggin's statement how the philosophies of materialism and individual degenerationism ("a depressed person as a *biochemically defective mechanism*") undergird biopsychiatry and the widely accepted medical model of mental illness. Believing that depression is a physical disease is primarily a belief in both individual degenerationism and materialism.

As earlier emphasized, depression is a suggested syndrome that groups together both metaphysical and physical symptoms. But the primary struggles that form the construct of depression are hopelessness, deep impairing sorrow, and guilt. The body is certainly affected and can be negatively altered by the soul's vexation, but this fact does not prove materialism or determine materialism to be necessary to approach and remedy impairment or distress. With both the individual's and society's condition consistently worsening since the early 1960s under this current medical model, it is clear that reductionism has failed.

Yet, most biopsychiatrists insist that the spiritual nature not be accepted or at least be minimized. If interpretations, explanations, and attempted remedies are restricted to biological presuppositions, then humanists must seek to explain and approach the metaphysical nature of hopelessness, sorrow, and guilt by only using biological terms, theories, and practices. Metaphysical processes which are understood to be mental/ spiritual must be attributed to the physical manifestation —

---

[202] Breggin, *Toxic Psychiatry*, 183.

typically in the nervous system, genomes, and neurotransmitters. If we are merely biological organisms, and it is assumed that we are normally able to resolve our own mental turmoil internally — that we are strong and not fallen, then any persistent distress or impairment which produces somatic effects must be viewed as a biological malady and physical substances and positive experiences be accepted as medicinal.

It is important to also realize that materialism dogmatically rejects the existence of spiritual realities except those allegedly created by material sources. Religious faith, for instance, is speculated by many secular neurologists to be an unwilled product of the brain.[203] True materialists do not consider the spiritual nature of mankind as a reality let alone its impaired and condemned state apart from God. They not only deny the gospel, but materialists also see no need for its consideration. Instead, scientism asserts scientific enlightenment as the new gospel. Harvard geneticist and self-proclaimed atheist Richard Lewontin both admits his commitment to materialism despite its failure and divulges why secularists must dogmatically cling to scientism in attempt to explain and remedy all aspects of human nature and life itself:

> Our willingness to accept scientific claims that are against common sense is the key to an understanding of the real struggle between science and the supernatural. We take the side of science in spite of the patent absurdity of some of its constructs, in spite of its failure to fulfill many of its extravagant promises of health and life, in spite of the tolerance of the scientific community of unsubstantiated just so

---

[203] V.S. Ramachandran and Sandra Blakeslee, *Phantoms in the Brain: Probing the Mysteries of the Human Mind* (New York: William Morrow and Company, 1998), 183.

stories, because we have a prior commitment, a commitment to materialism.[204]

The "prior commitment" of materialism which Lewontin sets forth is the same "metaphysical presupposition" or philosophy that Wilhelm Wundt insisted must undergird all psychological investigation. In other words, to accept materialism as best explaining human nature, including mental struggles, requires faith itself. Acclaimed neurologist V.S. Ramachandran agrees with Lewontin and affirms that upholding philosophies of human nature is high priority and a common practice within secular allegedly scientific research:

> Sometimes the new observation simply doesn't fit. It is an "anomaly," inconsistent with the existing structure. The scientist can then do one of three things. First, he can ignore the anomaly, sweeping it under the carpet — a *form of psychological "denial" that is surprisingly common even among eminent researchers* [emphasis added]. Second, scientists can make minor adjustments to the paradigm, trying to fit the anomaly into their worldview, and this would still be a form of normal science. Or they can generate ad hoc auxiliary hypotheses that sprout like so many branches from a single tree. But soon these branches become so thick and numerous that they threaten to topple the tree itself. Finally, they can tear down the edifice and create a completely new one that bears very little resemblance to the original. This is what Kuhn called a "paradigm shift" or scientific revolution.[205]

Too often, as Ramachandran and Lewontin both acknowledge, secular researchers choose to uphold their worldview or paradigm despite the many empirical discoveries that undermine their faith.

---

[204] Richard C. Lewontin, "Billions and Billions of Demons," review of *The Demon-Haunted World: Science as a Candle in the Dark*, by Carl Sagan, *New York Review of Books*, January 7, 1997, 31.

[205] Ramachandran and Blakeslee, *Phantoms in the Brain*, 222.

Rather than faith in God, materialists place their faith in the fallible creature (Romans 1:18-32). Biblical apologist John Haught remarks,

> If faith in God requires independent scientific confirmation, what about the colossal faith our new atheists place in science itself? Exactly what are the independent scientific experiments, we might ask, that could provide "evidence" for the hypothesis that all true knowledge must be based on the paradigm of scientific inquiry? If faith requires independent confirmation, what is the independent (nonfaith) method of demonstrating that their own faith in the all-encompassing cognitional scope of science is reasonable? If science itself is the only way to provide such independent assessment, then the quest for proper validation only moves the justification process in the direction of an infinite regress.[206]

While it appears that materialism is science driven, it is, in truth, a belief system of circular reasoning; it is an attempt to dismiss necessary faith in God and place faith in man's wisdom to explain and remedy human nature. Dr. Lewontin expounds further on why humanists must fully commit to materialism:

> It is not that the methods of and institutions of science somehow compel us to accept a material explanation of the phenomenal world, but on the contrary, that we are forced by our a *priori adherence* [presuppositional faith] to material causes to create an apparatus of investigation and a set of concepts that produce material explanations, no matter how counterintuitive, no matter how mystifying to the uninitiated. *Moreover, that materialism is absolute, for we cannot allow a Divine Foot in the door* [emphasis added].[207]

For secularists to deny materialism is to open the possibility that God exists, that He created us precisely as He claims in His Word (with dual natures), that He is precisely who He says He is, that He will do exactly what He declares, and that He alone

---

[206] John F. Haught, *God and the New Atheism: A Critical Response to Dawkins, Harris, and Kitchens* (Louisville, KY: Westminister John Knox Press, 2008), 45.

[207] Lewontin, "Billions and Billions of Demons."

can deliver our souls and restore us to spiritual health. To accept dualism over materialism is essentially to dismiss humanity as savior (humanism) and to confess the need to find a savior outside of one's own self. Stated differently, to deny materialism is to open the possibility of accepting the moral nature of humanity, the very bad news of who one truly is (both in weakness and wickedness), and to face the good news of Jesus Christ. Materialism, then, is a delusion — a philosophy which denies reality in order to sustain false belief.

The philosophies of humanism, materialism, and individual degenerationism are in direct opposition to the gospel and the knowledge of God. Yet, these philosophies are the foundational faith on which secularists base their widely accepted theory that depression constitutes a physical disease or is a product of physical disease.

Ironically, the biological paradigm lacks empirical evidence to prove that the body, apart from the spiritual heart, produces hopelessness, sorrow, and guilt when it allegedly malfunctions. These common features of human nature are all metaphysical realities that fall outside of valid scientific exploration, and therefore, they must be primarily approached by faith. It is not simply that the secular construct of depression has failed; the underlying faith that supports the Kraepelinian system has failed.

Despite their dogmatic loyalty to materialism, many prominent secularists, such as former president of the APA and head of psychiatry at Columbia University Jeffrey Lieberman, acknowledge that within the medical field, the mind and the brain, though regularly theorized to be the same substance, are approached differently because of their distinct natures:

> The discovery that some mental disorders had a recognizable biological basis — while others did not — led to the establishment of two distinct disciplines. Physicians who specialized exclusively in

disorders with an observable neural stamp become known as neurologists. *Those who dealt with the invisible disorders of the mind became known as psychiatrists* [emphasis added].[208]

Lieberman begins by indirectly asserting his belief that the mind and brain are one, but he ends the statement admitting that psychiatry exists as an attempt to heal the soul of its metaphysical problems. He explains this reality further:

> Psychiatry originated as a medical specialty that took as its province a set of maladies that, *by their very definition, had no identifiable physical cause* [emphasis added]. Appropriately, the term "psychiatry" — coined by the German physician Johann Christian Reil in 1808 — literally means "medical treatment of the soul." Like the Bering Strait, the schism between the neurological brain and the psychiatric soul separated two continents of medical practice.[209]

One might say, then, that psychiatrists are reductionistic and humanistic preachers who dogmatically cling to their faith, passionately evangelize, and make dependent disciples. But this type of soul care can never genuinely heal the soul.

Other prominent psychiatrists who dogmatically cling to materialism, as Lieberman does, admit that "the arrow of causality may travel the other way." Ronald Pies, for example, concedes that the soul's spiritual struggles can just as easily be producing the observable negative physical effects:

> An "association" is not a "cause." In fact, the initial formulation of Schildkraut and Kety allowed for the possibility that the arrow of causality might travel the other way; that is, that *depression itself might lead to changes in biogenic amines*, and not the other way around.[210]

[208] Lieberman, *Shrinks*, 26.

[209] Ibid., 26-27.

[210] Pies, "Doctor, Is My Mood Disorder Due to a Chemical Imbalance?"

"Biogenic amines" is a term that describes how the various bodily systems function together and change. In the medical model (and specifically in the construct of depression), these systems most often include the central nervous system (neurotransmitters such as serotonin), the digestive system ("gut health"), and more recently the cardiovascular system ("heart health"). Materialists regularly propose that chemical imbalances[211] and gut health, as examples, are causative for depression based upon the fact that these negative somatic features are common in people diagnosed. But as Pies rightly notes, these correlations do not equal causation and are just as easily explained as symptoms of one's thinking.

Researchers Joseph Schildkraut and Seymour Kety — whom Pies references — realized decades ago that the existence of abnormalities as observed in neuroimages does not imply a physical cause.[212] Yet, materialists insist that it does. Dr. Breggin comments,

> The fact that biochemical changes take place in the brain in association with intense moods proves nothing about which comes first. Yet the biopsychiatrists, without discussing it, usually assume that the brain is the egg from which the chicken — mental disorder — is born.[213]

Breggin later points out that

> there are no known biological causes of depression in the lives of patients who routinely see psychiatrists. There is no known genetic link in depression. There is no sound drug treatment for depression.

[211] For further study on the disproven theory of chemical imbalances, see Berger, *Reality of the Physical Nature*, 46-51; Berger, *Influence of Nurture*, 140-43; Berger, *Necessity for Dependence*, 24-33.

[212] Joseph J. Schildkraut and Seymour S. Kety, "Biogenic Amines and Emotion," *Science* 156 (1967): 21-37.

[213] Breggin, *Toxic Psychiatry*, 112-113.

The same is true for mania: no biology, no genetics, and little or no rational basis for endangering the brain with drugs.[214]

But many leading psychiatric researchers and neuroscientists are beginning to admit that the medical model of mental illness is scientism rather than science. For example, Drs. Jeffrey Lacasse and Jonathan Leo explain how research in both neuroscience and serotonin do not support the chemical imbalance theory:

> Contemporary neuroscience research has failed to confirm any serotonergic lesion in any mental disorder, and has in fact provided significant counterevidence to the explanation of a simple neurotransmitter deficiency. Modern neuroscience has instead shown that the brain is vastly complex and poorly understood. While neuroscience is a rapidly advancing field, to propose that researchers can objectively identify a "chemical imbalance" at the molecular level is not compatible with the extant science. In fact, there is no scientifically established ideal "chemical balance" of serotonin, let alone an identifiable pathological imbalance. To equate the impressive recent achievements of neuroscience with support for the serotonin hypothesis is a mistake.[215]

Psychiatrist, biomedical researcher, and director of translational medicine-neuroscience at Novartis Institutes Nassir Ghaemi describes well the scientism that sustains the biomedical model of mental illness:

> *By diagnosing patients within the DSM strictures only, we practice non-scientifically;* we use hundreds of made-up labels for professional purposes, without really getting at the reality of what is wrong with the patient. Sometimes those patients have diseases; we don't know what they are. Sometimes they don't have diseases; we don't know when that is. *And, because the whole process is "pragmatic" and made-up, we make no gradual progress in identifying when diseases are present,*

---

[214] Ibid., 183.

[215] Jeffrey Lacasse and Jonathan Leo, "Serotonin and Depression: A Disconnect between the Advertisements and the Scientific Literature," *PLoS Medicine* 2.12 (2005): e392. *PMC.*

and when they are not, and what the causes of those diseases (or non-disease conditions) might be [emphasis added].[216]

Former head of psychiatry at Duke University, Allen Frances, also comments,

> [It was] an unrealistic goal of transforming psychiatric diagnosis by somehow basing it on the exciting findings of neuroscience. This would be wonderful were it possible, but the effort failed for the obvious reason that it is still a bridge too far.[217]

The reason the entire system is pragmatic, an unrealistic goal, and a failed effort is that the core of depression (and other psychiatric constructs) is metaphysical, and neuroscience can only study that which is physically observed and material. Sorrow, hope, and guilt cannot be assessed through the scientific process or through neuroimaging, so biological changes can be viewed as either causes or effects depending upon which presuppositional faith is applied. But since sorrow, hope, and guilt are metaphysical, the burden of proof rests on materialists to supply empirical evidence that these mindsets are caused by physical mechanisms — an impossibility for sure. Dr. Breggin remarks,

> Despite all of this biopsychiatric propaganda . . . depression is a readily understandable expression of human despair that is frequently responsive to psychosocial help . . . . Many psychotherapists wouldn't dream of prescribing a drug for anything so obviously psychological and spiritual in origin.[218]

Simply stated, the secular claims that the metaphysical syndrome of depression is an abnormality that is physically

---

[216] Nassir Ghaemi, "One Step Back, Two Steps Forward: The Solution to *DSM* and drugs?" *Medscape Psychiatry Online* (January 15, 2013): http://boards.medscape.com/forums/?128@@.2a37df02! comment=1&cat=All.

[217] Frances, *Saving Normal*, 171.

[218] Breggin, *Toxic Psychiatry*, 122; 171.

caused, that neuroimaging proves it to be true, and that psychoactive drugs are medicines are all speculative and pragmatic beliefs based upon faith in materialism rather than founded in valid science.

In fact, it is widely recognized within the fields of psychoneuroimmunology, epigenetics, and the placebo/nocebo studies that the mind alters the body in positive and negative ways.[219] Psychiatrist Cynthia Geppert, who resides as director of ethics education at the University of New Mexico School of Medicine and serves on the U.S. National Center for Ethics in Health care offers one illustration of how materialists understand that mental processes change the body. Still, Geppert must attempt to frame biological changes as causative rather than as consequences of the soul's condition:

> Emerging evidence from brain imaging, animal studies, and psychometric testing converges on the dramatic and previously neglected points of how depression corrupts genetic processes, depletes neurotransmitters, alters neural functioning, distorts neuroarchitecture, and ultimately destroys neurons.

While Geppert asserts that brain imaging shows how hopelessness, sorrow, and guilt cause genetic variances and destroy the nervous system, she must remain loyal to her materialistic vantage point and insist these somatic changes are causative. She continues:

> This destruction is found in the crucial areas of the brain that govern emotion, cognition, endocrine homeostasis, and vitality and thus provides a link to the syndromic manifestations of poor

---

[219] For further study on how the spiritual nature directly controls and alters the physical nature, see Berger, *Mental Illness: The Reality of the Physical Nature*, 110-25.

concentration, depressed mood, insomnia, anhedonia, and even the psychic markers of guilt and pessimism.[220]

Following her logic, the syndrome of depression causes somatic changes ("depression corrupts genetic processes"), and these somatic changes cause a depressed mood ("syndromic manifestations of depressed mood"). With this attempt to acknowledge somatic changes while restricting her understanding to materialism, Geppert asserts a logical fallacy where alleged causes are really symptoms which create alleged causes. But logically, causes cannot create causes.

Sadly, many Christians place their faith in the medical model of mental illness and accept materialism and individual degenerationism without realizing their unbiblical faith and the theory's secular origin. One of the more common arguments that these Christians set forth in debating the nature of depression and the use of dangerous drugs for treatment is comparing depression to heart disease or another physical illness. Their narrative follows something like this:

> If you were diagnosed with heart disease, you would certainly not stay away from a doctor or not take your medicine. Just like the heart goes bad, the brain can go bad too. Depression is just like heart disease, and so the brain should be treated by a doctor who prescribes medications.

Ironically, these same Christians also regularly argue that a psychosomatic or dualistic approach to human nature must be accepted. Yet, they do not realize that their insistence that others view hopelessness, sorrow, and guilt together as a biologically caused disease comparable to heart disease is a materialistic/humanistic perspective that denies the psychosomatic reality of human nature and the metaphysical core of depression itself.

[220] Cynthia M. A. Geppert, "Damage Control," *Psychiatric Times Online* 23, no. 6 (May 1, 2006): http://www.psychiatric times.com/articles/damage-control.

Moreover, the Bible speaks with clarity on these matters and determines them to be central to the gospel rather than medical issues. These secular philosophies that support the many constructs of mental illness are not merely attempts to sustain evolutionary theory, they are also direct assaults on the knowledge of God, the true nature of mankind, and the gospel of Jesus Christ.

No one on any side of the debate over the true nature of depression denies that somatic changes occur, but what is a matter of contention is whether or not these physical changes cause mental distress or are the effects. Where one bases his/her faith — either in materialism or dualism — ultimately determines that person's position and pursuit of a remedy.

The Biblical Perspective

Because wisdom — either provided by God or asserted by humanity — creates and supports all understanding and approaches to human nature, the underlying philosophies of the construct of depression must be considered as important in determining how people view themselves and the remedies they pursue. By turning attention to the Scriptures to better discern God's wisdom and gain clarity in the truths He offers one can gain wisdom about human nature which the Bible explained thousands of years ago and modern neuroscience is now confirming. Gaining a deeper biblical perspective allows Christians to better discern what philosophies and theories are false.

Scripture describes humanity as having both soul (metaphysical) and body (physical) — the dualistic perspective (e.g., Genesis 2:7; Ecclesiastes 12:7; Matthew 10:28 etc.),[221] and it also indicates that

[221] For further study on our dual nature, see Berger, *Mental Illness: The Reality of the Spiritual Nature* and Berger, *Mental Illness: The Reality of the Physical Nature.*

the mind can control the body. Christian neurosurgeon Michael Egnor has come to believe over his decades of practice and research that valid neuroscience reveals three important things about the mind/soul:

> Remarkably, neuroscience tells us three things about the mind: [1] the mind is metaphysically simple, [2] the intellect and will are immaterial, and [3] free will is real [not in relation to pleasing God]. Materialism has limited the kinds of questions that we're allowed to ask, but neuroscience, pursued without a materialist bias, points towards the reality that we are *chimeras* [a single entity with a dual nature]: material beings with immaterial souls.[222]

That is, there is a very real part of human nature that is spiritual and functions on desire/value, produces thought, and is not at all morally controlled by the brain or other aspects of the physical nature.

Scripture says that hopelessness, sorrow and guilt, the core symptoms of depression, alter the physical body in a negative way. Proverbs 18:14 makes a clear distinction between physical sickness and the crushing/depressing of the spirit: "A man's spirit will endure sickness, but a crushed spirit who can bear?" Biblical commentator Tremper Longman comments on this verse that

> this proverb again makes an observation about the relationship between one's psychological state of mind and the health of the body. . . . The idea that a positive attitude can have a positive effect on a person's health is widely recognized even today, as well as the reverse idea that depression or anxiety can worsen a physical condition.[223]

Similarly, Proverbs 17:22 expresses how hopelessness (a crushed spirit) produces negative somatic changes: "A joyful heart is good medicine, but a crushed spirit dries up the bones."

[222] Egnor, "More Than Material Minds," *Christianity Today Online.*

[223] Longman, *Proverbs,* 349.

Denying that the mind has executive control over the body does not dismiss this reality. The body's production of tears and the restricted blood flow to the brain caused by sorrow of heart both provide indisputable empirical evidence of how the soul creates negative somatic changes.

As previously noted, biblical characters like King David and Job attest to their own bodily effects of sorrow and vexation. For example, Asaph states in Psalm 77:1-5 that

> my soul refuses to be comforted. When I remember God, I moan; when I meditate, my spirit faints. Selah You hold my eyelids open; I am so troubled that I cannot speak.

Asaph sees his soul as the metaphysical substance in trouble, and this struggle produces specific features that the APA has listed as depressive symptoms in the *DSM-5*. As Proverbs 15:13 relates: "A glad heart makes a cheerful face, but by sorrow of heart the spirit is crushed." The spiritual heart in joy or in sorrow alters the physical and spiritual natures. As one biblical commentator, Bruce Waltke, explains,

> Grief and joy are matters of death and life. Whereas v. 20 connected heart and tongue, this one connects heart and spirit. On its own the proverb admonishes the disciple to live in such a way that he experiences joy that revives and not depression that kills. . . . Even the most firm and powerful perish when they become depressed. As 15:15 (Cf 18:14) makes clear, the difference between exhilaration and depression depends more on a person's spiritual resources than on his circumstances (cf. Acts 16:25).[224]

As the result of the bad news of our hopeless, sorrowful, and guilty state (framed as depression) negatively affects our bodies, most certainly the result of the good news (the gospel) offers healing. Proverbs 15:30 states this truth precisely: "The light of the eyes rejoices the heart, and good news refreshes [makes

---

[224] Waltke, *The Book of Proverbs*, 60-61.

healthy or fattens] the bones [the body]." Proverbs 16:24 offers the same certainty: "Gracious words [both spoken by God and through people] are like a honeycomb, sweet to the soul and health [curative or medicinal] to the bones [lit. the body or physical substance]."[225]

Proverbs 3:7-8 affirms the same truth that God's wisdom is medicinal, but also the passage focuses on the destructive self-dependence/pride/moral failure of normal human nature — leaning unto one's own understanding (3:5-6):

> Do not be wise in your own eyes; Fear the LORD and turn away from evil. It will be healing to your body [*shor*; central "cord"[226]] and refreshment to your bones [bones or physical substance].

Dr. Cohen notes that the Hebrew word *shor* is a unique word[227] in Scripture denoting "the centre of the existence of the body."[228] *The Pulpit Commentary: Proverbs* explains,

> The navel is here regarded as the centre of vital strength. This is the only place in the Proverbs where this word is found. Gesenius, however, takes *shor*, or *l'shor'rekha*, as standing collectively for the nerves, in which, he says, is the seat of strength, and translates accordingly, "Health (i.e. refreshment) shall it be to thy nerves."[229]

---

[225] Proverbs 12:18 explains how the tongue can be used to destroy others or to heal them: "There is one whose rash words are like swords thrust, but the tongue of the wise brings healing."

[226] William McKane, *Proverbs: A New Approach* (Philadelphia: Westminster Press, 1970), 293.

[227] In Song of Solomon 7:2, *shor* is translated in context as the center of the woman's body. The only other usage is found in Ezekiel 16:4 where *shor* is translated as central life cord or what today is called the umbilical cord.

[228] Abraham Cohen, *Proverbs* (London: Soncino Press, 1946), 14.

[229] *The Pulpit Commentary: Proverbs* ed. By Henry D. M. Spence and Joseph S. Exell (Logos Research Systems, [orign. 1909] 2004), Proverbs 3:8.

Proverbs 3:8 likely references the central nervous cord that today is known as the central nervous system. Regardless of the word's nuance in this text, the Bible is clear that the body is affected by the soul's relationship with God – physical death being prime evidence. Depression is simply the normal impairing and destructive state of being apart from God's wisdom, and the good news – the hope of the gospel – is the metaphysical medicine that heals. Of course, until a person sees Christ face to face, the full dosage – which fully remedies the human condition – will not be realized.

Proverbs 3:7-8 also exposes that the negative effects, which the mind so often produces on the body, can be reversed by healthy (spiritually speaking) thinking. Secular physician Bruce Lipton offers one example from research of how faith can positively change the body and affect the central nervous system,

> A California interior designer, Janis Schonfeld, who took part in a clinical trial to test the efficacy of Effexor in 1997, was just as "stunned" as Perez when she found out that she had been on a placebo [a sugar pill]. Not only had the pills relieved her of the depression that had plagued her for thirty years, the brain scans she received throughout the study found that the activity of her prefrontal cortex was greatly enhanced. (Leuchter, et al., 2002) Her improvements were not "all in her head." When the mind changes, it absolutely affects your biology.[230]

As people's ways of thinking and faith change (for better or for worse), so too does their body – a point which neuroscience and secular descriptive psychology have both affirmed.[231]

---

[230] Bruce H. Lipton, The Biology of Belief: Unleashing the Power of Consciousness, Matter & Miracles (New York: Hay House, 2005), 111.

[231] Pert, Molecules of Emotion, 192-93.

As with sorrow, guilt caused by a person's individual sin also negatively affects the body. In Psalm 31:9, David shares his own experience: "my eye is wasted," "my strength fails," and my "bones waste away." David later conveys how his unconfessed sin both burdened him with guilt and negatively affected his body (Psalm 38:3-5):

> There is no soundness in my flesh because of your indignation; there is no health in my bones because of my sin. For my iniquities have gone over my head; like a heavy burden, they are too heavy for me. My wounds stink and fester because of my foolishness,

The *NIV* translates verse 4 this way: "My guilt has overwhelmed me like a burden too heavy to bear." Metaphysical guilt weighs heavily on the soul and alters the physical body. Sorrow, hopelessness, sin, and guilt all create negative somatic changes rather than their being caused by the body.

The American Psychology Association published a book in 2005 revealing which factors are most likely to influence therapy outcomes. Remarkably, one of the most powerful factors was the mind's ability to alter the body:

> The past 15 years have seen an explosion of research findings from the fields of behavioral medicine and psychoneuroimmunology demonstrating the effects of attitude, behavior, cognitive set, and unpleasant states of mind on physiology and illness. . . . Companion research also has shown, sometimes in dramatic and moving ways, how modifications of attitude, behavior, cognitive set, and unpleasant states of mind can promote healing.[232]

Observable neurological, genetic, and neurochemical variances are not validation of the medical model's theory that depression is a disease. Rather, these expected somatic changes are effects of the mind's executive control over the body and empirical

[232] Hubble, Duncan, and Miller, *Heart and Soul of Change,* 262-63.

evidence of the psychosomatic nature of mankind as God designed it to function.

The Integrational Perspectives

To be sure, there are many false claims currently being accepted as truth within the secular theory of depression. But even more disconcerting, these false theories have not only been propagated by some who claim to be Christians but also are spread by well-intentioned Christians who attempt to integrate biblical truths with secular theories.

As Christians react to secular theory which they know to be false and form theories which seem to be scriptural, altogether new theories are formed. These quasi-biblical theories are not primarily based upon the Word of God, but arise from the evolutionary philosophies of individual degenerationism, materialism, and the humanistic idea that normal people are not severely impaired or distressed in a persistent way. In essence, these false theories do not see Scripture as entirely sufficient to explain and remedy hopelessness, sorrow, and guilt, and thus, too often, they neutralize or undermine the work of the gospel in those who deeply sorrow.

Whereas the secular position attempts to substitute the gospel of Christ for a humanistic salvation, the integrationist attempts to wed both humanistic theory with Scriptural truths. The consistent pursuit that gives the integrationist away is seeking to discover what causes hopelessness, sorrow, guilt and the soul's vexation apart from the Genesis 3 account; an integrationist is one who attempts to interpret mindsets, emotions, and behavior according to the philosophies of individual degenerationism, materialism, and bio-determinism instead of according to biblical universal degenerationism, dualism, and moral determinism.

The Christian who starts with the philosophy of universal degenerationism to approach the human condition does not continue to seek for causes/etiologies of depression. Instead, he/she accepts both the Genesis 3 account as causative, and acknowledges the scriptural truth that sorrows can be multiplied or increased by many factors in life. Only when the biblical anthropology is denied or ignored in favor of the secular presuppositional philosophy do Christians begin to both accept the secular psychiatric constructs and to theorize about what causes depression apart from original sin. The integrationist must overlook biblical teaching that deep sorrow, hopelessness, guilt, and negative somatic changes and decline (as observed in death itself) are all caused by the original sin of Adam.

There are two prominent integrational perspectives which need to be addressed. Both false beliefs are based upon the humanistic philosophy of individual degenerationism and one also on materialism.

"Depression is Caused by Disease"

The first popular but false theory held by many well-meaning Christians is the idea that having a significant disease or a terminal illness causes depression in some. This seemingly biblical framework differs from modern secular theory in that secularists see depression as both its own disease entity (a disorder) as well as the symptom of various physical diseases. In the common Christian theory, depression is framed to be two types: (1) depression caused by a spiritual/internal struggle including sin (2) depression caused by physical disease. Essentially, this position eliminates the materialistic claim that depression is a disease itself, but accepts the materialistic claim that the body or physical diseases can cause hopelessness, sorrow, and guilt.

Many Christians promote the theory that there are two types of depression: depression as a symptom of either personal sin (internally caused by the heart's moral failure) or a symptom of physical disease (externally caused apart from the spiritual heart). But such a position is actually not new or based upon Scripture. In truth, Emil Kraepelin, the 19th century German psychiatrist who, based on his materialistic beliefs, created the construct of mental illness and transformed historic madness into a disease concept, promoted the assumption that depression was both "endogenous" (internally caused) and "exogenous" (externally caused).[233] While no evidence exists to prove two types of depression, there does exist a correlation (which does not prove causation) between depression and physical diseases.

It is true that depression is found as a "risk factor" or listed as a symptom in many physical illnesses such as heart, thyroid, and autoimmune diseases. However, as Charles Nemeroff, former president of the American College of Psychiatrists and current chairman of the Department of Psychiatry and Behavioral Science at the University of Miami acknowledges, depression (hopelessness, sorrow, and guilt) is a facilitator and can cause many physical diseases:

> [Depression] affects the whole body. Part of having depression is
> being very vulnerable for other medical disorders, including
> diabetes, heart disease, certain forms of cancer, stroke. Depression is
> a killing disease. Not only does it kill you by suicide, it kills you
> because your life expectancy is shorter because of the biology of the

[233] Kraepelin searched for internal biological causes. Kenneth Davison, "Historical Aspects of Mood disorders," *Psychiatry* Vol. 5 (4) (2006): 115–18 available from doi:10.1383/psyt. 2006.5.4.115. Though Kraepelin first suggested the two types of depression, it was another German psychiatrist, Kurt Schneider, who coined the terms *endogenous* and *exogenous* depression (Schneider, "Zeitschrift für die Gesante," *Neurological Psychiatry* 59 (1920): 281–86).

illness. What I mean by that is the biology of depression is not just in the brain. It's in the whole body.[234]

Nemoroff—who holds to the evolutionary philosophies of materialism and individual degenerationism—believes that depression itself is a disease. But here he presents depression as biological in the sense of its effects on the body rather than it being biologically caused—a point that can be agreed upon.

The American Psychology Association has discovered in studying a wide range of research that hopelessness precedes heart disease, heart attacks, cancer, and even death:

> Compared with low scorers, moderately hopeless men were at more than twice the risk and highly hopeless men more than three times the risk of death, primarily due to cardiovascular disease and cancer. High levels of hopelessness also predicted incidence of first heart attack in men with no history of angina, and moderate and high hopelessness significantly predicted incident cancer. Strikingly, these relationships held even when adjustments were made for other medical, demographic, and behavioral risk factors, including depression and availability of social supports. [235]

Heart disease does not cause depression; conversely, hopelessness stresses the heart. Such a reality is also why powerful psychiatrists, such as Nemoroff, have negotiated depression into lists of "risk factors:"

> For many years, I conducted research on trying to understand why depressed patients were at risk for heart disease. . . . It took almost 20 years of negotiating with the American Heart Association before they were willing to actually list depression as a risk factor for heart disease.[236]

[234] Nemeroff, "Depression: A Killing Disease."

[235] Hubble, Duncan, and Miller, *Heart and Soul of Change*, 268.

[236] Nemeroff, "Depression: A Killing Disease."

The major features of the construct of depression are metaphysical, but their many negative effects are regularly observed in the body. Former chief of brain biochemistry at the NIH and materialist Candace Pert also remarks on how emotions produce physical ailments,

> Although we don't know what the role of the emotions is in all this, epidemiological evidence suggests there is a link. It's well documented, for example, that people have more heart attacks on Monday mornings (when the work week begins) than any other day of the week, and that death rates peak during the days after Christmas for Christians and after Chinese New Year for the Chinese. Since these are all days with high emotional valence, one way or another, it seems clear that the emotions in some way correlate with the state of people's hearts.[237]

What both the Bible and scientific evidence reveal is that emotions and hopelessness can and regularly do bring about biological diseases.

Not only does one's mind bring about physical ailments and diseases, but so also can physical diseases expose a person's true nature. When a person is diagnosed with a terminal or chronic disease, it is expected to feel mentally/emotionally deflated. Nehemiah 2:2a illustrates this understanding: "And the king said to me, "Why is your face sad though you are not sick? This is nothing but sadness of the heart." Temporal hopelessness and sorrow are not symptoms of physical diseases, but the common and expected spiritual responses to human fragility:

> Studies have documented that a cancer diagnosis results in high levels of emotional distress. Patients go through an adjustment period for about 4 to 6 weeks after diagnosis. *Cancer for many patients is synonymous with death* [emphasis added] and debilitating treatments, with images of a prolonged painful dying process. Patients often say they feel overwhelmed trying to assimilate medical information and make treatment decisions — all while

---

[237] Pert, *Molecules of Emotion*, 189.

continuing to manage family, work, and other responsibilities. However, for the majority of patients, once they receive a plan of action and begin treatment, their emotions tend to level out.[238]

If a person regains hope in this life after this initial period of emotional distress and deflation, there is a better chance of recovery and less of depressive symptoms. Also new treatments with good results offer renewed hope and allow people diagnosed with cancer to see it less as "a terminal illness to more of a chronic illness."[239] Those who receive a diagnosis and lose their hope in this life have lower rates of recovery and are regularly diagnosed as depressed. If a person is mentally forced to face death — which diseases can do, that person must also consider his/her own true nature (Ecclesiastes 7:2-3).

What also regularly increases the risk of "depressive symptoms" are the side-effects of the drugs prescribed to treat physical illnesses such as heart disease.[240] This reality highlights one of the problems with creating syndromes out of symptoms: symptoms are shared by many constructed syndromes and brought on by many factors apart from the alleged syndrome. Consequently, causes, effects, and correlations are often confused.

In truth, diseases do not cause hopelessness, sorrow, or guilt. Instead, diseases multiply sorrows, expose human nature to be

[238] Christina Pozo-Kaderman, "Depression and Anxiety Disorders in Patients with Cancer," *Psychiatric Times Online* Vol. 34 (3) (March 31, 2017): http://www.psychiatrictimes.com/ depression/depression-and-anxiety-disorders-patients-cancer.

[239] Ibid.

[240] "Sometimes medications taken for these physical illnesses may cause side effects that contribute to depression" (National Institute of Mental Health, "Depression," *NIMH* [2018]: https://www.nimh.nih.gov/health/topics/ depression/ index.shtml).

weak and dying, and regularly reveal the vanity of trusting in the false hope of health and this life. Framing depression as a disease or caused by disease is to fail to understand the normal human state recorded in Genesis 3 and throughout Scripture and to view humanity through the philosophy of individual degenerationism and materialism.

"Sorrow is a Sin"

In addition to attempting to integrate the humanistic medical model with the biblical approach, the belief that depression — specifically sorrow — is sinful has done great damage to those who are hurting and has perverted the gospel. The position that sorrow is sinful is, sadly, one of the most accepted and destructive Christian reaction theories; it is a legalistic mindset and detestable theology. Instead of being gospel-centered, this common belief is derived in part from the false philosophy of individual degenerationism and in part from the true Genesis 3 account.

It is upon this theory that we can again observe how it is many times necessary to separate hopelessness, sorrow, and guilt rather than always view them together in a social construct such as depression. Personal sin relates to hopelessness, sorrow, and guilt because they are all a part of fallen human nature. But struggling with one of these features — especially sorrow — does not mean that one's own sin is the primary cause of a person's struggle.

As related in chapter 3, the subjective nature of the psychiatric construct of depression allows clinicians to diagnose people as depressed when they are simply struggling with guilt or sorrowing too deeply in a way that goes beyond what the clinician feels is appropriate. This wrong approach to people who struggle with deep sorrow has infiltrated the church and is observed in the idea that being in deep sorrow is sinful or exposes someone who is not right with God.

As I have had opportunity to speak around the world, I have met many Christians who have genuine hope in Christ and are not struggling with guilt, and yet clinicians diagnose them as being depressed. More often than not, there is a legitimate reason their sorrow has deepened. These people are primarily sorrowful because of the fallen nature of the world and not from being sad as a consequence of their own sinful choices.

By way of illustration, years ago I was speaking at a conference and met a mother of four children. She had lost her husband who had died at war, was herself diagnosed with a rare form of cancer, and lacked sufficient income to provide for her large family. Several people in her church had told her that she needed to "get over her husband's death," since it had been more than two years since he passed. In tears, she shared with me that some in the church had even suggested that she could not be right with God and still continue grieving, while others suggested that she needed to "get help." The book of Job came to my mind as I talked with her, as Job, in the middle of his own sorrow and losses, received similar counsel, which God rebuked.

Moreover, dozens of people, who as children were tossed around in the foster care system and eventually adopted, have regularly been diagnosed as having the psychiatric constructs of depression, bipolar, and schizoid-affective disorder (to name a few) because of their understandable struggle with the trauma of abandonment and the sorrow of their lives. Psychiatrists have even developed a construct that they refer to as "attachment disorders" to explain the depression, anxiety, and emotional struggles that these children rightly experience. Psychiatrist Joanna Chambers remarks,

> Attachment theory was developed in the 1950s by John Bowlby, a
> British psychiatrist and psychoanalyst who studied children left by

159

their parents in post-World War II England. In his work with these children, Bowlby found that they were not only attached to their parents, but indeed became depressed when they were separated from them.[241]

The children's struggles with hopelessness, sorrow, and false guilt due to abandonment should be expected rather than viewed as abnormal. These struggles are real no matter how loving and gracious an adopted family may be or how much the adopted child loves God. These sorrows are understandable considering the degree of distress; therefore, these sorrowful responses — even extreme and impairing cases — are indeed normal human responses, not biological disorders or indications of sin.

Sorrow

It is important to understand that though hopelessness, sorrow, and guilt are all features of normal human nature and caused by Adam's fall, personal sin/idolatry does increase sorrow, guilt, and hopelessness. Psalms 16:4, for instance, states that "the sorrows of those who run after another god shall multiply" (see also Proverbs 23:29-30 and Psalm 16:4; 32:10). The verse assumes that sorrows are a part of human nature and that they are multiplied with idolatry and sinful behavior. A person's sorrows can multiply from the death of a loved one or the anticipation thereof (John 20:11), the sins and abuses of others, rejection, and the fallen nature of this world, including tragedy, change of seasons, and lack of sleep (to name a few). As Solomon stated, life is full of sorrows.

---

[241] Joanna E. Chambers, "Perinatal Psychiatry: Where Psychoanalytic Theory, Neuroscience, and Integrated Clinical Psychiatry Meet," *Psychiatric Times Online* Vol. 34 (3) (March 24, 2017): http://www. psychiatrictimes.com/ depression/perinatal-psychiatry-where-psychoanalytic-theory-neuroscience-and-integrated-clinical-psychiatry.

The sorrow that parents incur from their children's foolish choices and rejection of God's wisdom provides another prime example. Proverbs 17:21 states, "He who sires a fool gets himself sorrow, and the father of a fool has no joy" (see also 17:25; 10:1). Though sorrow increases with personal sin, being in sorrow is not sinful and should be the expected norm. It is a hurtful but all-too-common error to assume that everyone who is struggling with deep sorrow is struggling with sorrow related to his/her own sin. It is also an error to assert that being sorrowful is sinful, and that people who are in sorrow need to get out of it.

The Example of Christ

As previously noted, Jesus himself — who was without personal sin — is described in Scripture as being a man well acquainted with sadness and identified as a "man of sorrows" (Isaiah 53:3). To say that being in sorrow is sinful or is caused by individual sin is to create a legalistic concept of sorrow and to deny the exemplary life of Christ. Charles Spurgeon noted that it is most often those who are walking with God and not opposed to God who experience the most sorrow:

> A great number of God's best servants have trodden the deeps of the valley of the shadow; and this ought to comfort some of you. The footsteps of the holy are in the valley of weeping . . . . No sin is necessarily connected with sorrow of heart, for Jesus Christ our Lord once said, 'My soul is exceedingly sorrowful, even to death.' There was no sin in him, and consequently none in his deep depression . . . . In grief itself there is no necessary cause of sin.[242]

The theory that sorrow is always caused by one's sin or that it is a sin to be sorrowful is not merely based upon a wrong philosophy; it is also an unbiblical theology.

---

[242] Charles H. Spurgeon, *The Metropolitan Tabernacle Pulpit: Sermons Preached and Revised* Vol. XXVII (London: Passmore & Alabaster and Sons, 1882) 234.

The sorrow of Christ was persistent, was severe, and was endured throughout His life. In Matthew 26:38 Christ expresses to Peter and to the others who were with him that, "My soul is very sorrowful [spiritual pain], even to death; remain here, and watch with me." Christ was in such distress that He was close to death, and He experienced extreme somatic symptoms of sweating drops of blood (Luke 22:44) — a medical condition known as *hematohidrosis*. While I have counseled numerous people who experienced incredibly deep sorrow and painful rejection, I have never met a person who suffered with such severity as Christ did.

If Jesus, suffering with intense sorrow and distress, went to a modern clinic to get help, He would likely be diagnosed with major depression or with bipolar I, since He would meet all three axioms within the psychiatric constructs. Because Christ experienced severe, distressful, impairing, and persistent sorrow with somatic symptoms and spent his life and energies proclaiming His gospel, many secular psychiatrists believe that His life and sacrificial death provide a case study in mania.[243] Clearly, though, Jesus was not hopeless or deceived, nor was He guilty of any sin or pride.

The Example of King David

In contrast to the perfection of Christ, King David provides a great illustration of one who multiplied his sorrow with his own sinful choices (Psalm 38:1-22). David's sorrow was so impairing that Editor in Chief Emeritus of the *Psychiatric Times* Ronald Pies

---

[243] Several secular psychiatrists have in hindsight diagnosed Jesus to have had bipolar depression among other alleged disorders (Evan D. Murray, Miles G. Cunningham, and Bruce H. Price, "The Role of Psychotic Disorders in Religious History Considered," *Journal of Neuropsychiatry and Clinical Neurosciences* 24 [2012]: 410-26).

and psychiatrist Cynthia Geppert[244] insist that David was clinically depressed:

> The distinction between clinical depression and ordinary grief seems as old as recorded history. In Psalm 38, the psalmist laments his sins. He tells us that "there is no soundness in my flesh . . . no health in my bones because of my sin. . . . My wounds grow foul and fester because of my foolishness, I am utterly bowed down and prostrate; all the day I go about mourning. . . . I groan because of the tumult of my heart." Psychiatrists today would likely recognize in this description clinical symptoms of major depression, such as psychomotor slowing ("utterly bowed down") and severely depressed mood. The psalmist's sense of bodily decay and self-loathing [guilt] are more suggestive of clinical depression than of grief, in which the sense of self-worth is usually intact. [245]

According to these psychiatrists' professional opinions, David was clinically depressed because of his "low self-worth," "severely depressed mood," and "psychomotor slowing." But under inspiration, David confessed that his sin had multiplied his sorrow, brought about his negative somatic symptoms, and was responsible for his guilt:

> Be gracious to me, O LORD, for I am in distress; my eye is wasted from grief; my soul and my body also. For my life is spent with sorrow, and my years with sighing; my strength fails because of my iniquity, and my bones waste away (Psalm 31:9).

Was not David's guilt, distress, and sorrow in this case — though all impairing — right ways of thinking about his life?[246] Would

---

[244] Geppert works as director of ethics education at the University of New Mexico School of Medicine and serves on the U.S. National Center for Ethics in Healthcare.

[245] Pies and Geppert, "Clinical Depression or 'Life Sorrows'?

[246] Research reveals that adolescents who engage in deviant sexual behavior (e.g., transgenderism and homosexuality) are more likely to experience depression and self-harm (e.g., cutting, eating disorders, and suicide) (George W. Citroner, "Sexual Minorities More Likely to Self-Harm," *Medscape Psychiatry Online* [December 21, 2018]: https://www. medscape.com/

these honest mindsets not eventually lead him to repentance and desired fellowship with God?

The suffering of Jesus and David offers two examples to consider. On one hand, there is Christ who was without sin, and on the other hand, there is David who committed much sin. Yet both shared deep impairing sorrow, and some secularists have diagnosed both in hindsight as being clinically depressed. To assume that every secular diagnosis of depression is caused by sin is both to embrace a Christianized individual degenerationism as well as to dismiss the reality that the syndrome of depression is a subjective construct.

The Example of the Church

Another reason that being sad is not a sin is that the Bible admonishes Christians to participate in others' sorrow. The Bible tells us to "rejoice with those who rejoice, weep with those who weep" (Romans 12:15). Scripture nowhere admonishes believers to rescue people out of their sadness or send the sad away to get help. Rather, Christians are to actively sorrow with those who are sad, and they are to do so to the point that they physically engage by weeping with others who are weeping.

In 2 Corinthians 7:8-9, Paul expresses joy that the church is grieving over the letter he wrote, since they "became sorrowful as God intended." The church has become so influenced by secular thinking that it has failed to see sorrow as God intends as something positive, but instead, the church has insisted that sorrow be viewed as bad/sinful, while constantly searching for its cause and removal. Sorrow in an individual or in the local

viewarticle/906924?nlid=126852_2051&src=WNL_mdpls news_181228_mscpedit_psyc&uac=264124BV&spon=12&impID=1846389&faf= 1#vp_2).

body of believers is intended by God for the good of all His people.

If being deeply sorrowful were sinful, then the Apostle Paul, under inspiration, would be encouraging believers to participate in sin. These verses also reiterate the truth that if sorrow is accepted in accordance with God's will, then it is something positive to be engaged in rather than something to escape or from which to save others. It is probable, then, that some Christians frame sorrow as sinful or as a sickness in order to excuse their own failure to love others as Christ desires. It is much easier to set people aside by telling them that they need to go get help or declaring that they are wicked or abnormal then it is to graciously engage in their lives and understand God's intent for their sorrow.

Worth also noting from 2 Corinthians 7:8-9 and many other passages is that sorrow is most often relational and an aspect of discipleship that is regularly ignored. Sorrow is the human condition from Genesis 3 because humanity is naturally alienated apart from God's covenant grace received in "the hope of the gospel" (Colossians 1:20-23). Even the sorrow of Jesus is explained in Isaiah 53:3 to be in large part due to humanity's rejection of Jesus as Messiah. If someone is defrauded, abandoned, rejected, or abused, and has lost a loved one or friend, or has been hurt by another, he/she is not in sin for being deeply saddened. Sadly, it is within the relationships of the family and the church where hurts and sorrows are regularly multiplied.

These truths have major impact on how the church (Christians) counsels those in sorrow. For one, Christians must understand and set forth that sorrow is the normal and right way of thinking about the fallen world in which all live. People who are struggling with deep sadness, whether or not they understand or can explain why they are sad, are thinking truthfully about their own soul's condition and life after the Fall. Understanding one's own identity from the biblical perspective is vital to the soul in deep sorrow.

Secondly, no counselor (or physician) should attempt to remove sorrow from a person's life. Any attempt to change the normal spiritual condition of sorrow apart from God's work of grace is a failing effort. Keep in mind that Christians are to participate in others' sorrow not try to pull others out of this mindset or convince them to get over their sadness. To insist that Christians ought not to sorrow goes against the very words of Christ (John 16:20) and against His plan to restore regenerates and provide delivering hope. Christians are, however, to point others to the time when Christ will fully deliver us from our sorrow, pain, and death—" the hope of the gospel" that Revelation 21:4 explains will occur in eternity.

Likewise, Christians are not searching for what causes sorrows, but what multiplies them—never assuming that a person's deep despair is caused by his/her personal sin or caused by a physical disease. The cause of sorrow is found in the Genesis 3 account, and the increases of sorrow are found in each person's life history and heart's desires. Removing factors which multiply sorrows (such as sin, sickness, seasons, broken relationships etc.) can temporarily ease sorrow in our lives, but it will not remove our sorrowful condition on this side of eternity. Any promise or attempt to remedy sorrow in this life, whether spiritual or physical in nature, is a false hope that cannot genuinely and permanently remove sadness of heart.

The biblical perspective is that universal sin has caused the human condition which secularists have framed as depression, and experiences (including death of a loved one, lack of sleep, diseases, and trauma, etc.), bad behaviors, mindsets, and relationships will multiply sorrows. From a scriptural view, depression (a pained and crushed spirit) is a distressing spiritual

166

reality of normal human nature that negatively alters the physical nature, but which God in His mercy can use to lead people out of their fallen condition and into faith in the hope of Jesus Christ.

CHAPTER 6

RECONSIDERING EMOTIONS

"Depressed *feelings* are signals of underlying frustration and despair, and can provide a window in [sic] the sources of the problem."[247] —Peter Breggin, psychiatrist and former consultant for the NIMH

The subject of emotions both in the construct of depression and also within the church has elicited much attention and controversy in recent years. Often people prefer the terms *feelings* and *moods* instead of emotions, and many people believe that the idea of emotions is a free-standing aspect of humanity that differs from the spiritual heart and observable behavior. In fact, the description of human nature typically includes mindsets (cognition), emotions, and behaviors. But are emotions something distinct from mindsets and behavior, are they spiritually or physically caused, and are they realities approachable with science?

In order to answer these questions, it is imperative to examine the source of the concept of emotions. One of the original terms used to describe what is now framed as emotions was *affects or affections*. The word "*affect* is based on a Latin word [*Ad* + *facio*]"

---

[247] Breggin, *Anti-Depressant Fact Book*, 193.

that means "act on, have influence on, to do something to."[248] Protestant theologian Jonathan Edwards wrote in 1746,

> Holy affections are not heat without light, but evermore arise from some information of the understanding, some spiritual instruction that the mind receives, some light or actual knowledge.[249]

Edwards recognized that affections arose or came out of a spiritual reality. Similarly, the terms that would become widely accepted in today's society *emotions* or *emote* are based upon the Latin *ēmōtus*, which means "to move out, move away."[250] Likewise, *Mod* is the Old English word for "heart," "frame of mind" or "spirit,"[251] and it is the root of another synonym for emotion that is commonly used in secular psychology: *mood*. What secularists have framed as *mood disorders* are simply the heart's destructive responses (according to its values) to circumstances, and these responses have manifest into common patterns of behavior; they are physical signals or signs of a person's metaphysical reality. Secular psychiatrist Peter Breggin explains,

> Depression is, above all else, a signal that our lives are not going well. . . . The depth of our despair often reflects the contrasting desire that we have to live a more joyful, creative, and meaningful life.[252]

---

[248] N.S. Gill, "What is the Difference Between Affect and Effect?" *Thought Co.* (October 23, 2018): https://www.thoughtco.com/difference-between-affect-and-effect-118479.

[249] Jonathan Edwards, *A Treatise Concerning Religious Affections.* (Philadelphia: J. Crissy, 1821. Reprint, New Haven, CT: Yale University Press, 1959), 266.

[250] "Emotion," https://en.wiktionary.org/wiki/ emotion.

[251] "Mood," *Online Entomology Dictionary* (2018): https://www.etymonline.com/word/mood.

[252] Breggin, *Anti-Depressant Fact Book*, 25.

Secular psychologist Gregg Henriques concurs:

> Depression and anxiety are, for the large majority of cases, emotional signals that one's psychological [soul] health is not ideal and that one's psychosocial/relational needs are not being met. Indeed, the first place that I look when I see depression and anxiety is the need for relational value.[253]

Depression and anxiety are sourced in the heart's values or treasures and are expressed in accordance with how people perceive their life situations and relationships.

Both the words *affections* and *emotions* signify that there is an acting or motion (a behavior) that arises from something. What, then, causes *moods/emotions*?

There are two prominent theories about what causes emotions. The Bible teaches that the spiritual heart produces affections/ emotions whereas materialists theorize that emotions are sourced in the body. Both perspectives agree that within the concept of emotions some physical changes can be observed and approached by applying the scientific method. But emotions are also at their core metaphysical (without physical characteristic or property) — only the bodily manifestations are observable and objectively measurable.

Secular Perspective

It is helpful to examine the perspective of leading materialists and how they utilize the foundational philosophies that govern today's medical model of mental illness to frame the construct of emotions. Candace Pert, a materialist who served as the former chief of brain biochemistry research at the National Institutes of

---

[253] Gregg Henriques, "Anxiety and Depression Are Symptoms, Not Diseases," *Psychology Today Online* (March 26, 2016): https://www.psychology today.com/us/blog/theory-knowledge/201603/anxiety-and-depression-are-symptoms-not-diseases.

Health (one of the highest neuroscientific achievements one can obtain) writes in her book *Molecules of Emotion: The Science Behind Mind-Body Medicine* that

> we can no longer think of the emotions as having less validity than physical, material substance, but instead must see them as cellular signals that are involved in the process of translating information into physical reality, literally transforming mind into matter. [254]

Pert realizes that emotions are a construct which people regularly utilize to describe how the spiritual and physical natures relate. She also states,

> It is the emotions, I have come to see, that link mind and body. This more holistic approach complements the reductionist view, expanding it rather than replacing it, and offers a new way to think about health and disease—not just for us scientists, but for the lay person also.[255]

While she denies that she is accepting a dualistic approach to human nature in accordance with her reductionist faith and attempts to explain the biological process of how the body receives metaphysical input, Pert admits in her book that the construct of emotions best describes how the spiritual and physical natures are connected.

In secular psychology and psychiatry *emotion* is a relatively new "theoretical keyword." Historian Thomas Dixon remarks,

> The word "emotion" has named a psychological category and a subject for systematic enquiry only since the 19th century. Before

---

[254] Pert, *Molecules of Emotion*, 189.

[255] Ibid., 18-19.

then, relevant mental states were categorized variously as "appetites," "passions," "affections," or "sentiments."[256]

Emotion is a fairly young social construct that is an attempt to explain the metaphysical reality of human nature. Dixon also recognizes that the word *emotion* is a subjective construct,

> "Emotion" has, since, been a theoretical keyword at the heart of modern psychology. In that year William James wrote an influential article in *Mind* entitled "What Is an Emotion?" A century and a quarter later, however, there seems to be little scientific consensus on the answer to his question, and some are beginning to wonder whether it is the very category of "emotion" that is the problem. [257]

But within secular thinking — especially in the last century — the category or construct of emotions began to be viewed less as a metaphysical reality which translates into the physical realm, and more of a bodily function entirely. In materialists' view, sorrow, anger, anxiety, and hopelessness are born not out of the heart, as the Bible states, but out of biological processes.

Since materialists cannot deny the reality of emotions, they must seek to fit these mindsets which become behaviors into a scientific framework. During the 19th century, Edinburgh professor of philosophy Thomas Brown was one who sought to establish emotions as a major tenet in the "science of the mind":

> [Brown] subsumed the "appetites," "passions," and "affections" under a single category: the "emotions." The word "emotion" was already in wide usage, but in Brown's lectures, first published in 1820, *the term took on a newly systematic theoretical role in the science of the mind* [emphasis added]. This innovation proved to be popular. In arguably the first modern psychological book about the emotions, the incredibly wide reach of the new category was made explicit:

[256] Thomas Dixon, "'Emotion': The History of a Keyword in Crisis," *Emotion Review: Journal of the International Society for Research on Emotion* 4, no. 4 (2012): 338-44.

[257] Ibid.

> "Emotion is the name here used to comprehend all that is understood by feelings, states of feeling, pleasures, pains, passions, sentiments, affections" (Bain, 1859, p. 3).[258]

The word *emotion* is again utilized as a construct in attempt to explain the spiritual heart's manifestation in the physical realm.

Since throughout history, the idea of affections or emotions has included the observable-outward manifestations, *sensible* was another utilized synonym.[259] Today, emotions are regularly referred to as *feelings*—a word that also highlights how metaphysical emotions can stir the physical senses and affect the body. The outward manifestations of the inward desires seemingly offer materialists the ability to frame emotions as entirely approachable within the field of science, though they are not. In this paradigm, the physical phenomenon is studied, even back to the smallest neurological and chemical changes that can be observed, and the most minute changes are theorized to be the cause/etiology of mood states. Neurites, cells, chemicals, genes, and even entire regions of the brain and other bodily systems are all theorized to cause emotions. However, although the behaviors and physical changes that occur certainly are observable windows into the unobservable psyche/soul, framing emotions as only somatic realities limits their nature to exclude their metaphysical source.

Since the early 1800s, humanistic psychiatrists and psychologists alike have utilized negative emotions or affections to build their constructs of mental illness or perceived abnormalities. For example, what the APA now calls depressive and bipolar disorders, or more broadly "mood disorders," was a construct

[258] Ibid.

[259] J. H. Diller, "'Emotion' vs. 'Passion': The History of Word-Use and the Emergence of an A-Moral Category," *Archive für Begriffsgeschichte* 52 (2010): 127–51.

created by the German psychiatrist and father of the current medical/biological model of mental illness, Emil Kraepelin. Kraepelin called his theorized disorder *affective psychosis* (the "emotional condition of the deceived soul").

Once again, the term *emotions* represents a construct which attempts to describe a metaphysical reality of the soul with physical effects that can be observed in measurable behavior and somatic changes. But as observed in the previous chapter, materialists have no use or room within scientism to actually consider the soul or its emotions as real or relative. Dr. Pert explains,

> Measurement! It is the very foundation of the modern scientific method, the means by which the material world is admitted into existence. Unless we can measure something, science won't concede it exists, which is why science refuses to deal with such "nonthings" as the emotions, the mind, the soul, or the spirit.[260]

Secularists must deny the soul's existence and significance apart from the physical nature or must open wide the door to the gospel.

True to a reductionist position, Dr. Pert describes her own definition of emotions,

> When I use the term *emotion*, I am speaking in the broadest of terms, to include not only the familiar human experience of anger, fear, and sadness, as well as joy, contentment, and courage, but also basic sensations such as pleasure and pain, as well as the drive states," studied by the experimental psychologists, such as hunger and thirst.[261]

Dr. Pert has skillfully progressed from listing metaphysical thoughts that reflect the heart's passions to including physical

---

[260] Pert, *Molecules of Emotion*, 21.

[261] Ibid., 131.

sensations and drives (pleasure, pain, and drive states). By grouping physical sensations and needs (e.g., hunger and thirst) together with the spiritual desires' produced behavior, secularists are more easily able to assert and classify metaphysical emotions as only biological processes. Since materialists are only able and willing to trace causes back to the physical nature, they are unwilling to see beyond molecular structures and neuroreceptors in order to acknowledge that it is the metaphysical heart that produces the metaphysical mindsets, which in turn, produce bodily changes. Dr. Pert notes this struggle in secular research:

> If psychological contributions to physical health and disease are viewed with suspicion, the suggestion that the soul — literal translation of psyche — might matter is considered downright absurd. For now we are getting into the mystical realm, where scientists have been officially forbidden to treat ever since the seventeenth century.[262]

Reductionists — those who attempt to reduce all human nature to material causes and explanations — rightly observe the physiological changes that occur as a person desires and thinks, but they fail to accept or acknowledge the soul's control and involvement in governing the physical nature. In a sense, emotions are the empirical evidence of the soul's existence and its executive control over the body.

Since materialists have no use for or belief in the spiritual heart/metaphysical soul, not only must they explain the soul's control over the body as a biological process, but also they must insist that emotions are determined products of biological functions. Secularists remove responsibility for one's emotions and actions from a person's spiritual heart and reassign responsibility to a person's body — usually a part of the brain. When emotions are seen to be negative and impairing, they are

---

[262] Ibid., 18.

framed as mental illnesses according to which cognitions and behaviors are most prominent.

Along this line of thinking, secular psychiatrists theorize that an invisible disease of depression causes these unwanted "feelings" of sadness, hopelessness, and guilt rather than being the true substance of a person's depression. The APA offers this common-speculative belief on its website:

> Depression (major depressive disorder) is a common and serious medical illness that negatively affects how you feel, the way you think and how you act. Fortunately, it is also treatable. *Depression causes feelings of sadness and/or a loss of interest in activities once enjoyed* [emphasis added]. It can lead to a variety of emotional and physical problems and can decrease a person's ability to function at work and at home.[263]

In this theory, emotions that are considered bad (impairing or distressful) come out of a theorized disease rather than the person's spiritual heart.

Depression, then, in the bio-medical paradigm, is not related to a person's moral will according to Scripture but to a biological force — something in the brain or body, which controls people against their will. Joseph LeDoux remarks on this popular materialistic/evolutionary perspective:

> With the rise of experimental brain research in the late 19th century, emotion was one of the key topics that early neuroscientists sought to relate to the brain (see LeDoux, 1987).[264]

---

[263] APA, "What is Depression?" *American Psychiatric Association Online* (December 2018): https://www.psychiatry. org/patients-families/depression /what-is-depression.

[264] Joseph E. LeDoux, "Evolution of Human Emotion: A View through Fear," *Progress in Brain Research* 195 (2002): 431-42.

Dr. LeDoux later compares emotions to small preprogrammed microorganisms in nature that react instinctively to their environments. Within evolutionary reductionistic thinking, emotions are viewed as unwilled thoughts and reactions to circumstances that are predetermined by biological processes in the body rather than sourced in the spiritual heart. This widely held secular belief is referred to as *biodeterminism.*[265]

Humanist, materialist, and prominent psychiatric theorist Robert Berezin holds to genetic determinism so rigidly that he refers to human consciousness as an "engrained play" and to psychiatric disorders as "genetically determined temperaments":

> We are all participants and observers in our plays. Our primary orientation is just a matter of where on the axis we fall. I have mentioned some of the major symptoms that are generated by our specific genetically determined temperaments. Different combinations of temperament and trauma create the entire fabric of psychiatric nosology: obsessive, compulsive, anxiety, depression, paranoia, panics, phobias, and delusions. People have character behaviors that get them into trouble — drinking, drugs, gambling, eating (anorexia, bulimia, overeating, bingeing), sexual perversions, impulsivity, rages, emotional isolation, narcissism, echoism, sadism, masochism, low self-esteem, and psychotic and manic states. They may have crises in their lives — divorce, death, loss, illness, rejections, failures, disappointments, traumas of all kinds, and posttraumas.[266]

Berezin's belief in determinism represents a key aspect of the medical model of mental illness, and it excludes the very real possibility that these psychiatric labels describe people's common reactions rather than a group of predetermined character roles in the fictional play of evolution. The genetic

[265] Biodeterminism includes *genetic determinism* and *neurodeterminism.*

[266] Robert A. Berezin, "How Our Genomes Shape Psychiatric Symptoms," *Medscape Psychiatry Online* (November 9, 2018): https://www.medscape.com/viewarticle/904589?nlid=126054_424&src=WNL_mdplsfeat_181113_mscpedit_psyc&uac=264124BV&spon=12&impID=1799736&faf=1#vp_3.

theory of mental illness is not new, but is Francis Galton's and Emil Kraepelin's unsubstantiated theories of eugenics repackaged.

Ironically, Berezin continues in the same article to point out that the brain is not as pre-determined as he at first insists, and "problematic mapping" can be reversed through simply talking — the brain has plasticity:

> Psychotherapy (talk therapy) works by deactivating these problematic limbic mappings in the chain of memory. When a problematic mapping is deactivated, these neurotransmitters are no longer operative, and new, more positive, memory mappings take their place. What changes our play of consciousness is mourning a problematic memory in psychotherapy, and allowing for real brain change.[267]

Other prominent neuroscientists, like Candace Pert, have concluded from their own clinical research that hugs have the same healing effect on the brain and nervous system as prescribed drugs.[268] Biodeterminism is not as determined as secularists wish everyone to believe.

A great illustration of how prevalent emotional biodeterminism is can be observed in the Pixar movie *Inside Out*. The movie presents emotions (sadness, anger, joy, fear, and disgust) as living entities — animated characters — in the brain that control the person. As the emotions make mistakes or malfunction within the animated brain, so too do the emotions of the main human character in the movie (Riley). In context of the movie, however, Riley is going through various trials and somewhat traumatic situations in her life. According to this secular perspective, Riley's poor choices are the result of her body's emotions — housed in her brain — malfunctioning rather than

[267] Ibid.

[268] Pert, *Molecules of Emotion*, 271.

being the product of her heart's desires responding to her life's circumstances. Ironically, while the movie indoctrinates the viewer with biodeterministic ideas and introduces children to the medical model of mental illness, the storyline also emphasizes that sadness has meaning and purpose in a person's life and should not be discarded, minimized, or escaped.

Materialists have theorized and invented various types of biodeterminism over time, but all theories, including the construct of mental illness, have shown themselves to be fallacies. As neurosurgeon Michael Egnor asserts,

> The materialist insists that we are slaves of our neurons, without genuine free will [not in relation to God]. Materialism comes in different flavors, each having passed into and then out of favor over the past century, as their insufficiency became apparent. Behaviorists asserted that the mind, if it exists at all, is irrelevant. All that matters is what is observable—input and output. Yet behaviorism is in eclipse, because it's difficult to deny the relevance of the mind to neuroscience.[269]

Valid science, rather than proving that all truth can be explained within a metaphysical framework, reveals that human nature and the universe consist of both spiritual and physical realities.

A Biblical Perspective

While the Bible does not utilize the term *emotion*, it does speak at great length about the realities that this construct seeks to explain. The modern term *emotions* translates in the biblical understanding to the heart's treasures/affections/pursuits/ desires/lusts/love being made manifest in mindsets, behaviors, and somatic changes. For example, the Bible tells us in Matthew 6:20-32,

---

[269] Egnor, "More than Material Minds."

Do not lay up for yourselves *treasures* on earth, where moth and rust destroy and where thieves break in and steal, but lay up for yourselves *treasures* in heaven, where neither moth nor rust destroys and where thieves do not break in and steal. *For where your treasure is, there your heart will be also.* . . . No one can serve two masters, for either he will hate the one and *love* the other, or he will be *devoted* to the one and despise the other. You cannot *serve* God and money. Therefore I tell you, do not be anxious about your life, what you will eat or what you will drink, nor about your body, what you will put on. Is not life more than food, and the body more than clothing? . . . Therefore do not be anxious, saying, "What shall we eat?" or "What shall we drink?" or "What shall we wear?" For the Gentiles *seek after all these things*, and your heavenly Father knows that you need them all [Emphases added].

Where is the metaphysical heart located? According to Christ, the spiritual heart is exactly where a person's treasures are. When Christians use or hear the term *emotion(s)*, they should understand that a person's treasure(s)/desire(s) are being expressed in an observable, physical way. Through words, facial expressions, and other behaviors, the human body offers insight into the soul's affections and pursuits.

James 4:6-10 shows that as a person begins to value God over self, so too will the emotions change:

But he gives more grace. Therefore it says, "God opposes the proud but gives grace to the humble." Submit yourselves therefore to God. Resist the devil, and he will flee from you. Draw near to God, and he will draw near to you. *Cleanse your hands, you sinners, and purify your hearts, you double-minded. Be wretched and mourn and weep. Let your laughter be turned to mourning and your joy to gloom.* Humble yourselves before the Lord, and he will exalt you.

As the heart is purified and the mind changed to think truthfully, to prefer oneself less, and to establish right pleasures, the body will reflect these changes in what is commonly referred to as emotions and behaviors. As the passage also highlights and has been previously noted, sorrow is a central feature of the heart's change toward godliness.

When people act on their natural feelings rather than on a renewed mind, they are thinking and acting according to the flesh. Biblical counselor and director of Reigning Grace Counseling Center Julie Ganschow offers a list of pertinent verses from 1 and 2 Peter in her book, *Seeing Depression through the Eyes of Grace*,[270] in which she encourages people to not live according to their natural fleshly desires (feelings). The list she presents highlights the moral nature of the desires/values/ treasures of the heart:

> *1 Peter 1:14* – "As children who are under obedience, don't shape your lives by the desires that you used to follow in your ignorance" (*CCNT*).

> *1 Peter 2:11* – "Dear friends, as resident aliens and refugees, I urge you to keep at a safe distance from the fleshly desires that are poised against your soul like an expeditionary force" (*CCNT*).

> *1 Peter 4:2* – "As a result, it is now possible to live the remainder of your time in the flesh no longer following human desires, but following God's will" (*CCNT*).

> *2 Peter 1:4* – "Since His divine power has given us everything for life and godliness through the full knowledge of the one Who called us by His own glory and might, through which He has given to us valuable, indeed, the greatest promises of all, in order that through these you might have become partakers of a divine nature, having escaped from the corruption that is in the world because of desire" (*CCNT*).

> *2 Peter 2:10* – "Especially those who are following the polluted desire of the flesh and despise ruling authority" (*CCNT*).

> *2 Peter 2:19* – "Through uttering impressive-sounding clap-trap, by an appeal to fleshly desires and to impure practices, they bait a trap for persons who have barely escaped from those who live in error" (*CCNT*).

---

[270] Julie Ganschow, *Seeing Depression Through the Eyes of Grace* (Kansas City, MO: Pure Water Press, 2015), 21-22.

Many of these passages also denote that desires produce corresponding behavior: right treasures produce right actions and fleshly desires produce destructive lifestyles. Second Peter 2:11 expresses that the true force against the soul is one's natural desires and not the effects (emotions) the wrong desires create. The *ESV* translates the verse this way: "Beloved, I urge you as sojourners and exiles to abstain from the passions of the flesh, which wage war against your soul." Natural human lusts not only wage war against God and others, but they also attack one's own soul. Clearly, the depraved heart's inability to overcome wrong desires apart from regeneration and sanctification through Jesus Christ creates patterns of wrong emotions and behaviors, and these destructive lusts are an unfortunate characteristic of all people and not an abnormality. Sorrow, anger, and anxiety (to name a few) are normal responses of each person's human nature, because life does not go according to one's desires.

The greatest loss the heart faces — though often people do not realize it — is the loss of fellowship or peace with God that every person contends with because of the fall of Adam (Genesis 3) and the resulting self-centered desires thereafter. Physician and minister of the gospel Martyn Lloyd-Jones once said,

> There are so many people trying to diagnose the human situation; and they come to the conclusion that man is sick, man is unhappy, man is the victim of circumstances. They believe therefore that his primary need is to have these things dealt with, that he must be delivered from them. But I suggest that that is too superficial a diagnosis of the condition of man, and that man's real trouble is that he is a rebel against God and consequently under the wrath of God.[271]

In previous chapters, it was observed from Isaiah 53 that Jesus came into the world to save sinners, to take away sorrows, to

[271] Martyn Lloyd-Jones, *Preaching and Preachers* (Grand Rapids, MI: Zondervan, 1971), 27.

offer genuine hope, and to provide a perfect guilt offering. But in order to accomplish all of this, Christ needed to offer Himself as the perfect sacrifice to appease the wrath of God and restore peace between God and man. Ephesians 2:13-16 is one passage which discusses this truth:

> But now in Christ Jesus you who once were far off have been brought near by the blood of Christ. For he himself is our peace, who has made us both one and has broken down in his flesh the dividing wall of hostility, by abolishing the law of commandments expressed in ordinances, that he might create in himself one new man in place of the two, so making peace, and might reconcile us both to God in one body through the cross, thereby killing the hostility.

Though Christ's atoning work is finished, the full benefits will not be realized until we are face to face with God (Revelation 21:3-5ff). Sorrow and pain will one day be eliminated and our souls will be restored to a full relationship with our Creator and Redeemer. This salvation is a sure promise.

A Moral Issue

While materialists and Christians disagree on what causes emotions, they do agree that emotions carry with them a moral tone. That is, emotions are considered good or bad/positive or negative/pleasurable or displeasureable: "Emotion is any mental experience with high intensity and high hedonic content (pleasure/displeasure)."[272] In this way, emotions are expressions of approval or disapproval of how life is going according to one's affections, desires, or values. Emotions are evidence that all people have a value/moral system written into the very fabric of their nature. Whether it be in relationships, in perceived needs, or in circumstances, everyone must judge and react to all of life according to one's own established values or desires.

---

[272] Michel Cabanac, "What is Emotion?" *Behavioural Processes* 60, no. 2 (2002): 69-83.

Sadly, society in general has accepted biodeterminism as explaining emotions, and even many Christians believe that emotions are a biological experience that a person has no control over and to which he/she is a victim. For example, many people, when they express their anger by yelling, say about their behavior afterward: "That wasn't really me; I am not really an angry person." But, in fact, emotions are revealing the treasures of a person's heart and his/her soul's true nature. Matthew 12:33-35 offers this biblical perspective:

> Either make the tree good and its fruit good, or make the tree bad and its fruit bad, for the tree is known by its fruit. You brood of vipers! How can you speak good, when you are evil? For out of the abundance of the heart the mouth speaks. The good person *out of his good treasure brings forth* [ekballo; emotes or produces] good, and the evil person *out of his evil treasure brings forth* [ekballo; emotes or produces] *evil*. I tell you, on the day of judgment people will give account for every careless word they speak, for by your words you will be justified, and by your words you will be condemned.

What controls a person, according to Scripture, (for good or for bad) is his/her affections/desires. One's "emotions" (that which emotes) allow a person's moral nature to be observed in the physical world; they provide a window into the soul rather than an etiology of a person's problems.

The Heart's Inescapable Morality

It is also helpful to utilize the "emotion" of anger to compare the biblical moral perspective with the biodeterministic view of humanism. When life does not go according to one's desires or lusts, that individual must respond. People may either fight with others in anger or passion, lose passion and become sad, or alternate between both responses as the secular construct of depression acknowledges. James 4:1-5 explains the common human tendency to become angry and fight with others when a person's desires are not realized:

> What causes quarrels and what causes fights among you? Is it not this, that your passions are at war within you? You desire and do not have, so you murder. You covet and cannot obtain, so you fight and quarrel.

According to Scripture, anger, disagreements, fights and even murders are all sourced (*ek*; "out of") in the natural desires (*hēdonōn*; passions) of spiritual hearts. If we have treasures or desires, then we also experience anger and sorrow according to our own value system, fear according to our heart's resources, hope according to our heart's faith, and have guilt according to the law written on our hearts.

One might say, then, that a person's affects produce his/her affections. Good moods and bad moods are not biologically caused, but spiritually produced in accordance with moral desires/treasures; "mood disorders" are literally spiritual heart (*mod*) problems. This truth is also why secularists view depression as *anhedonia* ("diminished interest or loss of pleasure")[273] and mania as *hedonism* ("the pursuit of pleasure or self-indulgence").[274] As a person's heart is crushed, that individual should lose faith in self and what normally interests them. Without the soul's naturally destructive desires being crushed and turned from self-dependence, Christ cannot be established as the highest value and pursuit.

In contrast to Scripture, humanists see anger, hatred, and other negative emotions as being pre-determined abnormalities and sourced in the brain or in genomes. Ronald Pies, Editor and Chief of the *Psychiatric Times*, discusses his shared perspective on

[273] "Depression," *Medscape Psychiatry Online* (August 29, 2018): https://emedicine.medscape.com/article/286759-overview.

[274] A. Gonzalez-Pinto and the Santiago Psychiatric Department, Vitoria Spain, "Dimensions of Mania: Differences between Mixed and Pure Episodes," *European Psychiatry* 5 (August 19, 2004): 307-10.

research—conducted by professor of neurology, neurosurgery, and evolutionary biology at Sandford University, Robert Sapolsky—which allegedly shows that hatred and prejudices are hard-wired into people's brains:

> To be sure, there is substantial evidence that our brains are biologically predisposed to distinguish "Us" from "Them" . . . . Our brains may well predispose us to see "Them" as people to be hated or feared. But these same brains allow us to think and "feel" our way out of that mindset, and to behave with compassion and decency—and, as physicians, to do our duty.[275]

Are people merely mechanical computers that are preprogramed by evolution, or are people souls who are naturally predisposed toward pleasure and self-gratification/esteem? Christians are faced with two opposing moral systems to choose from: either accepting what God says and acknowledging universal depravity and fragility as Genesis 3 establishes, or placing one's faith in man's wisdom and accepting bio-determinism, individual degenerationism, and materialism to explain human nature.

Biodeterminism not only attempts to remove personal responsibility for people's moral emotions, but it also seeks to assuage appropriate guilt. In accordance with this secular perspective, all guilt is viewed as false guilt. If spiritual hearts, however, rather than people's bodies, are responsible for their spiritual condition, then people must also deal with guilt. In this sense, emotions serve as signs of the heart's condition and pursuits but are not the underlying problem, merely the symptom or observable signal. However, if people are only products of their bodies, then there is no morality or guilt, and

---

[275] Ronald Pies, "Are We 'Hardwired' for Hatred?" *Psychiatric Times Online* (December 6, 2018): http://www. psychiatrictimes.com/couch-crisis/are-we-hardwired-hatred/page/0/1?rememberme=1&elq_mid=4742&elq_cid=893295.

social control mechanisms like communism, Nazism, and psychiatry make sense. Dr. Egnor comments,

> Under the visions of Communism and Nazism, we are mere instruments of historical forces, not individual free agents who can choose good or evil. Without free will, we cannot be guilty in an individual sense. But we also cannot be innocent. By contrast, the classical understanding of human nature is that we are free beings not subject to determinism. This understanding is the indispensable basis for human liberty and dignity. It is indispensable, too, for simply making sense of the world around us.[276]

Without some type of moral system, attempting to establish differences between good moods and bad moods is illogical. On the other hand, if people are individually responsible for their moral nature, then everything that enters and comes out of each person's spiritual heart matters. No wonder Proverbs 4:23 admonishes the wise to "keep your heart with all vigilance, for from it flow the springs of life." The word translated *keep* here in Hebrew is also used of guarding a city gate to illustrate how the heart allows wisdom (God's or man's) in and allows responses/behaviors out. Both of these functions of the heart have major impact on the physical nature as well.

The observable bodily changes brought about by mindsets led Charles Darwin, in his book *The Expression of the Emotions in Man and Animals*, to focus on facial expressions as the best way to understand emotions. Though he was ignorant of where emotions were sourced, Darwin realized that these somatic expressions were universal to mankind and communicated a message.[277] Emotions are universal and alter the physical nature, not because of evolution as Darwin theorized, though, but

---

[276] Egnor, "More than Material Minds."

[277] Charles Darwin, *The Expression of the Emotions in Man and Animals* (1872), 3rd edition edited by P. Ekman (New York: Oxford University Press, 1998), 29-30.

because we all have a metaphysical psyche/soul that is created in the image of God and physically revealed in our created temporal bodies. The Bible established that facial expressions reveal the condition of the heart long before Darwin's observation.[278] The Jewish commentator Abraham Cohen offers this insight on Proverbs 15:13: "The heart of a man changeth his countenance, whether it be for good or for evil. A cheerful countenance is a token of a heart that is in prosperity."[279] Good or bad emotions come from the moral heart and are manifested in the physical nature.

Since emotions are always reflections of one's moral condition and affections, the moral law — which God has written on every heart and which produces guilt — is relevant. The fact that people express emotions is evidence that their spiritual hearts function by approving and disapproving (judging) life's experiences. People look on the outward appearance (countenance, words, behaviors, and lifestyles) to judge one's heart, whereas, God looks at the actual spiritual heart.

When Christ preached the Sermon on the Mount (recorded in Matthew 5), He undermined the popular view of that time, which viewed the law as something external that people could choose to behaviorally conform to or act against. Instead, Christ taught that the law is first and foremost a heart issue. In Matthew 5:21, for example, Christ discusses the emotion of anger:

> You have heard that it was said to those of old, "You shall not murder; and whoever murders will be liable to judgment." But I say to you that everyone who is angry with his brother will be liable to judgment.

[278] Proverbs 15:13a, "A glad heart makes a cheerful face." Nehemiah 2:2: "And the King said to me, why is your face sad, seeing you are not sick? This is nothing but sadness of heart."

[279] Cohen, *Proverbs*, 98.

In the same manner, Jesus comments on lust (5:27-28):

> You have heard that it was said, "You shall not commit adultery."
> But I say to you that everyone who looks at a woman to lust after
> her has already committed adultery with her in his heart.

Desires which please God and uphold His moral law produce
corresponding behavior, but desires that reflect one's natural
bent toward pleasing self, produce lawless manifestations.
Anger, sorrow, lust, and every other emotion reflect the moral
heart and not an imposing external force apart from one's
character.

The Heart's Default Position

Scripture declares that all people begin their lives with a
spiritual heart that is morally opposed to God and that pursues
desires that are destructive after the fall of Adam and Eve.
Theologians call this default position moral depravity, but it
could also be referred to as moral-determinism. This natural
moral bent inevitably produces worldly anger, sorrow, and other
emotions accordingly. As already noted, Scripture expects the
unregenerate heart to produce sorrow that leads to death as a
person reacts to fallen life according to their fallen moral nature.

One of the major problems of human depravity that the gospel
remedies is the natural desire to treasure and worship one's self
above all else — our moral starting point. People are skilled at
pleasing themselves and esteeming themselves highly above
God and others (Philippians 2:1-11) — a point already noted in
the construct of bipolar disorders (classified as a "mood
disorder"). When life does not go our way, and it certainly will
not, we find ourselves in distress. Attempting to constantly
change life to fit one's treasures is madness/mania and vanity as
Solomon explains in Ecclesiastes 1-2, and attempting to change
or deny one's treasures by human effort (stoicism) is also
madness and futility. Assuredly, a person cannot genuinely
change his/her emotions to be pleasing to God without a

genuine spiritual heart change by the grace of God (the gospel revealed). Titus 2:11-14 explains,

> For the grace of God has appeared, bringing salvation for all people, *Training* [disciplining or making into disciples] us to *renounce ungodliness and worldly passions*, and to live self-controlled, upright, and godly lives in the present age. *Waiting for our blessed hope*, the appearing of the glory of our great God and Savior Jesus Christ, who gave himself for us to redeem us from all lawlessness and to purify for himself a people for his own possession who are zealous for good works. [Emphasis added.]

Emotions do not control one's character and behavior or make anyone feel hopeless and guilty. Those who do not treasure Christ cannot be expected to have emotions that please God, self-control that the Spirit gifts (Galatians 5:22-23), or genuine hope.

Understanding and accepting God's wisdom about human nature also offers clarity as to why the number of people being diagnosed with so-called mood disorders has increased dramatically over the last four centuries. As society increasingly dismisses God and accepts humanistic values/affections — encouraging mindsets and lifestyles of self-fulfillment and self-focus, moods can only reflect these destructive changes. As God has been devalued and humanity worshiped within a society's moral system (idolatry), people become all the more aware of their anxiety, sorrow, guilt and hopeless/lost state. Ironically, humanist psychologist, Rollo May realized the connection of human vexation with establishing a humanistic value system. He said in 1953,

> It may sound surprising when I say, on the basis of my own clinical practice as well as that of my psychological and psychiatric colleagues, that the chief problem of people in the middle decade of the twentieth century is emptiness . . . . The upshot is that the *values and goals* which provided a unifying center for previous centuries [Judeo-Christian] in the modern period no longer are cogent. We have not yet found the new center which will enable us to choose our goals constructively, and thus to overcome the painful bewilderment and anxiety of not knowing which way to move.

Another root of our malady is our loss of the sense of the worth and dignity of the human being [emphasis added].[280]

In truth, however, the sense of worth and dignity was lost in the Garden of Eden when Satan convinced Adam and Eve that they should regard themselves apart from God and His Word. This loss of viewing themselves in truth — as God's unique creation and in His image, as eternal souls that relate to a Creator rather than as merely evolved particles living for self — is responsible for all people's unsatisfied souls, painful bewilderment, and many vexations. When people naturally suppress the truths about God that are written on their hearts, pursue their own lusts, and worship the creation instead of the Creator, all sorts of wrong and destructive thinking, passions, and behavior result (Romans 1:18-32).

All emotions are undeniable windows into our moral souls. Becoming a disciple of Christ through God's grace allows every person to set aside the naturally destructive godless desires/ treasures, to live self-controlled lives, to be found innocent rather than guilty, and to have genuine hope in this hopeless world. Without a heart change, people are predetermined and predisposed to pursue all that their hearts desire, which is observable in negative emotions/behavior and leads to destruction.

Secularists have transformed the word *emotion* into a social construct that attempts to describe and explain how a person's spiritual heart is revealed in the physical world, and this construct has become a key term in humanistic psychology with much controversy and no valid empirical evidence. If one wishes to call sorrow, guilt, and hopelessness emotions, he/she must

---

[280] Rollo May, *Man's Search for Himself* (New York: W. W. Norton & Company, 1953), 13; 49.

understand that these mindsets and physical manifestations are an honest reflection of everyone's spiritual condition. Emotions are evidence that God created mankind in His own image and are a constant reminder that humanity is degenerate (the bad news). If the human conditions, which secularists have constructed as unipolar and bipolar depressions, must be viewed as mood disorders, then these constructs should be understood as revealing the heart as God describes it to be in Genesis 3 and throughout the Bible. Emotions — whether good or bad — are not forces outside of one's self or biological phenomenon which act apart from one's spiritual nature as secularists and some Christians presume. Instead, emotions are an honest reflection of a person's heart — a picture of what he or she truly treasures/worships.

CHAPTER 7

DISCOVERING GOD'S REMEDY

"The LORD has promis'd good to me,

His Word my hope secures;

He will my shield and portion be as long as life endures.

Yes, when this flesh and heart shall fail,

and mortal life shall cease;

I shall possess, within the veil,

a life of joy and peace."[281]

- John Newton, from "Amazing Grace"

No matter our belief system or field of study, we all agree that those struggling with depression desperately need deliverance from their hopeless condition, guilt, and sorrow, and that hope provides this remedy. Hope goes to the heart and deals with these very real problems by addressing the division between humanity and its maker created at the fall of the first man Adam. The healing of this spiritual separation creates the environment

---

[281] John Newton, "Amazing Grace," *Olney Hymns* (Britain, 1779), stanzas 5-6.

necessary for hope to take root and flourish and for endurance in life to be enabled.

The Humanist's Claims

Leading secular theorists, clinicians, and researchers across all fields of anthropological and medical study understand that hope is essential to remedy the human condition — especially the symptoms framed as depression. For example, former research professor and head of placebo studies at Harvard University Irving Kirsch conducted an investigation and a corresponding controlled study to discover if drugs labeled as antidepressants were effective, and if so, what chemical mechanism underlined their healing effects. After scouring through all the pharmaceutical research both published in prestigious medical journals and those submitted to the FDA without being published, Kirsch realized that the vast majority of studies revealed that the placebo pill (a pill form filled with sugar)[282] was just as effective in clinical trials as these so-called antidepressants for helping people through their depression. He also noted that the majority of documented research which exposes this reality was purposely withheld from the public's knowledge and left unpublished:

> Antidepressants are supposed to work by fixing a chemical imbalance, specifically, a lack of serotonin in the brain. Indeed, their supposed effectiveness is the primary evidence for the chemical imbalance theory. *But analyses of the published data and the unpublished data that were hidden by drug companies reveals that most (if not all) of the benefits are due to the placebo effect* [emphasis added].[283]

[282] For further study on the placebo and nocebo effects and the importance of hope, see Daniel R. Berger II, *Mental Illness: The Reality of the Physical Nature* (Taylors, SC: Alethia International Publications, 2016), 141-51.

[283] Irving Kirsch, "Antidepressants and the Placebo Effect," *Zeitschrift fur Psychologie* 222, no. 3 (2014): 128-34.

Both the placebo and antidepressants work by providing hope.

In his extensive research, not only did Kirsch discover that the chemical imbalance theory was false — a position now widely recognized, but he also decided to conduct his own controlled studies to better understand if the powerful drugs which so many people consume are truly antidepressants. More specifically, Kirsch and his Harvard University research team sought to know if these psychotropic drugs healed depression through their chemical processes, or whether these chemicals were helping assuage depression through factors apart from their physical nature and the drugs' chemical actions.

As with most pharmaceutical testing and research, Kirsch utilized the placebo study, and his experiments confirmed time and again that a sugar pill is just as therapeutic in relieving depression as the drugs framed as antidepressants. The reason, he explains, is that the framing of these drugs as healing medicines provides hope:

> Whereas hopelessness is a central feature of depression, hope lies at the core of the placebo effect. Placebos instill hope in patients by promising them relief from their distress. Genuine medical treatments also instill hope, and this is the placebo component of their effectiveness. *When the promise of relief instills hope, it counters a fundamental attribute of depression. Indeed, it is difficult to imagine any treatment successfully treating depression without reducing the sense of hopelessness that depressed people feel. Conversely, any treatment that reduces hopelessness must also assuage depression.* So a convincing placebo ought to relieve depression. [Emphases added.][284]

This same type of controlled study has been repeated time and again and has consistently yielded the same result, thus influencing most educated psychiatrists to deny or abandon the

---

[284] Irving Kirsch, *The Emperor's New Drugs: Exploding the Antidepressant Myth* (New York: Basic Books, 2011), preface 3.

notion of chemical imbalances altogether.[285] But the damage has been done to the extent that a great portion of society still believes that drugs like *selective serotonin reuptake inhibitors* (SSRIs) are valid medicines that treat an alleged chemical imbalance responsible for sadness.

Empirical evidence confirms that the syndrome of depression is significantly helped with faith that produces some type of hope and that the therapeutic benefit of antidepressants is not their chemical structure but their dose of metaphysical hope. Notably, the undeniable power of faith to heal even the physical body has caused hardened materialists, such as Ted Kaptchuk current head of placebo studies at Harvard and administrator at Beth Israel Deaconess Medical Center as well as Dr. Franklin Miller of the NIH, to recognize faith's importance in medicine:

> Research has revealed placebo effects [the power of faith and hope] to be genuine biopsychosocial phenomena representing more than simply spontaneous remission or normal symptom fluctuations.[286]

The secular scientific community — though they deny dualism — cannot discuss healing the body within a medical context without also considering the reality and necessity of faith and hope.

But secularists still do not want to view faith and hope as a metaphysical reality and frame them only as a reality accessible by the senses and within science. For example, Scientific Director of the Imagination Institute in the Positive Psychology Center at the University of Pennsylvania, Scott Barry Kaufman, comments on hope's importance: "Science is on the side of hope. . . .

[285] Pies, "Psychiatry's New Brain-Mind and the Legend of the 'Chemical Imbalance.'"

[286] Ted J. Kaptchuk and Franklin G. Miller, "Placebo Effects in Medicine," *The New England Journal of Medicine* 373 (July 2, 2015): 8.

Whether measured as a trait or a state [of mind], hope is related to positive outcomes.[287] Scientific evidence is on the side of hope, but hope — that which is not seen but in which a person places his/her faith (Hebrews 12:1) — cannot be approached through scientific processes alone. In reality, the placebo effect is a scientific way of describing a metaphysical feature of human nature (a noumena) that cannot be denied because of its powerful physical effects (phenomena). Attempting to frame faith and hope as material realities makes them appear to be approachable with science. But only the effects of faith and hope can be observed and measured, and they are so powerful that secularists can no longer deny faith's relevance to spiritual and physical health. Dr. Candace Pert of the NIH remarks,

> [Patients] are here because they need to have hope . . . . They know I've been on the cutting edge with my research, crossing disciplines and researching for breakthroughs in cancer, AIDS, mental illness. I always feel a little nervous when I see them sitting in my audience. Are they expecting me to deliver their miracle cure like a preacher at a revival meeting? Hope is a dirty, rarely uttered word in the circles I frequent, and it still tugs uncomfortably at my self-image as a scientist. To think I'm being viewed as a healer — God forbid, a faith healer! Yet I can't ignore the expressions of desperation and suffering that I see on their faces.[288]

Science cannot explain how or why metaphysical faith alters human nature, but scientists know well that it does and that hope is a necessity of all people.

If faith, which is foundational to any hope, can alter the physical nature, what do faith and hope do to the spiritual nature? Senior scientist at Gallup and humanist author of the 2013 book *Making*

---

[287] Scott Barry Kaufman, "The Will and Ways of Hope," *Psychology Today Online* (December 26, 2011): https://www. psychologytoday.com/us/blog/beautiful-minds/201112/the-will-and-ways-hope.

[288] Pert, *Molecules of Emotion*, 15.

Hope Happen: Create the Future You Want for Yourself and Others,
Shane Lopez states,

> How we think about the future — *how we hope* — determines how well
> we live our lives. . . . Our relationship with the future determines
> how well we live today. [289]

Lopez continues,

> Although some people still believe that hope is too "soft" to study
> scientifically, other researchers and I have convincing evidence that
> hopeful thoughts and behavior propel everyone toward well-being
> and success; that hope underlies purpose-driven action.[290]

Hope and purpose, though, better fit into the category of
philosophy and religion rather than science. Yet, each of these
materialists acknowledges that one's metaphysical nature alters
his/her physical nature and observable lives and that hope is the
key to success and establishing drive and purpose. This
understanding, however, denies the scientism to which they
cling.

The amount of available research showing how hope is central to
what secularists categorize as emotional distress and bad moods
and how hope is both preventative and healing for what they
claim as depression is overwhelming. For example, one group of
medical researchers explains their own findings:

> Possessing hope and resilience positively affect mood and
> functioning. Hope and resilience have been associated with better
> physical and mental health outcomes in undergraduates as well as
> better health and well-being and lower psychological distress in
> adults. In addition, Ryden, et al. found that resilience is a protective
> factor against depression and the impact of stress. Gooding, et al.
> indicated that higher levels of hope countered the negative effects of

---

[289] Shane J. Lopez, *Making Hope Happen: Create the Future You Want for
Yourself and Others* (NY: Simon & Shuster, 2014), 9-10.

[290] Ibid., 11.

depression on resilience related to emotional regulation. Additionally, patients who report higher levels of hope and resilience are less likely to show mood disturbances and tend to possess higher self-esteem. By contrast, low levels of hope have been associated with depression.[291]

As these findings acknowledge, both the physical and metaphysical natures are altered with the presence of hope. Professor, researcher, and editor and chief of the *Archives and Neurology and Psychiatry*, Dr. Harold Wolff, stated in 1957 that

hope, like faith and a purpose in life, is medicinal. This is not merely a statement of belief, but a conclusion proved by meticulously controlled scientific experiment.[292]

While Dr. Wolff understands the power of hope, he — like most every other materialist — fails to realize that faith is the substance of things hoped for and that having hope and purpose are not disconnected. Psychiatrist Peter Breggin also realizes that people who see no hope in the future or who believe themselves to be defeated rightly fit into a diagnosis of depression:

Depression is more common everywhere that choices and opportunities are stifled, and where people are taught that they do not deserve or cannot achieve anything.[293]

After rigorous studies and well-documented research, the American Psychological Association concluded in its book, *The Heart and Soul of Change: What Works in Therapy*, that the efficacy realized in the 200+ types of psychotherapies rests not in the

[291] Devika Duggal, Amanda Sacks-Zimmerman, and Taylor Liberta, "The Impact of Hope and Resilience on Multiple Factors in Neurosurgical Patients," *Cureus*, 8(10) (2016): e849. doi:10.7759/cureus.849.

[292] Harold G. Wolff, "What Hope Can Do for Man," *Saturday Review*, 40 (1957), 42.

[293] Breggin, *Anti-Depressant Fact Book*, 16.

various techniques or approaches but primarily in establishing hope:

> Research confirms the importance of hope and expectation in psychotherapy. Already potent ways for therapists to facilitate hope and positive expectations for change have been presented (i.e., forming strong therapeutic relationships, identifying goals, and incorporating client's strengths into the treatment). The suggestions and 'techniques' now sampled possess no special curative powers on their own. Instead, their value resides in the extent to which they facilitate hope and a positive expectation for change.[294]

Hope, even false hope, assuages depression, since within its metaphysical fabric is the promise of salvation from one's condition of hopelessness, guilt, and sorrow. Establishing goals and purpose, authoritative and caring relationships, therapeutic promises, and patient expectations are all a part of extending hope that will help those who feel hopeless. But false temporal hope, while it may help for a time, will inevitably fail and cause greater damage and destruction.

Whether one prefers the medical model to understand, approach, and attempt to remedy depression or, instead, accepts the biblical worldview, both perspectives recognize that supplying hope is necessary to treat people who have become aware of their hopeless condition. But what differs drastically between these two perspectives is the assertion of what constitutes valid and reliable hope and where it can be found.

False Hopes

Whereas Scripture presents a clear and singular hope, secularists have numerous theories and subsequent objects of hope to choose from. But as we will see, it is not just having hope in this life that is needed; hope in an immutable truth that extends beyond this life and offers eternal security is vitally important.

---

[294] Hubble, Duncan, and Miller, *Heart and Soul of Change,* 418.

Unfortunately, people are skilled at both creating and accepting false hopes which cannot save humanity from their hopelessness, sorrow, guilt, and spiritual struggles. Within secular thinking, various models of hope exist, but the most widely acclaimed are based upon the humanistic idea that people create their own particular hope from within themselves. The preferred popular humanistic model or concept of hope was developed by C.R. Snyder,[295] author of the book *The Psychology of Hope: You Can Get There from Here.* It is in his book *Handbook of Hope: Theory, Measures, and Applications*[296] that his basic model is presented. Snyder (and humanists in general) defines hope as an "energy" or mindset that (1) believes in one's self (humanistic agency), (2) is able to establish goals (purpose), (3) figures out "pathways" (means), and (4) overcomes barriers in order to attain desired goals (resilience/endurance).[297] From these humanistic "characteristics of hope" was developed "the hope scale" in attempt to measure how hopeful people are when they enter a clinic for help and to measure their perceived progress. Psychologist Scott Barry Kaufman explains this popular position:

> Simply put: Hope involves the will to get there, and different ways to get there. *Why is hope important? Well, life is difficult.* There are many obstacles. Having goals is not enough. One has to keep getting closer to those goals, amidst all the inevitable twists and turns of life. Hope allows people to approach problems with a mindset and strategy-set suitable to success, thereby increasing the chances they will actually accomplish their goals. *Hope is not just a feel-good good emotion, but a dynamic cognitive motivational system.* Under this conceptualization of hope, *emotions follow cognitions,* not the other

[295] Hubble, Duncan, Miller, *The Heart and Soul of Change,* 267.

[296] C.R. Snyder, *Handbook of Hope: Theory, Measures, and Applications* (San Diego: Academic Press, 2000).

[297] Http://positivepsychology.org.uk/hope-theory-snyder-adult-scale/.

way around. Hope-related cognitions are important. [Emphases added.][298]

Kaufman notes several biblical truths concerning hope, though he denies Scripture's authority. Hope is necessary because life is difficult—or as Scripture states: life is full of sorrows and vexations. Kaufman also points out an important truth relating to emotions and the previous chapter's discussion: people's mindsets precede their emotions. How people view themselves, God, those around them, and life itself determines their emotional responses and behaviors. Having right hope establishes desires, purpose in life, direction, motivation, emotions, and fulfillment of goals.

But Kaufman, utilizing Snyder's model, also promotes belief in humanism that displaces God and exults mankind. As aforementioned, faith is the substance of all things hoped for. The humanistic model is founded on two faith agents: internal and external objects of faith. The first agent is faith in oneself—a faith that encourages people to look inward in order to find or create hope and obtain goals. This wrong perspective is used in most psychotherapies; it has created claims of reliability, and it is seen as a valid pathway to achieve happiness and discover meaning in life. This hope is limited to both the person's abilities and to his/her temporal life. But as previously noted, a crushed spirit is one that acknowledges that turning inward for strength and deliverance will not work.

Therefore, another agent of hope is necessary within humanistic thinking. The second agent of humanistic hope is an external faith in something that is temporal or allows a continuous pursuit in this life. These external mechanisms include countless self-help cures for depression which focus on the senses and physical health (e.g., take this pill, follow this diet, do this

[298] Kaufman, "The Will and Ways of Hope."

exercise, move your eyes back and forth, drink this mix, smell these scents, repeat these sayings, etc.). These and many other suggestions of external hope are at their core a hope in science (scientism) and the medical model; they are practical applications of the gospel of humanism and materialism.

Assertions of various inward and outward hopes abound, and most of these so-called hopes come packaged with claims of scientific reliability and empirical evidence which suggest that they work. These claims further people's faith in these suggested hopes as well as in materialism, but they only sustain false hopes that cannot truly deliver a people from their brokenness.

In reality, it is not the techniques, the experience, the substance, or the application that is therapeutic as is regularly claimed. Instead, the supplying of hope—a hope that cannot genuinely and permanently remedy hopelessness—explains these many accepted treatments for depression. The list of temporal hopes that eventually fail include but is certainly not limited to: special diets,[299] psychoactive drugs, psychedelic drugs, psychotherapies,[300] exposure to sunlight or blue light,[301] physical exercise,[302] special oils,[303] unique drinks,[304] forms of

[299] Mark L. Fuerst, "3 New Studies About Depression," *Psychiatric Times Online* (October 18, 2018): http://www.psychiatrictimes.com/ major-depressive-disorder/3-new-studies-about-depression-and-lifestyle. See also Amanda Macmillan, "Mental Health: A New Understanding," *Time Magazine* Special Edition (November, 2018), 66-67.

[300] Hubble, Duncan, and Miller, *Heart and Soul of Change.*

[301] Amanda Macmillan, "Mental Health: A New Understanding," *Time Magazine* Special Edition (November, 2018), 64.

[302] Ibid.

hypnoses,[305] vitamins,[306] electric shock treatment,[307] tapping on the body,[308] and countless other hopes based upon the humanistic doctrines of materialism and individual degenerationism that exist and will be suggested for decades to come. All of these popular treatments share the common element of hope, which provides their vendors/distributors with empirical evidence for claiming their efficacy. But some of them are not as simple as sugar pills; some are quite elaborate and/or affect the physical body in extremely harmful ways.

At times, some doctors utilize the power of placebo by performing medical procedures while knowing full well that no

[303] Hannah Nichols, "Can Essential Oils Treat Depression?" *Medical News Today Online* (December 3, 2018): https://www.medicalnews today.com/articles/315481.php.

[304] Plexus VitalBiome, "Healthy Gut. Happy Mind," *Plexus*: https://plexusworldwide.com/product/plexus-vitalbiome.

[305] EMDR Institute, "What is EMDR?" *EMDR*: http://www.emdr.com/what-is-emdr/.

[306] Daniel K. Hall-Flavin, "Vitamin B-12 and Depression: Are they related?" *The Mayo Clinic Online* (December 2018): https://www.mayo clinic.org/diseases-conditions/depression/expert-answers/vitamin-b12-and-depression/faq-20058077.

[307] Charles H Kellner and Max Fink, "ECT for Catatonia and Melancholia: No Need for Ambivalence," *Psychiatric Times Online* Vol. 34 (9) (September 28, 2017): http://www.psychiatrictimes.com/depression/ect-catatonia-and-melancholia-no-need-ambivalence.

[308] Dawson Church, "You Don't Have to be Depressed! Science Shows EFT Tapping Successfully Treats Depression," EFT Universe: https://www.eftuniverse.com/depression/depression.

medical benefit exists for the physical surgery itself.[309] In one particular study conducted at the world-renowned research center at McGill University, a non-functional MRI was used as a prop to study the power of suggestion to heal mental conditions framed as psychiatric disorders. The children who were studied were told that the MRI would heal them, and over the course of treatments all the children came to believe that it did. But there was no medicinal benefit to the fake MRI; it was, as the host stated, "faith in science—the power of thoughts to heal"[310] that delivered the children from their poor thinking and bad behavior. The power of metaphysical hope to alter the physical and spiritual nature is undeniable and explains why hopeless people can have temporary relief from their hopelessness by accepting any number of false hopes. False hopes do relieve depression for a time, but they cannot genuinely heal anyone's human condition.

Psychoactive/Psychotropic Drugs

Many people believe that the solution to depression is psychotropic drugs commonly known as antidepressants.[311] These drugs are widely accepted and used, but a growing number of humanistic psychiatrists and physicians question their effectiveness and safety. For example, psychiatrist, biomedical researcher, and director of translational medicine-neuroscience at Novartis Institutes—the second leading pharmaceutical company in 2018 based on sales, Nassir Ghaemi

---

[309] Beryl Lieff Benderly, "Placebo Effect Stronger Than We Thought," *Pacific Standard Online* (January 4, 2012): https://psmag.com/social-justice/placebo-effect-stronger-than-we-thought-38717.

[310] "The Power of Suggestion," *Mind Field* S2 E6: https://www.youtube.com/watch?v=sMWoyAUrxcM.

[311] For a more detailed discussion, see *Mental Illness: The Necessity for Dependence,* volume 5.

confesses the scientific nature of psychopharmacology and the chemical imbalance theory of depression:

> 20th century treatment is the giving of pills for symptoms, augmented by the giving of counseling for everything. If depressed, give antidepressant; if anxious, give anxiolytic; if labile or psychotic, give neuroleptic; if insomniac, give sedative; if cognitively impaired, give amphetamine. *And we justify this highly simplistic symptom-based approach with a pseudoscience of neurotransmitters* going up or down based on animal studies which are hardly proven or disproven or unclearly related to the human conditions we are treating. *Our best-selling psychopharmacology textbook consists of pure speculations* presented as pretty pictures with color-coded synapses, and key-lock receptors and chemicals, which we mistake for science. . . . *We have a huge amount of neurobiology research now to conclude that the 20th century neurotransmitter theories of psychopharmacology basically are false. The dopamine and monoamine hypotheses of schizophrenia and depression are wrong, and thus using our drug classes to increase or decrease neurotransmitters is wrong-headed* [emphasis added].[312]

Dr. Peter Breggin proposes his conclusions:

> The term "antidepressant" should always be thought of with quotation marks around it because there is little or no reason to believe that these drugs target depression or depressed feelings. In fact, I find considerable evidence that these drugs have little or no therapeutic effect on feelings of depression.[313]

Psychiatrist Joanna Moncrieff, who serves as the senior lecturer for the Department of Mental Health Sciences at the University College London, offers her own criticism. Moncrieff has published numerous articles and books on this subject, including *The Myth of the Chemical Cure*, which emphasizes that no drug exists which can cure the human condition:

> This book exposes the traditional view that psychiatric drugs target underlying diseases, or correct chemical imbalances, as fraud. It

---

[312] Ghaemi, "One Step Back, Two Steps Forward."

[313] Breggin, *Anti-Depressant Fact Book*, 14.

traces the emergence of this view and suggest that it was adopted not because there was any evidence to support it, but because it served the vested interest of the psychiatric profession, the pharmaceutical industry and the modern state.[314]

These powerful drugs and other material substances and practices can offer false hope, but no drug exists to assuage guilt, or to provide joy and genuine lasting hope.

The therapeutic benefits that SSRIs, SNRIs, and other so-called antidepressants provide are (1) blunting feelings by suppressing a person's awareness, (2) offering hope of healing, and (3) allowing those who have not slept because of their distress to sleep better. These benefits do not address depression; they simply cover up the struggle by suppressing or chemically dehumanizing the individual so that they do not have to consider their true condition. Psychiatrist Joanna Moncrieff explains,

> The emotional detachment produced by selective serotonin reuptake inhibitors (SSRIs) and similar drugs may reduce or blunt negative emotions, so people will rate themselves as less depressed. The sedative effects of the tricyclic antidepressants can improve sleep and reduce anxiety. Since these factors feature prominently in depression-measuring scales, these effects will produce an apparent improvement in depression, despite the fact that there may be no change in the individual's actual mood (although of course feeling less anxious and sleeping better might improve one's mood too).[315]

But drugs which psychiatrists claim to be antidepressants, within their chemical properties, are not healing anything. In fact, they work by attacking or working against healthy function

---

[314] Joanna Moncrieff, *The Myth of the Chemical Cure: A Critique of Psychiatric Drug Treatment* (New York: Palgrave Macmillan, 2008), book summary: https://joannamoncrieff.com/upcoming-talks/.

[315] Joanna Moncrieff, "Why There's No Such Thing as an 'Antidepressant,'" November 27, 2013, https://joannamoncrieff. com/2013 /11/27/why-theres-no-such-thing-as-an-antidepressant/.

of the nervous system and suppressing mental awareness — they are antagonists. Former chief of brain biochemistry at the NIH, Candace Pert, discusses these dangerous drugs' true action,

> As a researcher on the drug frontier for over twenty years, I have to depart from the opinion of most of my colleagues in the mainstream ["medical model"] and say that less is best. The implications of my research are that all exogenous drugs [such as antidepressants] are potentially harmful to the system, not only as disrupters of the natural balance of the feedback loops involving many systems and organs, but because of the changes that happen at the level of the receptor. Each of us has his or her own natural pharmacopoeia — the very finest drugstore available at the cheapest cost — to produce all the drugs we ever need to run our bodymind in precisely the way it was designed.[316]

Pert notes that the body responds naturally and produces or blocks chemicals based upon how one is thinking. The drug action of "antidepressants" is, ironically, to depress the nervous system by blocking selective neurotransmitter reuptake. People allegedly feel better because their ability to feel is suppressed by the drug.

But the drug's suppressing effects and the false hope they offer regularly wear off and leave the hopeless and sorrowful person in a worse mental and physical state. In her report to the annual congress of the European College of Neuropsychopharmology in 2017, researcher Markku Lähteenvuo admitted about these powerful drugs, "We were actually surprised to find that SSRIs and other antidepressants aren't really very effective at keeping depressed patients out of [the] hospital."[317] It is hope, and not

---

[316] Pert, *Molecules of Emotion*, 271.

[317] Markku Lähteenvuo quoted by Bruce Jancin, "Rethinking Lithium: It keeps patients with unipolar depression out of the hospital," *Clinical Psychiatry News Online* (October 29, 2017): https://www.mdedge.com/psychiatry/article /150510/ depression/rethinking-lithium-it-keeps-patients-unipolar-depression-out.

the chemicals or drug's action in "antidepressants" and placebos alike which offers the primary benefit to its struggling consumer. Dr. Pam Harrison discusses this reality in *Medscape Journal Online*:

> People's expectations about how effective their antidepressant medication is going to be almost entirely predicts their response to it, such that giving patients a placebo pill as active therapy during an 8-week period results in very similar reductions in symptoms.[318]

Chair of the *DSM-IV* task force Allen Frances discloses,

> There is another historical precedent — a much older one going back all the way to shaman times. The wisdom of the ages is that whenever they feel bad, people want to take something to feel better. The five-thousand-year-old mummified man, wonderfully preserved in the ice of the Alps, was carrying his little bag of plant medicine — the Prozac of his day. As we have seen, most medicine taken for most illnesses, most of the time, since the dawn of time, has at best been of very little specific help, usually has been completely inert, and very often has been directly harmful, even poisonous. But shamans, priests, and doctors prescribed them and patients dutifully took them and seemed to benefit. The magic of medication manages to survive its ineffectuality and potential harm. The popularity of placebo seems to be built into our DNA.[319]

Researcher at Harvard University, Irving Kirsch, published his own findings in a German psychiatric journal in 2014:

> Some antidepressants increase serotonin levels, some decrease it, and some have no effect at all on serotonin. Nevertheless, they all show the same therapeutic benefit. Even the small statistical difference between antidepressants and placebos may be an enhanced placebo effect, due to the fact that most patients and doctors in clinical trials successfully break blind. *The serotonin theory is as close as any theory in the history of science to having been proved wrong. Instead of curing depression, popular antidepressants may induce a*

---

[318] Pam Harrison, "Patient Expectations Largely Dictate Antidepressant Response," *Medscape Online* (September 15, 2014): https://www.medscape.com/viewarticle/831689.

[319] Frances, *Saving Normal*, 156.

biological vulnerability making people more likely to become depressed in the future [emphasis added].[320]

As Breggin, Moncrieff, and Kirsch note, "antidepressants" is a misnomer, since these drugs are not healing mechanisms, and they regularly worsen a person's condition. The reason is simple: hopelessness is one of the underlying struggles of depression, and both temporary hope and dehumanization through chemical suppression are the true therapeutic substances in psychoactive drugs. When the hope of "antidepressants" is realized to be false, the person is left in a worse hopeless state of mind. Pharmaceutical companies market and psychiatrists assert that antidepressants are the best and most reliable available treatment for depression. When their best available hope fails, what hope is left within a medical framework?

But more and more influential psychiatrists admit that research reveals how alleged antidepressants create a resistance to healing rather than being a mechanism of health. Psychiatrist James Phelps, for example, noted in 2017 that "the more antidepressants [prescribed and consumed], the lower the change of response or remission."[321]

Considering the attack on the nervous system and the false hope that "antidepressants" provide, it is no surprise to learn that these powerful mind-altering drugs increase suicidal ideation. So much so, that the Federal Drug Administration requires the black box warning to be printed on all prescribed "antidepressant" labels:[322]

[320] Kirsch, "Antidepressants and the Placebo Effect," 128-34.

[321] James Phelps, "Might Antidepressants Create Treatment Resistance? *Psychiatric Times Online* (April 11, 2017): http://www.psychiatrictimes.com/depression/might-antidepressants-create-treatment-resistance.

[322] See Berger, *Necessity for Dependence*, 159-66.

In 2004, the FDA issued a black box warning for all antidepressants indicating an association with an increased risk of suicidal thinking, feeling, and behavior in young individuals . . . . According to the package labeling for antidepressants, patients of all ages who are started on antidepressant therapy should be monitored closely for emergence and worsening of suicidal thoughts and behaviors.[323]

False hopes do not just fail, but as with mania, they also leave the consumer with less hope and further promote sorrow that leads to spiritual and physical death.

Psychedelic Drugs

The clear failure of psychoactive drugs to treat depression has forced many secular theorists to turn to alternative and new hopes. One of the most controversial and debated new hopes is psychedelic drugs. Well-known psychedelic drugs, such as LSD, ketamine, psilocin, MDMA, DMT, and noribogaine are all being studied for their potential, and secularists are hopeful that a synthetic version of these drugs can soon be manufactured and sold as the new hope for depression and trauma. Researcher at University of California (Davis), David Olson explains:

"Mood and anxiety disorders are some of the leading causes of disability worldwide," says Olson. "We need to use every tool at our disposal — including psychedelics — *to better understand the fundamental neurobiology of these diseases,* so we can help those who are suffering [emphasis added]."[324]

[323] Timothy O'Shea, "10 Black Box Warnings Every Pharmacist Should Know," *Pharmacy Times Online* (March 14, 2016): https://www.pharmacy times.com/contributor/timothy-o-shea/2016/03/10-black-box-warnings-every-pharmacist-should-know?p=5.

[324] David E. Olson quoted by Katherina Lindemann, "Psychedelic Drugs Could Inspire New Medications to Treat Depression and Anxiety," *Research Gate Online* (June 12, 2018): https://www.researchgate.net/blog/post/psychedelic-drugs-could-inspire-new-medications-to-treat-depression-and-anxiety.

Reductionists continue to justify their own assumptions and dogmatic assertions that depression is a disease and that searching for physical and/or chemical remedies is a necessity. As Olson's comments convey, asserting mind-altering drugs as medicines does more for sustaining the false belief that depression is a neurobiological disease than it does to heal the metaphysical problems of sorrow, hopelessness, guilt, and the spiritual heart's many struggles.

Since psychotropic drugs are unable to truly treat depression or any of the soul's problems, humanists must now look for a replacement means of supplying hope to those in need. But secular theorists and researchers alike are unwilling to replace the false philosophy of materialism itself and consider a proven metaphysical solution. The new proposed replacement theory, which will likely secure funds for research and eventually produce a synthetic version of a naturally found psychedelic substance, is the theory that the brain can be fixed by supplying euphoric experiences through the use of psychedelic drugs. Ketamine, one of the most-favored psychedelic drugs, creates a sense of euphoria and offers false hope in the form of a spiritual experience to its consumer:

> Another arc to the ketamine story dates back to a decades-old era of psychedelic research and search for medications with transformative power. Indeed, although primarily conceptualized today as a dissociative anesthetic, ketamine has also been classified more broadly as a hallucinogen. *Hallucinogens function by various pharmacological mechanisms of action but exhibit similarities in their ability to occasion temporary but profound alterations of consciousness,* involving acute changes in somatic, perceptual, cognitive, and affective processes. *Current biological theories involving ketamine's antidepressant effect may be inseparable from these non-ordinary experiences of consciousness* [transcendence, "to go beyond normal"] [emphasis added].[325]

[325] David S. Mathai, Matthew J. Sanjay, Eric A Storch, and Thomas Kosten, "A Case Built on Current Research Findings," *Psychiatric Times Online* 35, no. 6

In many ways, ketamine and other psychedelic drugs are chemically induced manic episodes which attempt to provide pleasurable and euphoric experiences whereby the consumer can theoretically escape sorrow.

Psychoactive and psychedelic drugs further highlight that the ancient shaman and the modern psychiatrist share the same destructive philosophies and practices. If trauma or life's burdens cause negative neurological changes, the theory is that supplying euphoric and altered states of consciousness should heal those biological impairments. In a biological explanation, if researchers can heal the atrophied neurites in the brain, induced by sorrow and trauma, or new neurites can be grown through a euphoric experience, then secularists can sustain hope that the brain and ultimately depression will be healed:

> The next step will be to determine whether the psychedelics' ability to stimulate growth is linked to their hallucinogenic properties. "Our ultimate goal is to engineer a drug that side steps the hallucinations while still producing the desired effects on *neural plasticity* [the brain's ability to heal]."[326]

But both Scripture and neuroscience agree that offering good news and hope produces desired and healing neural plasticity. People do not need to chemically or electrically address the side-effects of atrophied brains when they can receive genuine healing through safe and effective means. Therapies such as electroconvulsive therapy (ECT), transcranial magnetic stimulation (TMS), and eye movement desensitization and reprocessing (EMDR), like psychoactive and psychedelic drugs, provide temporary false hopes and faith in the medical model and materialism. Many of these also destroy the nervous system or are easily traced back to shamanism.

(June 26, 2018): http://www.psychiatrictimes.com/depression/revisiting-hallucinogenic-potential-ketamine.

[326] Olson quoted by Katherina Lindemann, "Psychedelic Drugs."

These secular ideas of hope cannot truly heal the soul, though their placebo effects can certainly make positive changes in one's thinking and in the brain's structure. However, treating the physical symptoms that hopelessness and sorrow produce via material means does not prove that depression is physically caused or even that physical remedies that address the core issues of depression actually exist.

Biblical Hope

Because the Bible presents sorrow, hopelessness, guilt, and trials as normal aspects of fallen nature, it also addresses how we should deal with them. The Bible does not just describe the fallen state with clarity, but also establishes the only genuine and reliable hope able to deliver people's souls. Discovering this hope, though, requires that one first accept both that God created mankind as an embodied spirit as well as the moral view of human nature established in Genesis 3. Dr. Martyn Lloyd-Jones once proclaimed,

> We do not begin to understand the New Testament doctrine of "the hope" until we realize that this present world is completely under condemnation.[327]

"The hope" which delivers humanity from its brokenness that Dr. Lloyd-Jones references is not merely possessing hope or establishing just any hope. What people need is a sure hope—a hope that genuinely saves people from their fallen and condemned state. As Dr. Breggin understands, "There is no substitute for confronting how and why our lives have become so depressing to us."[328] While each person has his/her own story

[327] Martyn Lloyd-Jones, *Studies in the Sermon on the Mount* (1959). Reprint (Grand Rapids, MI: Inter-Varsity Press, 2000), 112.

[328] Breggin, *Anti-Depressant Fact Book*, 25.

as to why he/she is struggling with deep sorrow and feelings of guilt, all stories are born out of the history of Adam and Eve in Genesis 3. It is at this historical fall that human lives became so depressed, vexed, and condemned. Everyone living apart from Christ is hopeless, experiences sorrow and vexation, and has a price to pay for his/her own moral failures, as each one's own heart confirms. All people share the same broken condition whether or not they wish to acknowledge this truth.

There is a model of genuine hope presented in Scripture, but it is not a system or a temporal hope that people can generate within themselves or create by their own efforts. Instead, the Bible offers Jesus Christ as the model or agent of hope — the only one who both endured severe sorrow and also provided the perfect sacrifice to pay for the sins of His people.

The Reliability of Genuine Hope

Though leading secular researchers are well aware of how beneficial faith in God is to the soul on this side of eternity, they must suppress this truth in order to maintain the medical model of mental illness. Former president of the Royal College of Psychiatrists, Andrew Sims, offers his own confession:

> What I have written is an attempt to portray the difficulties between psychiatry and Christian faith. . . . The advantageous effect of religious belief [Christianity] and spirituality on mental and physical health is one of the best-kept secrets in psychiatry and medicine generally. If the findings of the huge volume of research on this topic had gone in the opposite direction and it had been found that religion damages your mental health, it would have been front-page news in every newspaper in the land![329]

Dr. Breggin also remarks,

> The individual in a *euphoric or manic state* is an extreme challenge to clinicians who do not want to involuntarily hospitalize patients or to

[329] Sims, *Is Faith Delusion*, preface xi.

use drugs as chemical restraints. In the era of Moral Therapy in the 18th and 19th century, *these individuals were successfully treated* without resort to drugs in genuine asylums that provided round-the-clock monitoring, caring social interactions, and moral support, *often in the form of religious persuasion.*[330]

After comparing the results of counseling done from a biblical perspective with secular *cognitive behavioral therapy* (CBT) and other types of counseling in treating depression, a research team of leading psychologists overseen by former president of the American Psychology Association, John Norcross, concluded that

> Clients in both religious CBT [Cognitive Behavioral Therapy] and PCT [Person Centered Therapy] reported significantly lower post-treatment depression and better social adjustment than did clients in either the nonreligious CBT or WLC [wait list conditions] . . . . While clients in all the treatments decreased in depression, the least effective condition was the nonreligious therapists doing standard CBT. . . . The Christian [treatment] complemented standard RET [Rational Emotive Therapy] by using Christian beliefs to dispute irrational beliefs, encouraged the use of Christian imagery homework, and utilized brief prayer in session. At post-treatment, both treatments had reduced client's depression and automatic negative thoughts, while the Christian therapy was also effective in reducing clients' irrational beliefs (but standard RET was not).[331]

Research, also published by the American Psychology Association, shows the power and importance of religious faith and hope to remedy valid physical illnesses:

> The loss of hope — hopelessness — has been associated with health complications and poor treatment outcomes. For example, hopelessness has been related to greater tumor progression and earlier death among cancer patients, and to increased morbidity and

---

[330] Peter Breggin, *Psychiatric Drug Withdrawal* (New York: Springer Publishing, 2013), 177.

[331] John Norcross, Everett L. Worthington Jr., and Steven J. Sandage, *Psychotherapy Relationships That Work: Therapist Contributions and Responsiveness to Patients* (New York: Oxford University Press, 2002), 392.

mortality from ischemic heart disease. In a related study, Oxman, Freeman, and Manheimer (1995) examined the relationship between response to cardiac surgery and religious conviction, recognizing the powerful experience of hope and optimism that religious faith affords patients confronting serious illness. Even after controlling for the effects of prior surgical history, presurgical functional impairment, and age, Oxman et al. found that the absence of strength and comfort in religion was related to risk for death during the 6 months postsurgery.[332]

Metaphysical hope is spiritually and physically healing.

Scripture also speaks to the reliability of faith in Christ to produce genuine saving hope. Though many view Hebrews 11 as the "hall of faith," the passage of Scripture should also be regarded as the "hall of hope," as it emphasizes the reliability of biblical hope. The *New Living Translation* highlights this truth (34b-35b): "Their weakness was turned to strength. . . . They placed their hope in a better life after the resurrection." The last verses in the chapter declare further (39-40),

> And all these, though commended through their faith, did not receive what was promised, since God had provided something better for us, that apart from us they should not be made perfect.

Biblical hope does not falsely anticipate deliverance from weaknesses on this side of eternity. Instead, reliable hope longs for the full deliverance and restoration which occurs in eternity. Such hope supernaturally turns human fragility — such as sorrow — into strengths and accomplishments observed in the hall of hope (Hebrews 11).

Not only is history full of examples that reveal the Bible's ability to deliver people from their hopeless condition, but also biblical counselors today are witnessing great numbers of people shedding psychiatric labels and finding genuine help and deliverance for their many vexations and struggles in the hope

[332] Hubble, Duncan, and Miller, *Heart and Soul of Change,* 267.

of the gospel of Jesus Christ. As the aforementioned secularists and many others attest, the Bible through the supernatural work of the only God of hope is fully able to restore the soul to mental health and turn weaknesses into eternal values.

If people desire genuine hope for their true fallen state — what secularists have framed as depression, they will only find it by placing their faith in the authority of the one true God as described in the Bible.

The Core of Genuine Hope

Hope, as with sorrow, is never separate from a person's spiritual heart and specifically his/her desires, treasures, and pursuits. Recalling Proverbs 13:12, "Hope deferred makes the heart sick, but a desire fulfilled is a tree of life." The biblical commentator Bruce Waltke remarks,

> An evil desire would never be equated with the tree of life. The righteous may find their hopes deferred for a while, but their hearts never grow sick, for they know the Lord who upholds his promises. Though tried, they are never disappointed in their faith. . . . The proverb is an index of lives that are moving either toward final despair of every expectation in death or toward a fulfillment of every desire in the everlasting presence of the Lord.[333]

A person who finds him/herself to be hopeless is not abnormal but experiencing the point where the fallen world in which he or she lives joins together with his or her own misplaced and temporal desires. Lamentations 3:25 shows this same connection between a person's pursuits and hopes, "The LORD is good to those whose hope is in him, to the one who seeks him (*NIV*)." What people treasure and pursue in their hearts is never disconnected from their hopes. In fact, hopes are most often established upon that which the spiritual heart treasures most. A wonderful marriage, children, fame and fortune, a career, or a

---

[333] Waltke, *Proverbs: Chapters 1-15*, 563.

trouble-free life are common treasures that shape many people's false hopes.

When God has genuinely saved a person, he/she has come to a place of repentance or change of heart. A Christian is one who is not perfect, but rather one who confesses/admits his/her hopelessness and justly condemned condition and by God's grace and mercy receives hope in Christ alone. But Christians who desire to love God and others and have placed their hope in Christ for all eternity still wrestle with the flesh and deal with both wrong and temporal desires. Christians can and regularly do set up false treasures and subsequent false hopes that direct them away from genuine hope. Peter explains in 1 Peter 1:13-15 that it is the turning back to fleshly desires — double-mindedness — that brings about the sense of hopelessness in believers who do have genuine hope in Christ.

> Therefore, preparing your minds for action, and being sober-minded, set your hope fully on the grace that will be brought to you at the revelation of Jesus Christ. As obedient children, do not be conformed to the passions of your former ignorance, but as he who called you is holy, you also be holy in all your conduct.

If Christians' treasures are corrupt because of double-mindedness, so too will be their moods, and they will feel hopeless and condemned, though they are not. When Christ is preeminent in Christians' heart and God is their only hope, they will still sorrow, but not according to the flesh. As the Apostle Paul stated in 1 Thessalonians 4:13, Christians sorrow, but not like those who have no hope. Paul also explains this reality and highlights this hope in 2 Corinthians 4:16-18:

> So we do not lose heart. Though our outer self is wasting away, our inner self is being renewed day by day. For this light momentary affliction is preparing for us an eternal weight of glory beyond all comparison, as we look not to the things that are seen but to the things that are unseen. For the things that are seen are transient, but the things that are unseen are eternal.

Having this sure hope in Christ enables people to bear the weight of sorrow in this life as they understand its purpose in revealing God's goodness to them. Charles Spurgeon once said,

> When we are so weak that you cannot do much more than cry, you coin diamonds with both your eyes. The sweetest prayers God ever hears are the groans and sighs of those who have no hope in anything but his love. There is music in our moaning to his kind and tender ears. He can restore you, even though you be as the marred girdle; and when he once puts you on again, you will cleave to his loins more closely than ever, praying that he will bind you fast about him.[334]

Destructive temporal desires and false transient hopes must be set aside if one is to have his/her eyes fixed upon genuine hope and be drawn near to Christ. People's lives here on earth, because of the fall of Adam, are not meant to be as in heaven and not meant to be without sorrow.

As observed in Hebrews 11, faith is the substance of reliable hope. But the next chapter of Hebrews (12:1-3) explains that the only genuine hope is found with faith in Christ — setting one's heart on Him:

> Therefore, since we are surrounded by so great a cloud of witnesses, let us also lay aside every weight, and sin which clings so closely, and let us run with endurance the race that is set before us, looking to Jesus, the *founder and perfecter of our faith, who for the joy that was set before him endured the cross*, despising the shame, and is seated at the right hand of the throne of God. Consider him who endured from sinners such hostility against himself, so that you may not grow weary or fainthearted. In your struggle against sin you have not yet resisted to the point of shedding your blood.

---

[334] Charles H. Spurgeon, "The Cast-Off Girdle," *The Complete Works of C. H. Spurgeon,* Vol. 29: Sermons 1698-1756 (Harrington, DE: Delmarva Publications, 2013), sermon no. 1706.

Temporal hopes may not always be sin, but they can be weights that shift a person's desires off of Christ and can cause Christians to become fainthearted and double-minded.

Jesus Himself looked ahead to the joy that was set before Him in order to endure His extreme sorrow and suffering on the cross. But Christ so treasured degenerates that He was willing to die and rise again to free mankind from their sins and vexations and provide hope that saves. When He returns again, His plan will be accomplished and full salvation will be realized: "Christ, having been offered once to bear the sins of many, will appear a second time, not to deal with sin but to save those who are eagerly waiting for Him" (Hebrews 9:28). Hope rests on both the completed work of Christ on the cross and the sure promise of His second appearance guaranteed in His resurrection. No other hope exists that can change the spiritual heart of degenerates, fully eliminate moral guilt, appease the wrath of God, explain the deep sorrows of this world, and supply delivering hope. Jesus is the author and finisher of faith. By this hope alone Christians are delivered from their hopeless reality for all eternity.

In truth, the construct of depression attempts to explain the natural longing/desire for heaven — especially God's presence, which God has written on each person's heart. Every person — though they may not realize it or acknowledge it — also desires the benefits of having both a perfect relationship with God and others and to be free from pain, guilt, heartache and death. In other words, each soul desires to live in a perfect condition as God intended, as Adam and Eve experienced prior to the Fall recorded in Genesis 3, and as God promises to reestablish for those who believe in Him (Revelation 21:4). Whether acknowledged or not, every person has this awareness, since God "has planted eternity in the human heart, but even so, people cannot see the whole scope of God's work from beginning to end" (Ecclesiastes 3:11). Charles Ellicott comments,

> Taking this meaning of the word [eternity] here (the only place where the word is used with the article), we may regard it as contrasted with that for "time," or season, immediately before. *Life exhibits a changing succession of weeping alternating with laughing,* war with peace, and so forth. For each of these God has appointed its time or season, and in its season, each is good. *But man does not recognize this; for God has put in his heart an expectation and longing for abiding continuance of the same, and so he fails to understand the work which God does in the world* [emphasis added].[335]

It is not only that God sovereignly controls all of human history, but that He governs in order to restore humanity to His original design — what God declared to be entirely good. Another commentator, Tremper Longman, explains,

> It is interesting to note the rather significant allusions to Genesis 1 in this verse. Even the vocabulary is reminiscent, though not identical, with that used in Genesis 1. For instance, in Genesis 1 God pronounces each step of his creation "good" (*tob*). Qohelet's word "beautiful" (*yapeh*) may also be a reflex of this divine pronouncement. Further, the placing of *aloam*, eternity, in human beings might be analogous to God endowing his human creatures with his image (Genesis 1:26-17).

The common pursuit of happiness reflects the natural desire that we all have to escape the fallen condition and to permanently live in a perfect state — to return to God's original design after His own holy image. The changes of life are not outside of God's control or plan, and trusting in His goodness over our understanding, though we often cannot perceive His plan, is essential to have a right eternal mindset and a healing change of heart. This important truth allows Christians to understand that seasons of sorrow — no matter how long they last — are purposed by God in order to restore individuals to His original design.

When the hope of full restoration in Christ is accepted by grace through faith, sorrow is also understood and reactions to life's

---

[335] Charles John Ellicott, *Ellicott's Bible Commentary on the Whole Bible,* vol. IV (Grand Rapids, MI: Zondervan, 1971), 370.

losses changed. Martin Luther King, Jr. understood this truth: "We must accept finite disappointment, but never lose infinite hope."[336] Sorrowing over the true condition of this life — including the tragedy of physical death — is normal and right, but Christians are those who sorrow differently than the world who has no hope and can only value temporal things (1 Thessalonians 4:13). Even secularists, such as prominent psychiatrist Peter Breggin, see people's love of life — and really their love of self — as the underlying reason why people become depressed or enter into despair:

> Always remember that unless people deeply cared about their lives, they wouldn't become so wretchedly disappointed and discouraged. In this vein, I tell my patients, "You wouldn't be so horribly depressed if you didn't have a sense of how good life can be. You're not indifferent toward your life — you hate it. That means you want something better — much, much better.[337]

In contrast to those without Christ, Christians understand that to live in this world is to set Christ as the highest treasure, and to die is far more valuable (Philippians 1:21) as they will be given full access to know God without restrictions or impairments. The "much, much better" life of a person who has placed his/her faith in Christ is to come when they are in God's presence rather than on this side of eternity. This reality is the Christian hope that fully delivers, and it is the joy set before us that comforts us and enables endurance despite the crushing nature of this life.

---

[336] Martin Luther King Jr. quoted by Vi-An Nguyen, "15 of Martin Luther King Jr.'s Most Inspiring Motivational Quotes," *Parade Magazine Online* (April 4, 2018): https://parade.com/2526 44/vianguyen/15-of-martin-luther-king-jr-s-most-inspiring-motivational-quotes/.

[337] Breggin, *Anti-Depressant Fact Book*, 193.

The Substance of Genuine Hope

Though obvious to some, it is important to reemphasize that hope is not a physical substance that can be placed in a capsule, a drink, or another physical object: hope is metaphysical. By definition, faith is the very substance of hope (Hebrews 11:1), and the object of faith determines the value and effect of hope. Biblical hope, then, is faith in the person, work, and promises of the one true God as presented in Scripture.

Romans 8:1-39 offers several characteristics of this unique hope that the Creator offers to degenerates (all people after the fall of Adam) in order to restore them: (1) Genuine hope not only assuages guilt fully, but it defeats sin and fulfills God's moral law perfectly (vs. 1-4):

> "For the law of the Spirit of life has set you free in Christ Jesus from the law of sin and death. For God has done what the law, weakened by the flesh, could not do. By sending his own Son in the likeness of sinful flesh and for sin, he condemned sin in the flesh, in order that the righteous requirement of the law might be fulfilled in us, who walk not according to the flesh but according to the Spirit.

Christ's righteous fulfillment of the law fully resolves guilt and provides peace between God and man.

(2) Genuine hope supernaturally enables degenerates' (the natural man) minds to be set on a relationship with God instead of on death and enslavement to sin (5-17a): "For those who live according to [their naturally destructive desires] set their minds on the things of the flesh, but those who live according to the Spirit [of God] set their minds on the things of the Spirit."

(3) Genuine hope does not remove sorrows, suffering, and current struggles in this world, but in the one to come (17b-24): "The sufferings of this present time are not worth comparing with the glory that is to be revealed to us"; genuine hope is a

promise received by faith, which enables the believer to rejoice in the midst of sorrow and trials (2 Corinthians 6:10).

(4) Genuine hope is dependence upon the supernatural work of the Holy Spirit and not something people create individually within themselves or corporately among themselves. It is the Godhead that is the agent of hope and is nothing within human nature (26-27):

> Likewise the Spirit helps us in our weakness. For we do not know what to pray for as we ought, but the Spirit himself intercedes for us with groanings too deep for words.

In contrast to humanistic teaching, believers understand that they are weak and fragile and not just depraved. We again revisit Romans 15:13, which also affirms that the supernatural work of the Holy Spirit provides hope:

> And again Isaiah says, "The root of Jesse will come, even he who arises to rule the Gentiles; in him will the Gentiles hope." May the God of hope fill you with all joy and peace in believing, so that by the power of the Holy Spirit you may abound in hope.

Only by faith through the supernatural work of the Holy Spirit can degenerates find genuine hope that resolves hopelessness, provides joy that makes sorrow bearable, and offers peace with God that assuages guilt. Hopelessness is normal, whereas genuine hope is supernatural.

This reality also determines that no one is an agent of hope apart from Christ and the work of the Holy Spirit. Those who wish to help others in deep despair must come to realize that nothing they can do will change the faith of the one struggling or cause them to embrace genuine healing hope. Likewise, counselors and physicians cannot permanently remove sorrow from another's life nor should they try. What people can do to help those in need is both to proactively teach others under their care God's wisdom concerning human nature before a crisis arises in their lives, and prayerfully depend upon the Holy Spirit, who both gives hope and intercedes on their behalf. Waiting until a crisis arises or a person is faced with understanding their crushed human condition is not the best strategy in helping them find joy; it is difficult and can be harmful to attempt to force the armor of the Lord onto a wounded soldier in the middle of battle. Pastors and parents alike must faithfully teach God's truth concerning the human condition so that the wise, through the ministry of the Holy Spirit, can take God's wisdom to heart and be prepared for life's battles when they arise. Without the Armor of God, we all are weak (Ephesians 6:10-18a):

> Finally, be strong in the Lord and in the strength of His might. Put on the whole armor of God, that you may be able to stand against the schemes of the devil. For we do not wrestle against flesh and blood, but against the rulers, against the authorities, against the cosmic powers over this present darkness, against the spiritual forces of evil in the heavenly places. Therefore take up the whole armor of God, that you may be able to withstand in the evil day, and having done all, to stand firm. Stand therefore, having fastened on the belt of truth, and having put on the breastplate of righteousness, and, as shoes for your feet, having put on the readiness given by the gospel of peace. *In all circumstances take up the shield of faith, with which you can extinguish all the flaming darts of the evil one; and take the helmet of salvation, and the sword of the Spirit, which is the word of God, praying at all times in the Spirit, with all prayer and supplication.* To that end, keep alert with all perseverance [emphasis added].

Depending upon the strength of God in every way allows the Christian to persevere through every circumstance in life.

It is God's truth (the Sword) which the Holy Spirit uses to enable faith, supply delivering hope, and offer encouragement. Romans 15:4 explains,

> For whatever was written in former days was written for our instruction, that through endurance and through the encouragement of the Scriptures we might have hope.

Saving faith, the very substance of hope, comes from hearing, and hearing from the Word of God (Romans 10:17). Degenerates cannot be regenerated (rebirthed spiritually) apart from a covenant relationship with Jesus as revealed in the written Word of God, and believers cannot be encouraged or comforted apart from God's good Word. All people lack strength within themselves to endure sorrow (Psalm 119:28).

(5) Genuine hope guarantees eternal security, forgiveness, regeneration (new birth), and glorification (28-39):

> And we know that for those who love God all things work together for good, for those who are called according to his purpose. For those whom he foreknew he also predestined to be conformed to the image of his Son, in order that he might be the firstborn among many brothers. And those whom he predestined he also called, and those whom he called he also justified, and those whom he justified he also glorified. What then shall we say to these things? If God is for us, who can be against us? Who shall bring any charge against God's elect? It is God who justifies. Who is to condemn? Christ Jesus is the one who died — more than that, who was raised — who is at the right hand of God, who indeed is interceding for us. Who shall separate us from the love of Christ? Shall tribulation, or distress, or persecution, or famine, or nakedness, or danger, or sword?

God's plan to prosper humanity and to provide hope is secure because Christ both died and rose again. Paul even references Genesis 3 and the curse of sorrow during childbirth as he describes the current vexed state of both physical creation and the inward spiritual nature after the Fall (8:22-23):

> For we know that the whole creation has been groaning together in the pains of childbirth until now. And not only the creation, but we ourselves who have the firstfruits of the Spirit, groan inwardly as we wait eagerly for adoption as sons, the redemption of our bodies. For in this hope we were saved.

In contrast to humanistic ideas of hope, the Bible presents hope as found in an intimate relationship with Jesus Christ that does not just defeat guilt, it perfectly fulfills the moral law of God apart from human effort. This saving hope also provides peace with God despite depravity, mercifully reveals God's goodness despite spiritual blindness, and supernaturally sets the mind on eternity rather than on temporal/failing hopes. True saving hope is not a human system or religion; it is faith in the person and work of the one true God.

Hebrews 10:21-23 echoes Romans 8 in expressing how the atonement of Jesus Christ clears one's conscience of guilt, provides stable hope, and produces changed behavior:

> And since we have a great priest over the house of God, *let us draw near with a true heart in full assurance of faith*, with our hearts sprinkled clean from an evil conscience and our bodies washed with pure water. *Let us hold fast the confession of our hope without wavering, for he who promised is faithful.* [Emphases added.]

Biblical hope guarantees deliverance in the age to come, unlike temporal false hopes that are limited to temporal timeframes and always fail. Genuine hope also does not falsely promise to remove sorrow and inward groanings during this life as false hopes do, and genuine hope does not rely on the ability or efforts of crushed spirits to rescue themselves as agents of hope. Instead, biblical hope is the supernatural work of God the Father, God the Son, and God the Holy Spirit who progressively changes believers' minds and behaviors. In Psalm 42:11, King David expresses his own faith in this hope alone for his soul's turmoil: "Why are you cast down O my soul, and why are you in turmoil within me? Hope in God; for I shall again praise Him, my salvation and my God." Hope that delivers people from their inward turmoil and crushed spirit is not a temporal object or system, but it is supplied by God to prosper humanity and to one day (in eternity) fully restore believer's souls and bodies to health.

If you sorrow because you are genuinely hopeless and have need to assuage your guilt, Christ is your only hope of Salvation. You are not abnormal for coming to a place of accepting your inability to live in this broken world apart from a Savior and questioning the purpose of your life. On the other hand, if you have placed your faith in Christ and deeply sorrow because of the fallen condition of this world and the circumstances you find yourself in rather than because of misplaced desires, your sorrow is a result of the fall of Adam and ordained by God for your good. You are precisely where you need to be, and just as with the saints who have gone before you, faith obtained in a relationship with God will sustain you (Hebrews 11-12:5).

No matter why a person sorrows, he or she is not diseased or abnormal because he or she has come to accept the true condition of the human soul in this fallen world and everyone's need as degenerates to be restored to the image of the Creator. What will determine whether a person's life heads toward life or death is based entirely upon the desires of the heart and the corresponding hope that one chooses to establish. Having Christ as the agent of hope or trusting in an idol of the heart will determine which path of sorrow an individual chooses, which remedy he or she pursues, and ultimately his/her final destination. Either way, every person alive must struggle with the reality of his/her own sorrow and heart's desires — there is no escape on this side of eternity. Having faith in Jesus Christ is the only hope that can comfort humanity, enable endurance now, and fully deliver believers in the age to come.

CHAPTER 8

CONCLUSION

"Our bodies had no rest, but we were afflicted at every turn —
fighting without and fear within. But God, who comforts the
downcast, comforted us." Apostle Paul, 2 Corinthians 7:5b-6

The secular psychiatric labels of unipolar and bipolar depression
seek to explain and treat genuine normal problems that arise
from the brokenness of our world and from human nature itself.
The construct of depression is simply the popularized term used
to describe the distressful struggles which stem from sorrow,
hopelessness, guilt and various trials. These roots are our true
problems, the unfortunate realities of human nature. Though
they are spiritually impairing, they offer us an honest assessment
of our own heart's depravity and fragility.

The American Psychiatric Association has popularized the
notion that deep persistent sorrow and a crushed spirit are
abnormal. But the Bible establishes from Genesis 3 to Revelation
21 that every person's spiritual condition apart from Jesus Christ
is utterly depressed: we are all in pursuit of happiness/joy,
living according to our desires, attempting to remedy our guilt
and find peace, and suffering the losses and heartbreaks of this
world. Of course, because of our deceived nature and the
world's established system, we regularly do not realize or admit
our brokenness.

To further mask our true condition, the American Psychiatric Association (APA) has developed a subjective system as an attempt to delineate who is sad in a normal way and who should be fit into a diseased or degenerate category. But the time, severity, and distress axioms the APA suggests do not yield objective means of diagnosing alleged disorders of depression. Because all sorrow, hopelessness, guilt, anxiety and other vexations of the spirit are distressful and destructive, secularists have attempted to medicalize these unfortunate features of human nature. But as numerous psychiatrists and clinical psychologist continue to admit, these seemingly negative emotions are not medical issues.[338]

The Bible and secular theorists not only utilize different words to describe the same struggles, but they also rely on opposing worldviews to explain, approach, and attempt to remedy the psyche/soul. To view people who have reached the end of themselves as abnormal and sick is to have faith in the secular philosophies of individual degenerationism, materialism, biodeterminism, and humanism. Whether a person chooses to view human struggles through the lens of the biomedical model or through the wisdom of Scripture, each person must base his/her decision upon a presuppositional faith. This faith is foundational, as it establishes everything from normalcy to the very substance of things hoped for. Therefore, truly rethinking the syndrome of depression calls for one to consider underlying faith as most important.

The reality of mankind's fallen condition — the very bad news — demands that everyone not only experience the sorrow of life, but also that each person respond to it. People must either set up false hopes that lead them to death and destruction or embrace saving hope that leads them toward God and His promise of

[338] Rapley, Moncrieff, and Dillon, *De-Medicalizing Misery*.

restoration and deliverance. But as Solomon explains in Ecclesiastes 1-2, there is absolutely nothing that mankind can do apart from God that can bring about hope which delivers the soul from destruction.

Though humanists insist that people are the greatest agents of hope and self-deliverance, the existence of the bipolar construct proves otherwise. Self-reliance, self-actualization, and self-esteem are not remedies to depression as the psychiatric concept of mania attests. Additionally, mania should be understood not as a sickness, but as a construct which seeks to explain all self-dependent effort—no matter how grand—to escape our human condition.

Likewise, the claim that enlightenment and scientific advancement are the keys to delivering the soul is squelched by the fact that one of the most advanced and enlightened countries in the world—the United States of America—is faced with an ever-escalating crisis of depression, unhappiness, and suicide. As Solomon said, "In much wisdom is much vexation, and he who increases knowledge increases sorrow" (Ecclesiastes 1:18). Turning inward or relying on self and placing faith in science will not deliver humanity from their desperate state.

Depression is considered by many to be an emotional sickness, but emotions are not bodily products as secularists have attempted to frame them. Instead, emotions are our spiritual hearts manifested in the physical world. As we desire, so we hope, and when our hopes are deferred or crushed, so are our desires. Our emotions are windows into our souls and not forces apart from our heart's treasures.

But since we are naturally bent toward evil and deceit apart from God's truth, the metaphoric bad tree (our spiritual hearts) will naturally bring forth bad fruit (our behavior). This bad fruit is destructive and impairing; our souls cannot do otherwise until

God regenerates us and gives us new desires reflecting our delight in Him (Psalm 37:4).

Although depression is primarily a spiritual condition of the soul, both the Bible and empirical evidence confirm that the spiritual nature has a direct impact on the body. In other words, somatic effects should be expected. But these physical effects are not a person's biggest problem, and somatic symptoms do not determine depression to be a physical disease. Likewise, as a person's thoughts change toward right thinking, and especially according to the mind of Christ, the body also responds in healing. Sadly, many people try to treat only somatic symptoms, and the proposed treatments regularly bring about a worse spiritual and physical condition. Only by addressing the spiritual heart's destructive treasures, condemned nature, and false hopes can a person truly be healed.

Everyone on every side of the debate over defining, studying, and attempting to treat depression agrees that hope is the essential remedy. But what saving hope consists of is a matter of disagreement. Secularists insist that hope can be produced within the individual and that other hopes such as drugs, diets, activities, and materials can supplement and help to foster hope within a person's soul. But these hopes are both temporal and failing, and when they fail they leave people far worse than they had been before attempted treatment.

There is a genuine hope, however, that is medicinal to both the body and the soul. This hope – as with every hope – is obtained by faith, but this genuine hope comes from hearing the Word of God rather than from listening to an inner voice, the heart's affections, or the world's many empty promises. This hope is not a system or a false promise of a quick fix. In fact, the only hope able to eliminate guilt and condemnation, conquer death, and make sense of the sorrow of this world is faith in Jesus Christ.

Hope is not a thing; it is faith in God — the only one qualified to be an agent of hope and enable hope. Jesus himself bore our sorrows, sin, and guilt/shame on the cross and conquered death (Isaiah 53). Jesus fulfilled his plan to prosper us and to give us hope (Jeremiah 29:11), is preparing a place for those who believe in him (John 14:3), and has sent the Holy Spirit to comfort and counsel us through this fallen world until He returns (John 14:26). While we live, He promises that we will experience deep sorrow, but that deliverance and restoration are surely to come (John 16:20-21). Only God, who created man in His own image, can take fallen degenerates and regenerate and sanctify them despite their brokenness. When we experience sorrow, it is not an indication that we are abnormal, but a clear sign that we are precisely as God describes us to be, and He is exactly who He says that He is. When we are sad, it is an indication that we need to further depend upon the one true God and forsake self-dependence.

Before we can make a clear assessment of the causes and remedies of depression, we have to understand what it is. To miss the true nature and cause of sorrow, guilt, anxiety, and hopelessness is also to dismiss their significant purpose and their only genuine remedy. If God allows and purposes sorrow for our good as the Bible declares, then seeking to escape sorrow causes us to miss His goodness. Sorrow, then, is not a human condition to be escaped in this life, but the necessary pathway to the cure for hopelessness, guilt, and death. This truth is precisely what the Bible asserts throughout its pages. We are not only to accept our own sorrow, but we are also to participate in the sorrows of others and take to heart our true condition. Sorrow can either lead us to spiritual death or it can lead us to a covenant relationship with Jesus Christ and to the desired and necessary place of restoration.

There is no doubt that each of us wants deliverance from sorrow because of its impairing, distressful, and destructive nature, but without truly recognizing and accepting the very bad news that spiritually and physically weighs on us, receiving the good news cannot occur. If we accept sorrow, hopelessness, and guilt as right mindsets that identify who we truly are rather than as detached forces that victimize us, then we are in the necessary place to receive the only remedy. Being depressed, then, is simply being honest about one's own fallen heart as it relates to this fallen world; it is a confession of our fragility and depravity as well as our need for a savior apart from ourselves; it is admitting that false hopes are futile and destructive and that we cannot bear our crushed mental state apart from a covenant relationship with the one true God through faith.

While this book is about the construct of depression, it is equally about the gospel of Jesus Christ, and how God alone provides hope able to resolve our fallen human condition. If we are to only rethink depression without shifting our paradigm or presuppositional faith from human theory and practices onto God's wisdom as presented in Scripture, then we will individually and corporately continue down the path to destruction and death. The secular construct of depression does not describe a sickness or a sin; it describes our true fallen state apart from salvation in Jesus alone. What each of us desires — whether realized or not — is for our souls to return to God's original design prior to Adam's original sin and as promised in the age to come to those who believe God's promises.

Our perspective on the syndrome of depression or any psychiatric construct emerges from our basic beliefs about ourselves, our world, and truth itself. The psychiatric construct of depression is not humanity's true problem; it merely represents a label, which asserts the humanistic perspective. Truly rethinking the construct of depression requires that we denounce false beliefs and humbly trust in God's wisdom and His sufficiency to perfectly restore our souls to health (Psalm 19:7).

SELECTED BIBLIOGRAPHY

American Psychiatric Association. *Diagnostic and Statistical Manual of Mental Disorders*. 5th ed. Washington, DC: American Psychiatric Publishing, 2013.

———. *Diagnostic Criteria from the DSM-IV-TR*. Washington, D.C.: American Psychiatric Association, 2000.

Bentall, Richard. *Madness Explained: Psychosis and Human Nature*. New York: Penguin, 2003.

Berger II, Daniel. *Mental Illness: The Influence of Nurture*. Taylors, SC: Alethia International Publications, 2016.

_____. *Mental Illness: The Necessity for Dependence*. Taylors, SC: Alethia International Publications, 2016.

_____. *Mental Illness: The Necessity for Faith and Authority*. Taylors, SC: Alethia International Publications, 2016.

_____. *Mental Illness: The Reality of the Physical Nature*. Taylors, SC: Alethia International Publications, 2016.

_____. *Mental Illness: The Reality of the Spiritual Nature*. Taylors, SC: Alethia International Publications, 2016.

_____. *The Insanity of Madness: Defining Mental Illness*. Taylors, SC: Alethia International Publications, 2018.

Breggin, Peter. *Psychiatric Drug Withdrawal*. New York: Springer Publishing Company, 2013.

————. *The Anti-Depressant Fact Book: What your Doctors Won't Tell you about Prozac, Zoloft, Paxil, Celexa, and Luvox.* Cambridge, MA: Da Capo Press, 2001.

————. *Toxic Psychiatry.* New York: St. Martin's Press, 1991.

Chesterton, Gilbert Keith. *The Well and the Shallows.* London: Sheed & Ward, 1935. Reprint, United Kingdom: Aziloth Books, 2012.

Cohen, Abraham. *Proverbs.* London: Soncino Press, 1973.

Dixon, Thomas. "'Emotion': The History of a Keyword in Crisis," *Emotion Review: Journal of the International Society for Research on Emotion* 4, no. 4 (2012): 338-44.

Edwards, Jonathan. *A Treatise Concerning Religious Affections.* Philadelphia: J. Crissy, 1821. Reprint, New Haven, CT: Yale University Press, 1959.

English Standard Version. Wheaton: Good News, 2001.

Frances, Allen. *Saving Normal: An Insider's Revolt against Out-of-Control Psychiatric Diagnosis, DSM-5, Big Pharma, and the Medicalization of Ordinary Life.* New York: HarperCollins, 2013.

Ganschow, Julie. *Seeing Depression Through the Eyes of Grace.* Kansas City, MO: Pure Water Press, 2015.

Goldberg, David. "The Heterogeneity of "Major Depression," *World Psychiatry: Official Journal of the World Psychiatric Association (WPA)* 10, no. 3 (2011): 226.

Group for the Advancement of Psychiatry. "History of Psychiatry 19th Century." YouTube video, 31.45. Posted May 3, 2015. https://m.youtube.com/watch?feature =youtu. be&v=TFoJ0b4v3hY: 18:45-55.

Healy, David. *Let Them Eat Prozac: The Unhealthy Relationship between the Pharmaceutical Industry and Depression.* New York: New York University Press, 2004.

Hubble, Mark A., Barry L. Duncan, and Scott D. Miller. *The Heart and Soul of Change: What Works in Therapy.* Washington, D.C.: American Psychological Association, 1999.

Insel, Thomas. "Transforming Diagnosis." National Institute of Mental Health. April 29, 2013. http://www.nimh.nih.gov/about/director/2013/transforming -diagnosis.shtml.

Kirsch, Irving. "Antidepressants and the Placebo Effect," *Zeitschrift fur Psychologie* 222, no. 3 (2014): 128-34.

————. *The Emperor's New Drugs: Exploding the Antidepressant Myth.* New York: Basic Books, 2011.

Lewontin, Richard C. "Billions and Billions of Demons." Review of *The Demon-Haunted World: Science as a Candle in the Dark,* by Carl Sagan. *New York Review,* January 9, 1997.

Lieberman, Jeffrey A. *Shrinks: The Untold Story of Psychiatry.* New York: Little, Brown and Company, 2015.

Lloyd-Jones, Martyn. *Preaching and Preachers.* Grand Rapids, MI: Zondervan, 1971.

Lopez, Shane J. *Making Hope Happen: Create the Future You Want for Yourself and Others.* New York: Simon & Shuster, 2014.

Longman III, Tremper. *Proverbs.* Baker Commentary on the Old Testament Wisdom and Psalms. Grand Rapids: Baker, 2006.

May, Rollo. *Man's Search for Himself.* New York: W. W. Norton & Company, 1953.

McKane, William. *Proverbs: A New Approach.* Philadelphia: Westminster, 1970.

Medscape Psychiatry. https://www.medscape.com

National Institute of Mental Health, "Depression." https://www.nimh.nih.gov.

Norcross, John, Everett L. Worthington, Jr., and Steven J. Sandage. *Psychotherapy Relationships That Work: Therapist Contributions and Responsiveness to Patients.* New York: Oxford University Press, 2002.

Pert, Candace B. *Molecules of Emotion: The Science behind Mind-Body Medicine.* New York: Scribner, 1997.

Pies, Ronald. "Psychiatry's New Brain-Mind and the Legend of the 'Chemical Imbalance.'" *Psychiatric Times,* July 11, 2011. http://www.psychiatric times.com/blogs/psychiatry-new-brain-mind-and-legend-chemical-imbalance.

Pies, Ronald, and Cynthia Geppert. "Clinical Depression or 'Life Sorrows'?: Distinguishing between Grief and Depression in Pastoral Care." *Ministry Magazine,* May 2015: 8-9.

Pinker, Steven. *Enlightenment Now: The Case for Reason, Science, Humanism, and Progress.* New York: Penguin Random House, 2018.

Psychiatric Times Online. www.psychiatrictimes.com.

Pūras, Dainius. "Depression: Let's Talk about How We Address Mental Health," *United Nations Human Rights Office of the High Commissioner* (April 7, 2017): https://www.ohchr.org /EN/NewsEvents/Pages/DisplayNews.aspx?NewsID=21480&LangID=E.

Ramachandran, V.S., and Sandra Blakeslee. *Phantoms in the Brain: Probing the Mysteries of the Human Mind.* New York: William Morrow and Company, 1998.

Rapley, Mark, Joanna Moncrieff, and Jacqui Dillon. *De-Medicalizing Misery: Psychiatry, Psychology and the Human Condition.* Hampshire, England: Palgrave Macmillan, 2011.

Reilly, Katie. "Mental Health: A New Understanding." *Time Magazine* Special Edition, November 2018.

Sacks, Oliver. *Hallucinations.* New York: Random House, 2012.

Shorter, Edward. *A History of Psychiatry: From the Era of the Asylum to the Age of the Prozac.* New York: John Wiley and Sons, 1997.

Simon, Sarah, Nicole M. Cain, Lisa Wallner Samstag, Kevin B. Meehan, and J. Christopher Muran. "Assessing Interpersonal Subtypes in Depression." *Journal of Personality Assessment* 97, no. 4 (2015): 364-73.

Sims, Andrew. *Is Faith Delusion? Why Religion is Good for Your Health.* London: Continuum, 2009.

Spurgeon, Charles H. *The Metropolitan Tabernacle Pulpit: Sermons Preached and Revised* Vol. XXVII. London: Passmore & Alabaster and Sons, 1882.

Waltke, Bruce. *The Book of Proverbs: Chapters 1-15.* New International Commentary on the Old Testament. Edited by R. K. Harrison and Robert L. Hubbard Jr. Grand Rapids: Eerdmans, 2004.

———. *The Book of Proverbs: Chapters 15-30.* New International Commentary on the Old Testament. Edited by R. K.

Harrison and Robert L. Hubbard Jr. Grand Rapids:
Eerdmans, 2005.

Weiss, Kenneth J., and the Group for the Advancement of
Psychiatry. "A Trip Through the History of Psychiatry."
Psychiatric Times Online, November 7, 2017.
http://www.psychiatrictimes.com/blogs/history-
psychiatry/trip-through-history-psychiatry?GUID
=31158D64-F01A-4DEA-AC1A-D3CE843FC9BC
&rememberme=1&ts=14112017.

Whitaker, Robert. *Anatomy of an Epidemic: Magic Bullets,
Psychiatric Drugs, and the Astonishing Rise of Mental Illness
in America*. New York: Broadway Books, 2015.

Yusim, Anna. *Fulfilled: How the Science of Spirituality Can Help
You Live a Happier, More Meaningful Life*. New York:
Grand Central Life and Style, 2017.

Made in the USA
Las Vegas, NV
22 November 2024

12397784R00142